Organized for Action

Commitment in Voluntary Associations

David Knoke & James R. Wood

Rutgers University Press

New Brunswick, New Jersey

Library of Congress Cataloging in Publication Data

Knoke, David.
  Organized for action.

  Bibliography: p.
  Includes index.
    1. Pressure groups—United States.   I. Wood,
James R., 1933–   joint author.   II. Title.
JK1118.K56   322.4'3'0973   80-26927
ISBN 0-8135-0911-4

For Joann and Margaret

For Myriam, Lillette, and Paul

Contents

List of Figures and Tables

Preface

Our purpose in writing this book is to enlarge scientific knowledge about an important kind of social organization—social influence associations. These voluntary citizen groups are important corporate actors at all levels of democratic government. Together with political parties, social influence associations are major means of aggregating and articulating citizen demands for specific public policies that elected and administrative officials may authorize. While the study of interest groups, particularly at the national level, has a long tradition in political science, analysis of the internal functioning of mass-membership social influence associations has not received comparable attention.

The research presented here draws upon data from thirty-two local chapters of a wide variety of social influence associations. Two basic questions guided the research:

What organizational conditions enable some groups to generate high levels of membership commitment to the collective enterprise?

What organizational characteristics are most effective in helping associations to attain their goals of influencing public policies in their areas of interest?

In seeking answers to these questions, we were confronted by a paucity of theory and previous research findings to guide our data analyses. We had to synthesize a theory with testable hypotheses from a variety of sources, primarily in the organizational literature.

The analyses presented in the following chapters are based on a simple model of social influence association behavior deduced from a few general premises. This simplicity, by deliberately limiting us to a few key variables, allows us to explore some fundamental relationships in an area of social behavior where relatively little is understood. Our theory and findings should interest not only sociologists, political scientists, and other social scientists, but also the vast array of leaders and participants in social influence associations and (not least) the numerous public officials who are the target of these associations' influence. Our fondest hope for this book is that people who read and think about our findings will be stimulated to continue the advancement of knowledge about social influence associations begun in this study.

In any large-scale research enterprise, a host of participants contribute in large ways and small to the ultimate outcome. By singling out some persons for explicit acknowledgment, we do not intend to slight the importance of the efforts of those who go unnamed.

Susan A. Stephens, as field director of the Indianapolis Area Project (IAP), played a critical role in organizing and supervising a complex data-collection process. The superior quality of the interviews and the coding of data testifies to the excellent standards she sought and obtained. The graduate student participants in the IAP who performed these labors under her direction and analyzed portions of the data include Norma Benton, Ted Bonstedt, Joel Devine, Sue Hall, Mike Hooker, Darla McKeeman, Bernard McMullan, Bruce Navarro, Rob Parker, David Prensky, Mike Wallace, Larry Wolfarth, and Molly Wong. The research assistants who performed many and varied tasks essential to the success of the project were Patricia Doyle, Suzanne Meyering, Jeff Shaul, and Tim Stearns. During the data-analysis stage, the efforts of Stearns and McMullan immensely eased the arduous task of making sense out of chaos. We were extremely fortunate to have available the many and varied talents of Felicia Fellmeth, our administrative secretary, during the entire period of the field work.

Additional interviews were conducted by students and residents of Indianapolis too numerous to list. We single out Nancy Vargus, Linda Copenhaver, and Terry Bierman for their productivity. Commendations go to Professors Bryan Vargus and David Ford for helping to organize the Indianapolis interviewers, and to Marlene Simon for training them.

We were especially fortunate to engage the services of Jackie Warriner during the writing stage of the project. Her patience and forbearance in typing numerous drafts were especially appreciated.

Several institutional sources of support for this research are gratefully acknowledged. The Indianapolis Area Project of the Indiana University Sociology Department, Elton Jackson, chairman, provided the initial funding to launch the research. The IU Biomedical Research Support committee gave a small but well-timed stipend to assist in the preparatory field work. The National Science Foundation granted a generous supplement (SOC76-81477), which greatly expanded the scope of the project. And the National Institute of Mental Health's research scientist development program's support of Knoke (KP2MH00131) enabled us to complete the project at a much earlier date than would otherwise have been possible.

Several scholars offered criticisms of earlier drafts, which helped immensely to improve this final version. Lynn Appleton, Christopher Winship, and Edward O. Laumann provided comments on the blockmodeling analysis that appears in Chapter Eight. Paul M. Hirsch and Mayer N. Zald read the entire manuscript and their written critiques were a paradigm of the friendly critic's art.

A final, but most important, acknowledgment of moral support—the elusive but vital ingredient of the success of any research undertaking—goes to our families.

Chapter One

A Theory of Voluntary
Association Behavior

On the night of January 17, 1977, a blizzard chased even the streetwalkers from the sidewalks of Indianapolis. But on that night, while the wind-chill factor reached twenty below, a small band of women stoically marched in front of the state capitol, their lonely, unobserved vigil occasionally punctuated by their chant of "Pass ERA now." For more than a year these women, members of the local chapter of Women's Rights Organization, or WRO (not its real name), had planned, organized, and conducted a public relations and lobbying campaign to try to get the twice-defeated Equal Rights Amendment passed by the Indiana state senate. Now, on the eve of the crucial ratification vote, the WRO hoped by a final public collective action to influence a wavering senator or two.

When the capitol doors opened the next morning, the hardy band dragged their sleep- and cold-benumbed bodies to the senate chamber; occupants of the gallery soon overflowed into the hallway, with pro- and anti-ERA placard-bearers fighting for attention as the final debate began. The spectators were not timid about expressing their feelings vocally, and on several occasions the senate president was forced to gavel for order. After two hours, during which the controversies that had surrounded ERA for the past five years were once again read into the record, the roll was called. With two votes to spare, the senate passed the amendment, and Indiana became the thirty-fifth state to ratify it. A huge cheer rang through the senate gallery. Supporters wept, cried, and hugged each other, while opponents silently buttoned their coats and walked out into the cold.

The struggle to ratify ERA in Indiana was a classic display of voluntary grass-roots political action. In public arenas and in private contacts, citizens aroused by an impending public policy decision had buttonholed legislators in an effort to implement or prevent social change according to their values. Most of the activists who demonstrated on the capitol steps and in the senate gallery belonged to various voluntary organizations that had mobilized them for political action. Whether the WRO's chilly watch had swayed any last-minute waverers or was mainly a symbolic witness of the group's own unity, the incident reveals dramatically the deep commitment to a cause and to a group that political controversy can evoke. While the WRO demonstration was an extreme example of commitment to political action by members of a voluntary association, such phenomena in milder form are not rare. In this book we propose and examine a theory of how social influence organizations arouse and channel their members' energies and other resources into activities designed to achieve collective public policies.

Theoretical Overview

Figure 1.1 displays in schematic form the major theoretical concepts of our theory and their presumed relationships. This model is especially applicable to the class of organizations we call *social influence associations*—voluntary groups that attempt to influence public policy in specific areas. In Chapter Two we will expand on this type in greater depth and show how it differs from other formal organizations. At a level of general premises about organizational behavior, the theory involves three components. The internal social control system plays an essential role in an organization's ability to acquire resources necessary to sustain collective life. Resources available to the organization, in turn, are crucial for the attainment of the group's external goals.

Each theoretical component at the general level is linked to one or more concepts specific to social influence associations. Starting

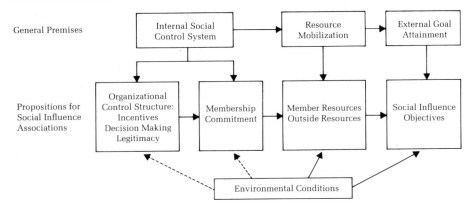

Figure 1.1. Schematic Representation of Relationships among Theoretical Concepts

at the left, the social control system of voluntary associations is composed of two broad components, one of which we take to be antecedent to and therefore partly determinative of variation in the other. Organizational control structures—broadly classified as incentive offerings, decision-making arrangements, and legitimacy patterns—are patterned interactions that affect the development of the membership's commitment. These commitments direct the participants toward collective interests rather than individual pursuits.

For social influence associations, the membership's commitment to the welfare of the collectivity is equivalent to the strength of the normative social control system. An organization with a weak normative control system would have many members who are not greatly concerned with the organization's performance and would readily abandon it when it got into trouble. A strong normative control system, however, exists when members show great loyalty and tenacity in fighting to keep the organization functioning even under conditions of great adversity. Thus, for our purposes, the terms *membership commitment* and *normative social control system* are interchangeable. In Chapter Two we will operationalize this concept by measuring the strength of a membership's commitment to the collectivity.

Voluntary associations acquire many of their essential resources from their members in the form of energy, skill, time, money, and support. Some resources, often substantial financial grants, may also be obtained from outside parties. The component of the social control system with the greatest impact on these resources is the membership's commitment. The particular type of goal attainment in which we are interested is the ability to influence social values, particularly public policies within the association's domain. The schematic model implies that the resources available to the organization will be a major determinant of such influence.

At the bottom of Figure 1.1 we have put *environmental conditions*, with arrows representing possible impact upon concepts internal to the association, thus recognizing another perspective on organizational behavior, one that has come into vogue in recent years. The causal sequence previously described is primarily one in which factors internal to the organization are the major forces shaping collective action. In contrast, much recent work in complex organizations and collective behavior pays considerable attention to factors outside organizational boundaries. The characteristic formal structures of organizations may reflect the historical conditions of its formative era (Stinchcombe, 1965; Aldrich, 1979). Contemporary events beyond an organization's control may also affect its capacity to mobilize members for action and to garner resources essential to pursue collective aims (Gamson, 1975).

Our analysis is designed to examine the relative merits of the internal organizational dynamics and its interplay with external environmental forces. We do not view these two perspectives on organizational behavior as contradictory, nor is the aim of our research to wholly reject one approach in favor of the other. But, given the different literatures, which emphasize one approach or the other, we believe a major task of this book is to sort out the relative contribution to collective action of internal and external influences. We are most concerned with the impact of the two sets of factors on organizational goal attainment and less interested in the effect of environment on internal structure (particularly since the data we use lack the historical dimension important to answering this question). Hence Figure 1.1 shows both solid and dashed arrows from environmental conditions to the internal properties.

The diagram shows no relationships between nonadjacent concepts. These links have been omitted for simplicity's sake, but their presence or absence remains an empirical question, to be determined in subsequent analyses.

The greatest drawback to pursuing research using this scheme lies in the ambiguity surrounding the causal sequence implied in the diagram. We postulate an order among variables that some may find arguable. We ignore the possibility of mutual feedback effects between concepts. Tests of relationships among empirical indicators will assume simple additive relations among the variables. Our diagram represents only one among many possible orderings of the five concepts. But it is the one we think is most defensible given the present state of knowledge about organizational behavior. Any proposed alternatives to the present scheme would likely contain equally problematic assumptions. We view this diagram as a heuristic device for guiding the selection of variables and estimating empirical relationships between independent and dependent measures. In the remainder of this chapter we will develop in greater detail the bases for expecting the relationships between concepts depicted in Figure 1.1.

Premises

Four premises assert the theory's basic concepts:

1. All organizations require social control of their participants.
2. All organizations require a continuous input of resources.
3. All organizations try to attain external (or output) goals.
4. All organizations operate in environments that necessarily constrain their ability to attain external goals.

These premises are sufficiently general to apply to a wide variety of social organizations such as families, churches, corporations, government agencies, and armies. As premises, they will not be subjected to direct observation or test. Instead, they make plausible statements about basic conditions that must be met if organizations are to continue to exist. Before stating propositions about the relationships among these four premises as they apply to voluntary associations, we will elaborate the assertions that social control, resource acquisition, environmental conditions, and external goals are fundamental features of organizational analysis.

Internal Social Control System

Whenever a collectivity is internally differentiated, it must coordinate members' activities toward common ends (Durkheim, 1933). Social control seeks to insure that collective rather than personal interests will be served by individuals' actions in the organization.

The term *social control* may conjure up an image of heavy-handed hierarchies in which top leaders constrain the behavior and life chances of the lower echelons but are themselves uncontrolled by subordinates (except perhaps through withholding of information, which can damage organizational performance; see Mechanic, 1962). This mechanistic model of control (Burns and Stalker, 1961) is common in military, prison, corporate, and other bureaucracies. A large literature on management problems in complex work organizations sees social control as a problem of supervisory constraints on subordinates' behavior. Similarly, in professional service agencies, control is commonly viewed as the exercise of professional constraint over client behavior.

Yet the study of social control cannot exclude consideration of constraints on the higher echelons' behavior. Historically, the sociological term *social control* meant society's capacity to regulate itself, not repressive or coercive control of subordinates by a superior stratum, as the term later came to denote. Janowitz's (1975, 1976, 1978) efforts to revive the earlier meaning of *social control* lie close to our understanding of membership commitment as normative social control in social influence associations: "Social control presents a format of influence based on the notion of interaction and mutual (two-way) relations among social groups" (Janowitz, 1975:87). Elimination or reduction of tensions and conflicts is a basic goal of social control. Success enables a collectivity to pursue a higher set of moral values than individual self-benefit.

While many voluntary associations explicitly pursue economic benefits for their members, the social influence associations stand in sharp contrast to economic-based associations. "From the point of view of social control, community voluntary groups operate from a different set of organizing principles—from a different set of goals which influence and rationalize their activities. They speak explicitly in the name of moral standards and of collective responsibility" (Janowitz, 1978:302). The self-regulation of social influence associations is obviously strengthened by personal control, "a person's capacity to channel his energies and to satisfy his needs and impulses while minimizing damage to himself and others" (Janowitz, 1978:324). In this intimate relationship between persons and groups, social influence association performance is improved to the extent that individual energies can be shunted away from self-centered pursuits and toward collective ends. By redirecting individual energies, a social influence association generates the membership commitment essential for its collective enterprise.

Social control arises whenever the diverse activities of a differentiated collectivity must be integrated around a common purpose or set of goals. Control seeks a common orientation toward the group, circumscribing idiosyncratic behavior that may threaten a social organization with dissolution or at least a drift away from its ostensible objectives. Control is problematic in complex work organizations. Such organizations often set up elaborate control mechanisms such as training and educational programs, supervisory and reporting systems, grievance committees, job descriptions, and other formalization of rules in an attempt to ensure greater faithfulness to organizational imperatives. But social control is also necessary in relatively simple collectivities. Given legal and moral limits on the use of sanctions (rewards and punishments) in voluntary associations, achieving social control may be more difficult than where money or coercion can also be readily applied to gain compliance (Etzioni, 1975). Social control analysis is concerned, then, not only with which organizational actors are to be controlled, but with the means used for control.

Several writers distinguish two ideal-typical mechanisms for social control in collectivities. March and Simon (1958:158–159) wrote of feedback and programming; Thompson (1967) discussed mutual adjustment and standardization; Hage (1974:28) used programming with sanctions and high feedback with socialization. These studies share the notion that control may be accomplished either by a prescribed set of rules enforced through hierarchical authority or by self-regulation, with participants continually monitoring each others' performances and socializing each other to adopt behaviors that sustain adequate organizational performance. Empirical organizations may blend both of these techniques of control and emphasize one over the other for different positions within the organization.

Regardless of the particular techniques of control, most writers agree that there must be some level of control among organizational participants if the collectivity is to persist.

Control in Voluntary Associations

Voluntary associations differ from formal work organizations in ways that imply that different means of social control are likely to be more appropriate. By *voluntary associations* we mean formally organized, named collectivities in which the majority of participants do not derive their livelihood from their activities in the group (see Smith et al., 1972, for extensive discussion of voluntary associations and volunteerism). Such organizations clearly differ from complex formal work organizations in the diffuse role expectations held for most members. No elaborate job descriptions exist, nor could they be developed for most participants. The voluntary association generally does not produce services or goods for the market. The major portion of its "output" is consumed by the members, although we shall examine specific voluntary associations that channel part of their collective efforts toward political action.

Unlike work organizations, which require substantial labor time and effort from their participants, most voluntary associations obtain only brief, episodic involvement from their members (there are obvious exceptions, such as social movement organizations). Thus, compared to work organizations, voluntary associations exert drastically lower levels of surveillance over members' behavior. Many fewer opportunities arise for voluntary association members to monitor and correct each other's beliefs and behaviors in order to keep them aligned in directions most suitable for collective interests. Many work organizations rely heavily on rules (formalization) to enable higher officials to control lower participants. Work organizations induce member contributions primarily through monetary exchanges in the form of wages, salaries, and perquisites. When utilitarian rewards predominate in participants' motives, organizational sanctioning of deviant behavior by manipulating rewards and punishments is more feasible. Legal and moral restrictions, as well as lack of extensive financial resources, prevent voluntary associations from using such sanctions to control most members (although withholding status recognition or expelling unsatisfactory members may be used by some groups).

Limitations on voluntary associations mean that the main mechanism for creating and maintaining social control over participants is the internalization of norms:

> Normative organizations are organizations in which normative power is the major source of control over most lower participants, whose orientation to the organization is characterized by high commitment. Compliance in normative organizations rests primarily on internalization of directives accepted as legitimate. Leadership, rituals, manipulation of social and prestige symbols, and resocialization are among the more important techniques of control used [Etzioni, 1975:40].

Though Etzioni emphasizes "control over most lower participants," normative controls also constrain elites' behavior.

Norms are symbolic values, shared by members of a social organization, that constrain them to believe and to act in the interests of the collectivity. Parsons (1937:75) defined a *norm* as "a sentiment attributable to one or more actors that something is an end in itself." He used norms as a basic component in a framework of normative regulation. Norms partly determine the ends of an actor's actions and set limits on the choice of means. Norms can be contrasted to interests: norms are imperatives, backed by informal and formal sanctions, that serve collective ends; interests are individual objectives that guide behavior without regard to collective considerations. A normative analysis of voluntary associations implies that members should act (and, indeed, have a moral obligation to act) on behalf of the collectivity. An interest analysis implies that members will act according to rational calculus (cost/benefit analysis) to further their individual well-being, even if that means sacrificing the welfare of the group as a whole.

Associations try to instill in their members the norm that the association's welfare is an end in itself. Norms are internalized prescriptions and proscriptions that influence a person's actions including participation in and psychological support for collective action. The creation of organizational norms and their inculcation in members change individual preferences (interests). Normative control by an association alters individual actions from those with high utility, or payoff, for the individual members toward those with high utility for the organization as a whole.

Through social support, shared values, and common expectations (consensus), conflict is minimized and the overt exercise of power and authority is less necessary to keep the organization operating. Normative coordination involves extensive persuasion, using information to focus participants' perceptions and preferences on association-centered beliefs and actions. Leaders originate much persuasive effort to socialize members to the importance of organizational objectives and the necessity of member participation to achieve these objectives. The degree to which norms are experienced and affirmed by members of an association is an empirical issue and cannot be decided a priori (Warner, 1978). To the extent that normative social control is successful, a voluntary association benefits from the unified and coordinated sentiments and actions of all participants on behalf of collective interests. But in associations where normative controls are absent, weak, or improperly inculcated, participants may pursue personal or idiosyncratic objectives to the detriment of the organization's performance.

Official leaders, perhaps more than members, are subject to

strong normative controls. Not only must leaders act as agents for the collectivity, but by striving to inculcate normative controls in other members they continually remind themselves of the importance of putting organizational interests ahead of personal interests. Elites are probably more, rather than less, obligated to adhere to fundamental norms than are rank-and-file members (Homans, 1950). Members expect their leaders to adhere to organizational norms, especially to procedural standards that ensure that collective rather than personal ends are pursued. In many instances, leaders are selected because they already exhibit strong adherence to the group's interests.

Successful inculcation of organizational norms should facilitate the emergence of an effective system of social control. The association in which norms are widely shared should be responsive to a broader range of member interests rather than to a limited set of interests by a subset (e.g., an organizational elite or a clique of members). Participants who internalize organizational norms will be more likely to support a wider range of concerns than those directly affecting their personal interests. They will be more willing to compromise, to seek collective goals and benefits, and to attempt to influence other participants to adopt these objectives. Thus, the successful transmission of norms ensures that collective interests will be served.

We shall refer to members' acceptance of association-regarding norms as the *membership's commitment to the association*. We view the membership commitment as one of two broad components making up an association's internal social control system. The other component encompasses a set of social control structures. Organizational control structures are relatively stable patterns of interaction and internal arrangements that may facilitate or impede the formation of the membership's commitment. A first major task in constructing a theory of voluntary association behavior is to establish the expected relationship between organizational control structures and the membership's commitment.

To identify the organizational control structures most relevant to membership commitment, we rely upon three sometimes divergent theories of organizational control: Clark and Wilson's (1961) incentive theory; Likert's (1961) theory of decision participation control (see also Tannenbaum, 1968); and a theory of legitimate leadership based on Weber (1968; see also Wood, 1981). Incentive theory holds that an organization's members contribute resources to it in exchange for various material, purposive, or solidary incentives. Material incentives are rarely available in large quantities in social influence organizations, but purposive incentives seem especially appropriate. Participative control stresses mutuality of influence among participants. This influence requires that members participate fully in the decision-making process. Because members have full opportunity to set and shape the organization's goals, they will develop positive normative beliefs about (that is, commitment to) the collectivity. Mutuality of influence leads to "a relatively high level of control by as well as over all organization members" (Tannenbaum, 1968:21). The legitimate leadership approach stresses the inculcation of a belief in the legitimacy of leaders who make decisions for the collectivity and interpret its core values. Leaders' claims to legitimacy may rest on traditional, rational-legal, charismatic, or value-rational grounds.

These three theories of organizational control sometimes anticipate different empirical outcomes, and sometimes they envision the same outcome but suggest different organizational control structures as explanations. Rather than treat them as competing theories, we reasoned that each might better predict organizational effectiveness under appropriate conditions. For example, an organization employing participative decision-making control might be more effective in mobilizing members toward a goal that requires members' activity. But when the goals could just as well be met by leaders' actions backed up with members' support, instilling a belief in legitimacy may be the most economical way to secure such support.

Increased organizational control—whether control by incentives, control by decision-making participation, or control by legitimate leadership—reduces strain and conflict among members, decreases the impact of irrational impulses, raises stability and calculability (rationality) in conducting organizational business, and enhances interpersonal communication of interests. In other words, increased organizational control enhances the self-regula-

tory aspects of social control. These control components lead to a stronger membership commitment to the collectivity.

Treating the membership's commitment as an outcome of variation in organizational control structures, we can state three general propositions to be examined empirically in three later chapters:

1. The greater the incentives offered by the association, the stronger the membership's commitment.
2. The greater the opportunities for participation in decision making, the stronger the membership's commitment.
3. The greater the leaders' legitimacy, the stronger the membership's commitment.

First, the use of incentives should measurably improve an organization's normative control over participants. Incentives are means of control used by organizations to induce member belief and behavior consistent with collective ends. We previously noted that many voluntary associations lack material inducements. Social influence associations are particularly likely to rely upon purposive incentives that stress organizational aims, community duty, collective ends, sacrifice, and altruism as membership benefits derived from commitment of personal resources. The greater use of such incentives, perhaps supplemented by social solidary ties among members, is more likely to create and to reinforce continually a common normative orientation among members. Incentives are exchanged in return for belief and behavior consistent with collective rather than individual interests. Organizations lacking incentives should have a membership less concerned with the welfare of the collectivity and more likely to pursue personal ends. The use of incentives is consistent with both the decision participation and legitimate leadership control perspectives mentioned earlier.

Second, decision-making patterns reveal to association members the extent of their control over programs and policies. A centralized organization in which decisions are made by a relatively small subset of members violates the ideology of member control inherent in participative control. If leaders can bind the organization to decisions without consulting members, compliance by

members is threatened. A decentralized decision-making process, on the other hand, implies the active implementation of the norm of member control. Widespread opportunity and actual involvement in decision making should, according to the decision-participation control theory, reinforce the internalization of normative controls over all participants.

Third, formal legitimacy gives leaders the right to set policies and to enforce those policies with sanctions backed up by higher authorities. In single-unit associations, legitimacy resides typically in the local unit, often in the entire membership rather than in any specific office. But in multiunit associations, the locus of authority may remain in the local unit or be lodged in supralocal bodies. Higher authority can be invoked to reduce the potential for local disagreements erupting into member rejection of binding decisions. Constitutionally based authority not only can sanction resisters but can also gain support from members who may disagree with the substance of organizational decisions yet be willing to uphold the authority structure that permitted these decisions in the first place. Extralocal authority also strengthens procedural norms of due process and orderliness that enable an organization to integrate its participants toward a common purpose, particularly when potentially divisive social policies are pursued. Associations with highly legitimated leadership are thus likely to develop memberships with more organizationally oriented social control beliefs (that is, with stronger commitment to the organization).

Resource Mobilization

Contemporary research on organizations embraces an "open systems" perspective (Katz and Kahn, 1978). Organizations are not self-contained entities but are embedded in larger social systems with which they interact continuously. Any organization is a bounded set of actors carrying on input, throughput, and output activities. Transactions between an organization and its environment are thus crucial to understanding many aspects of an organization's internal structure and behavior. Resource exchanges con-

stitute the main content of organizations' interactions with their environment.

Broadly defined, *resources* are any means or facilities potentially controllable by an organization that can be used in adaptations between the organization and its environment. A variety of items may serve as resources. Funds, personnel, information, and products or services (Aldrich, 1972); money and authority (Benson, 1975); money, information, legitimacy, and power (Parsons, 1966) have all been variously construed as essential elements for sustaining organized activity.

Differentiation and specialization by function in a complex environment reduce the chance for any organization to survive without entering into exchanges with others to obtain resources that cannot be generated internally. The premise that all organizations require resources assumes greater significance when resource acquisition is viewed as a main indicator of organizational effectiveness. A seminal statement by Yuchtman and Seashore (1967) suggested a system resource approach to organizational effectiveness that has gained popularity. Through competition for scarce and valued resources, a universal hierarchy emerges among social organizations. An organization's "bargaining position" in its environment is "an excellent yardstick against which to assess organizational effectiveness. . . . We propose accordingly to define the effectiveness of an organization in terms of its bargaining position, as reflected in the ability of the organization, in either absolute or relative terms, to exploit its environment in the acquisition of scarce and valued resources" (Yuchtman and Seashore, 1967:898). In this perspective, formally stated goals recede to mere strategies used by managers to enhance their organization's bargaining position. While we disagree with the last equation, we recognize the importance of resource acquisition in achieving organizational goals of survival and growth.

Various "political economy" models developed in the past decade stress resource acquisition as a driving factor in organization-environment relationships. Thompson (1967) captured the basic principle in his statement that resource scarcity precipitates organizational uncertainty, thereby stimulating mangerial efforts to

reduce uncertainty through structural arrangements and inter-organizational exchanges that negotiate relatively predictable environments. In one form or another, organizations' resource needs form a conceptual core of political economy models (Zald, 1970a; Benson, 1975), exchange models (Cook, 1977), resource-dependency models (Pfeffer, 1972; Aldrich, 1979), and strategic choice models (Hickson et al., 1971; Child, 1972) of organizational behavior.

For example, Benson (1975:231) asserted that "organization decision makers are typically oriented to the acquisition and defense of an adequate supply of resources." This motivation explains efforts to dominate the flow of money and authority in an interorganizational network or to avoid dependency on other organizations for these resources. Cook (1977:74) derived from exchange theory a proposition that "organizations seek to form that type of interorganizational exchange relationship which involves the least cost to the organization in loss of autonomy and power." Organization-environment transactions involve calculations of the relative gains and costs across a set of resources sought by an organization.

Resource considerations may affect the internal structure of organizations. The strategic choice hypothesis (Child, 1972) argues that units within an organization that deal directly with the most uncertain and problematic contingencies of the environment will become more powerful and thus able to control essential features of the organization's structure and process. The resource dependency perspective (Aldrich and Pfeffer, 1976:84) likewise asserts that administrative efforts to manage the environment are aimed at resource acquisition and organizational survival. An organization's agents actively select structures most compatible with environment constraints, contingencies, and uncertainties. Given this latitude for response, internal power configurations are decisive in organizational efforts to secure a predictable flow of resources from the external economy. Thus, Zald (1970a:229) attributed great importance to the organizational polity—"the whole web of groups and individuals, internal or external to an organization, that possess resources to sanction decisions"—in its relation

to the productive exchange economy inside and across organizational boundaries.

These various writers seem to have reached a consensus that an organization's ability to continue functioning in a competitive, resource-scarce environment depends on its ability to select an appropriate internal structure and to establish interorganizational relations that sustain a steady flow of resources. Ability to adapt organizational practice to the demands of resource acquisition ultimately means the difference between organizational survival or death. Thus our premise that all organizations require continuous input of resources lies at the heart of contemporary organization theory.

Resources in Voluntary Associations

Just as voluntary associations differ from work organizations in their means of social control, they differ in the nature and origin of their input resources. Work organizations obtain their raw materials either through exchanges in the labor, commodity, and credit markets or through transfer payments (taxation and subsidization). Legitimation and rationalization of external environments through political means are additional resources sought by both work organizations and voluntary associations (Zald, 1970a, 1970b; Benson, 1975; McNeil, 1978). Although some voluntary associations participate in an enrollment economy (e.g., the YMCA), most voluntary associations produce neither goods nor services for the market.

Consequently, members must provide the main input of resources in most voluntary associations. Even when financial aid comes predominantly from outside parties such as foundations or government agencies, voluntary associations rely heavily on members for other necessary resources, particularly labor power. Of course, in one sense, all corporate actors ultimately derive their resources from investments by natural persons (Coleman, 1974). But, by definition, such investment decisions in voluntary associations do not involve a direct financial inducement in return for participants' energy and time. Perrow (1970) aptly pointed out that members of voluntary associations are not only the primary source of raw materials, but they also consume a substantial share of the output. He cited four basic kinds of resources invested by members in the collectivity: names, money, manpower, and personality. Voluntary associations cannot compensate members financially for their commitment of resources, nor can the collectivity generally obtain them elsewhere if the membership is reluctant to make such investments. Thus we see the importance of normative controls in voluntary organizations for inducing members to relinquish personally controlled resources needed by the organization.

Member participation in various forms is obviously necessary to carry out both the daily and the special activities of the association. But leaders often need another resource that members can supply without becoming personally active: tolerance of leaders' actions as agents of the organization. Perrow's category of "names" comes close to this concept. If a membership will stand by its organization even when it acts in ways with which members disagree, the organization has an important resource to use in its political action efforts.

Voluntary associations can potentially use a variety of resource commitments from members. The perishability of some resources is greater than others: labor power cannot be stored like money. Convertability between resources also differs markedly (Clark, 1968a:61), constraining or facilitating the organization's application of input resources to its objectives. For example, in influencing politicians, money may be a highly useful resource in some circumstances (campaign contributions) but illegal in other situations (legislative bribes), where block votes may be more useful. Since no voluntary association can be completely sure which types of resources will be most useful in unforeseen circumstances, many types of resource commitments will be sought from members.

Energy in the form of human activity is perhaps the most vital and problematic resource required by voluntary associations. As Yuchtman and Seashore (1967:900) point out, "An 'effective' organization competes successfully for a relatively large share of the member's personality, engaging more of the personality in organizationally relevant ways, thus acquiring additional resources from its environment." Members exist only partially inside the organization, and an association will try to enlarge the proportion of a member's personally controlled resources relinquished for collective use. Although controversy exists as to whether human energy invested in one set of activities must necessarily be subtracted from other spheres of participation (Marks, 1977), voluntary associations are frequently at a competitive disadvantage with other social institutions. Work organizations and families usually provide stronger utilitarian and affectual incentives (Clark and Wilson, 1961) than do most voluntary associations. On the assumption that membership contributions are roughly proportional to organizational inducements (March and Simon, 1958:84), many voluntary associations will obtain only meager membership contributions of personal resources.

Important as member contributions of resources are, they are often not the sole source of support for social influence associations. An increasingly important phenomenon is assistance by outside organizations and institutions, as well as donations from unaffiliated persons. Other voluntary groups, churches, private foundations, and government agencies at various times provide facilities for meetings, mailing lists, staff workers for special projects, as well as sizable direct grants. Such outside resources are more likely to be forthcoming to associations that project an image of a dedicated, cohesive membership. Thus, taking both types of resources into account, we state the following proposition:

4. The stronger the membership's commitment, the more resources acquired by the association.

External Goal Attainment

The assumption that all organizations have external goals toward which they strive indicates how organizational resources are likely to be applied. Few organizations can persist merely to continue existing. Yet, of the three basic concepts, that of organizational external goals is the most slippery and the most controversial. We noted in the previous section that some contemporary writers, following the lead of Yuchtman and Seashore, wish to abandon the goal approach to organizational effectiveness and measure performance mainly as resource acquisition. We do not accept this equation, but argue instead that organizations have real, operant collective objectives that go beyond mere accumulation of resources for the sake of survival. Collective ends exist that are not the aggregate of individual participants' objectives and that can be distinguished from the objectives of subgroups such as production, sales, and distribution departments.

In conceptualizing organizational goals, we find the distinctions drawn by Perrow (1968) highly useful. He points out that a wide range of organizational behaviors can be classified as goal directed since there is only a relative distinction between ends and means. That is, almost any goal can also be viewed as a means to another goal. From this perspective, organizations pursue a variety of goals, many of which may be incompatible or in conflict with each other. Perrow classifies goals as having internal or external referents. Among external goals are those that distinguish organizations according to their output or general type of product. Their referent is "the public constituency of the organization" (306). In Blau and Scott's (1962:42–44) terms, output goals ask the question "Cui bono?" (Who benefits?). Output goals (also called the organizational "charter"; Pugh et al., 1968) are concerned with the application of organizational resources to achieving a characteristic product. Such goals need not be unchanging; Perrow gives the example of deviance control organizations (e.g., prisons or juvenile reformatories) whose emphasis shifts from incarceration to probation or preventive work.

External goals tell both outsiders and participants what the organization's basic purpose is all about. Although multiple objectives may be present, we usually have no trouble in daily life in distinguishing basic organizational objectives. General Motors makes cars and other vehicles; McDonalds sells hamburgers and fries; the NAACP influences public policy on racial matters through court cases. Goals can be transformed over an organization's lifetime, as in the classic case of the Townsend movement changing from old-age pension advocacy to recreational activities (Messinger, 1955), or in the case of the National Foundation's shift from polio to birth defect research (Sills, 1957). Of course, real or operant purposes must be distinguished from formal goals that serve merely as window dressing and do not explain organizational behavior. Thus, Joe's Newsstand and Sweetshop claims to sell newspapers and malteds, but its real objective is to make book for its regular customers. However difficult it is to identify organizational goals, their origins, and their attainment, we agree with Perrow that "the best work done in attempting to understand complex organizations has had to confront the question, 'To what variety of ends is organizational behavior patterned and motivated?'" (Perrow, 1968).

The concept of output goals is compatible with Parsons' (1956, 1960) perspective that goal orientation is the defining feature of a social organization. Goals are located within the boundaries of the collectivity, and the organization has some capaciy to resist environmental constraints and to set patterns of behavior that are most consistent with goal attainment. An organization's core tendency is to fulfill its goals and/or needs. "A collective goal here means a relatively optimal relation between the collectivity and some aspect of its intrasocietal situation (e.g., other collectivities) or its extrasocietal environment . . . a particular goal is not isolated; it is part of a system of goals. . . . [A collectivity] may be any system involving the coordinated action of a plurality of individuals oriented to the attainment of a collective goal or a system of collective goals" (1969:318). Thus, while acknowledging the existence of many objectives that may have individual participants or the organization itself as a referent, our concern is with those programs and policies that are oriented to the state of the environment (also called "transitive" goals; Mohr, 1973). As Simon (1964) pointed out, an organization's goals are constraints on behavior imposed by an organizational role. Higher-level executives seek out and support actions that advance these goals; subordinate employees do the same or tailor their choices to the constraints established by the higher echelons. Thus, organizational goals are articulated mainly at what Parsons (1958) called the "institutional," or executive, level of a collectivity rather than at the managerial or technical levels, whose objectives diverge in their efforts to meet the constraints set by collective goals.

In treating external goal attainment as a major component of organizational behavior we do not want to fall into the trap of assessing organizational effectiveness in terms of how well or how poorly an organization meets the target states implied in the goals. Under this criterion, most organizations probably fail to meet their goals fully and would be considered ineffective. A more realistic approach to goal attainment recognizes that not all organizations can direct their full effort toward achieving external goals. Some expend considerably more resources than others on maintenance and custodial activities, leaving fewer resources to pursue external objectives. Therefore, effectiveness in goal attainment should be assessed by "the degree to which an organization realizes its goals under a given set of conditions" (Etzioni, 1975:135), not by failure to achieve abstract performance standards that are unattainable given the internal and environmental constraints.

Although the "goal paradigm" remains dominant in the sociology of organizations, recent critics have challenged what they allege to be the reification of the organization as something more than a system of interacting individuals. These critics posit an alternative model in which an organization is a social construction based on certain actors' abilities to create and enforce their definitions of goals, needs, technologies, structural features, and the like (Benson, 1977; Meyer and Rowan, 1977). Power relationships are the "essential core" from which other organizational features proceed, and the organization reduces to "an arena within which the actions of social groups and individuals are carried out" (Benson, 1977:8).

We view this alternative paradigm as a less radical break with the goal-attainment models than do the critics. They basically argue that, through a political process, certain individuals or groups inside or outside the organization's boundaries (Thompson, 1967, called them the "dominant coalition") impose their notions of appropriate organizational objectives toward which a substantial portion of its participants' energies are directed. In the case of owner-controlled production organizations, the answer to the question "Cui bono?" usually is "A minority of the participants." But in the case of social influence associations, organizational goals may be more responsive to the interests of a larger constituency, whether members or nonmember publics served by the association. The extent to which association goals are shaped by other participants outside the dominant coalition is an empirical question. Certainly the ideology of democratic control leads one to hypothesize greater membership influence in shaping voluntary association goals than worker influence on the goals of production organizations.

Goals in Voluntary Associations

The external or product goals of work organizations typically involve physical goods or services and their distribution to a consumer market. Even government agencies are mainly concerned with the production and distribution of public goods. In contrast, the goals of voluntary associations are typically intangible or symbolic and are frequently consumed directly by the membership. Etzioni (1975 : 105) classifies the basic concerns of normative organizations as "cultural goals". "[These goals] institutionalize conditions needed for the creation and preservation of symbolic objects, their application, and the creation or reinforcement of commitments to such objects." For many voluntary associations, goal attainment occurs when members' values are altered in such a way as to conform to the organization's cultural precepts. For example, Alcoholics Anonymous wants its participants to view their drinking behavior as a disease and to stop imbibing completely. Fraternal and veterans' associations emphasize camaraderie and patriotism. Recreational groups devote considerable effort to getting members to adopt health- and fitness-oriented values. Parents' associations stress particular child-centered methods for raising children. These organizations consider their goals as having been attained when members' attitudes and behaviors toward the particular substantive focus are altered and maintained in accordance with the promulgated values.

The examples just cited are voluntary associations whose major emphasis is internal; that is, their goals emphasize changing the values held primarily by the members and only secondarily, if at all, by the larger nonmember public. But some associations' main goals stress the cultural values of nonmembership populations. These associations operate mainly through public opinion campaigns in mass media, attempting to broadcast their message and create a more favorable climate in which to carry out other programs. For instance, a "social health" association uses public service announcements and school and church forums to tell young people about venereal disease and attempts to modify their sexual activity, at least to the point of taking precautions to reduce the spread of infection. Similarly, a planned-parenthood association may attempt to influence popular attitudes toward birth control through various "public education" (i.e., propaganda) efforts. Many health-oriented voluntary associations (such as the cancer society, heart association, and various degenerative disease foundations) continually carry on public relations campaigns with two basic objectives: to alter population health behavior for detection and treatment and to raise funds for research and administration (both goals neatly summarized in the slogan "A checkup and a check"). Such associations consider their goals as having been attained if a major change in behavior of the general population occurs, for example, a decrease in cigarette smoking. (In fact, success is sometimes claimed in the face of no change in popular behavior by assertions that the situation would be "even worse" if the association's efforts had not been made.)

A third type of voluntary association—we call it the *social influence association*—seeks not only to change values of members or the mass public but to transform general societal values, primarily through new laws or social policies promulgated by the authority of other institutions. These associations try to institutionalize value changes by gaining the support of other organizations capable of legitimizing the behavioral and attitudinal changes sought by the social influence group. Perhaps the most notorious instance in American history was the "success" of the Anti-Saloon League and the Women's Christian Temperance Union in amending the United States Constitution to outlaw the manufacture and sale of alcoholic beverages. Despite their legal triumph, the associations' subsequent disinterest in enforcing conformity to prohibition revealed their goal attainment to be primarily symbolic rather than substantive (Gusfield, 1962). For some associations the goals to be implemented through institutional change involve all-or-nothing alterations in basic societal values that may be in conflict with other associations' goals (for example, the abortion decision, with so-called pro-life and pro-choice antagonists). For other associations, the goals can be implemented in incremental, piecemeal fashion with no overt opposition group (as in increased funding for mental health programs).

In many instances, even when goals have a substantial goods-and-services aspect, the major emphasis is on political action to transform the symbolic values of the society as a whole. These associations consider their goals attained if their values are incorporated into the core values of the society, as recognized by the support of legislatures, courts, government agencies, or corporate administrators. The initial thrust of the civil rights movement can be read precisely as an effort to transform the status of black citizens to full equality before the law, thereby bringing blacks symbolically into the mainstream of social and political life. Changing the attitude of the mass public, particularly its racist and segregationist elements, was secondary to the goal of changing legal values to acknowledge equality of citizenship.

Social influence associations may fruitfully be viewed as important corporate actors in society's political subsystem. Unlike voluntary associations with primarily internal goals, social influence groups have external goals that make joining the association a largely political act for most members. Social influence associations support the pluralistic bases of political power and group representation. They open up two-way channels of political communication between the association membership and political system elites. And they offer means for expressing personal political interests. Social influence associations embrace three distinctive types of organizations (Lane, 1959:79): political clubs, usually affiliated with a party; quasi-political organizations that take stands on public issues; and other types that serve to stimulate politically oriented discussion (see also Verba and Nie, 1972; and Olsen, 1972).

Parsons (1969:339–340) cited the associational subsystem as one of three key political "exigencies" in the society's goal attainment subsystem (the other two are the judiciary, concerned with legitimation of collective goals, and the bureaucratic agencies, which mobilize resources and implement policy decisions). The associational subsystem does not mobilize implementive resources but generates "constituent support and determination of the policies to be implemented." Social influence associations are publics that constitute the demand for particular policy decisions, and thus they function as interest groups. At the same time, however, an association may be a source of political support for institutional decision makers who must implement binding decisions for the society as a whole. Only part of that support may take the form of electoral backing. Some legislators and bureaucrats may welcome the information provided by influence associations and the "public opinion" they purport to represent because such pressures help justify political actions.

Given that social influence associations seek many goals attainable only within the political subsystem, the importance of resources in that process becomes obvious. We can thus state another proposition of our theory:

5. The more resources available to an association, the more effective its social influence.

Organizations and Their Environments

Organizations can be viewed as adaptive organisms in a threatening environment, but this point of view has only begun to inform the major efforts of organizational sociologists in the past decade. Ironically, one reason for the late development of this approach, which in retrospect appears a natural one for sociologists, was the preoccupation with characteristics of bureaucracy as the most rational structure for an organization. Yet for Weber (1968), so often quoted on this subject, bureaucracy was rational in part because it coped effectively with environmental pressures. To cite just one example, the establishment of credentials such as exam scores or diplomas as a basis for selecting bureaucratic incumbents was a way of coping with pressures from prominent families for positions for their sons. Despite theoretical work by Barnard (1938) and Hawley (1950; see Duncan and Schnore, 1959, for an appeal for wider use of Hawley's perspective) and despite Selznick's (1949) powerful empirical study of the Tennessee Valley Authority's struggle with and adaptation to its hostile environment, not until recently did organizations' interaction with their environments become a major research subject.

The explosive take-off of the organization and environment literature around 1970 may have been ignited by the appearance of two convincing arguments for an open-system approach to the study of organizations. Significantly, one of these books was written by a sociologist in a business school (Thompson, 1967) and the other by a pair of psychologists (Katz and Kahn, 1978). (As one indication of the increasing complexity of studies in this field, compare Terreberry's [1968] three types of organizational environments with Jurkovich's [1974] 64-cell typology.) Aldrich (1979), a principal contributor to the recent literature on organizations and environments, has provided an excellent review and synthesis of that now extensive literature (see also papers in Meyer and Associates, 1978).

Voluntary Associations and Their Environments

Many organizational types face similar pressures from the environment and use comparable strategies for coping with those pressures, but voluntary associations' relationships to their environments are especially precarious. Unlike business organizations, for example, voluntary associations cannot bind members to the organization with money incentives while weathering a storm resulting from low morale or a bad public image. They rarely have adequate funds for "market research" on how to attract new members (although a marketing literature for nonprofit organizations is developing; see Kotler, 1974). And, because members' incentives are often derived from the quality of interpersonal relations, voluntary groups cannot use advertising as a means of building a corporate image independent of the character of their personnel (Roe and Wood, 1975).

Of the many possible elements of voluntary associations' environments, we will focus on three. The first is a combination of the stability and complexity of the environment. Jurkovich (1974) included complexity as one of the six most important elements of organizational environments. He also included both stability and rate of change, but in measuring these elements he limited his attention to goal change. Complexity and instability were also implied in Terreberry's (1968) discussion of the "turbulence" of the environment. We reason that organizations with stable and simpler environments should be better able to calculate external contingencies and deal with them appropriately. Hence, such organizations are expected to attain their external goals better. The first of three propositions about the relationship between the environment and goal effectiveness follows from this logic:

6. The more stable and simple an association's environment, the more effective its social influence.

A second aspect of the environment is the extent to which an organization has opportunities to mobilize its membership for social influence attempts. Just as a combat unit may be in danger of losing the fine-honed edge of both its skills and its discipline when there are no battles (hence, maneuvers are devised to simulate battles), associations in environments that seldom require the exercise of social influence may be unprepared to take advantage of any opportunities that do arise. Hence:

7. The more often the environment provides opportunities to mobilize an association's membership for social influence, the more effective the association's social influence.

Finally, Thompson and McEwen (1958) argued for a direct relation between goal setting and interorganizational strategies for coping with the environment. They discussed competition, bargaining, cooptation, and coalition as basic strategies for gaining security to pursue organizational goals. Since Thompson and McEwen wrote their article, the analysis of interorganizational relationships has become increasingly more sophisticated (see the literature discussed in Chapter Eight). An association may achieve a particular place in a larger organizational network as the result of a conscious strategy (as implied by Thompson and McEwen), or the association's position in the network may be forced upon it by circumstances—including the strategies of other organizations seeking secure positions for themselves (Galaskiewicz, 1979). In either case, at any given moment an association's position in a community's organizational network is both an environment and an opportunity structure for exercising social influence in a larger environment. Accordingly, the third environmental proposition may be stated as follows:

8. The more favorable an association's position in the inter-organizational network of its community, the more effective its social influence.

Chapter Two

Social Influence Associations

On April 5, 1977, fifty people with varying disabilities—wheelchair-bound, blind, deaf, or retarded—crowded into the offices of Health, Education, and Welfare Secretary Joseph Califano, demanding that he implement a four-year-old law extending civil rights guarantees to the handicapped. Handicapped protesters sat-in during the next three weeks in a dozen cities from New York to San Francisco. By the end of the month, Califano capitulated and signed the regulations despite HEW's estimate that it would cost up to $2.4 billion a year to sweep away architectural barriers, litigate discrimination in employment, and redesign schools and training programs. A blind spokesperson for the American Coalition of Citizens with Disabilities, which coordinated the demonstrations, hailed the victory as a signal that a militant new minority had found its voice.

Protest, demonstration, and orderly petitioning for social change by disaffected Americans has become almost an evening-news ritual. Such visible, dramatic gestures are less spontaneous emotional eruptions than careful tactics by formal social organizations mobilizing their resources against the status quo.

The prevalence and importance of formal voluntary associations in stimulating collective political action is acknowledged in recent sociological theories (Tilly, 1978; Wilson and Orum, 1976; McCarthy and Zald, 1977). In this book we deal not with collective protest in general but with those voluntary associations most likely to provide the social support basis for political action efforts on behalf of constituent members or clientele. These voluntary associations have been variously called "instrumental voluntary associations" (Jacoby and Babchuk, 1963); "interest groups" (Zeigler, 1964; Holtzman, 1966); and even "political organizations" (Wilson, 1973). However, following Arnold Rose (1967), we shall refer to them as *social influence associations.* Such organizations typically have an interest in changing or preserving social conditions that either affect members directly (e.g., a labor union seeking higher wages for members) or affect others in whom the members have an interest (e.g., a group seeking better facilities for the mentally retarded). Our attention centers on formal organizations—those with a clearly definable membership and consciously adopted name—whose members are generally neither full-time employees nor otherwise dependent on the organization for their livelihood (Smith, Reddy, and Baldwin, 1972). A more precise definition of the organizations selected for analysis appears later in the chapter.

Social influence associations may be contrasted with "sociable" (or "expressive") voluntary associations, whose primary purpose is to provide members with direct means to gratify their affiliative needs (Aldrich, 1971). Sociable organizations such as fraternities and service clubs generally do not need to influence persons outside the organizational boundaries to achieve their primary formal goals. For example, a recreation club can usually provide its members with organized activities without the cooperation of other institutions. Social influence associations, however, cannot change conditions solely by their own efforts. They must influence decision makers in other social institutions (legislatures, government agencies and executives, courts, schools, corporations) to apply *their* authority to implement desired policies.

Social influence associations embrace a wide variety of functional, or "common-sense," types of voluntary associations. Almost every area of organized social life contains a host of such organizations designed to advance the aims of some segment of the population. In terms of sheer numbers of members, churches are the most prevalent voluntary association in America, although many do not engage in social influence in the way we described.

Economic associations—including trade councils, labor unions, and professional societies—constitute another large portion of the voluntary association population. Their primary goal is to further the economic well-being of their members, typically through influencing government to intervene favorably in the marketplace. Health and medical voluntary associations are a third major group. Many of their activities revolve around fund raising for research or direct patient services, but influencing public health policies is also an important objective. Another, and growing, type of voluntary association is the neighborhood or community organization dedicated to preserving or improving local conditions. Other associations try to improve the condition of racial and ethnic minorities, women, students, criminal offenders, amateur athletes, draft evaders—virtually any group seeking solutions to its problems through collective action.

Indianapolis and Indiana

Mention Indianapolis to any non-Hoosier and the first thing likely to come to mind is the annual "500" auto race. As a site for research on social influence associations, Indianapolis has much to recommend it besides easy access from Indiana University fifty miles away in Bloomington. Planned in 1820 as the state capital at the geographic center of the state, Indianapolis in 1970 had a population of 744,624. According to the 1970 census, Indianapolis was the nation's eleventh largest city (behind Cleveland and ahead of Milwaukee), situated in an eight-county standard metropolitan statistical area (SMSA) of 1,109,882 people, the twenty-ninth largest in the country. The discrepancy between city and SMSA rankings comes from the absence of any other large central city in the immediate vicinity.

If population composition is a sound basis for generalization, Indianapolis would appear an ideal research locale. As Table A.1 in Appendix A makes clear, Indianapolis closely approximates the national and the all-SMSA averages for a variety of descriptive statistics. The major departure is the proportion of the population with foreign origins (foreign-born or second generation). One-fifth the population of an average SMSA has foreign origins, but only one-twentieth of the Indianapolis SMSA population is so counted. Unlike Chicago, New York, Buffalo, Boston, and many other industrial cities, Indianapolis never attracted a large immigrant stream during the late nineteenth and early twentieth centuries. No ethnic groups are large enough to produce identifiable ethnic neighborhoods, and local politics is largely devoid of the social cleavages (other than black-white conflict) that once characterized the older cities of the eastern United States.

Indianapolis is a multifunction city. Besides serving as the state capital—one-seventh of its labor force is in government work—it boasts a diverse manufacturing economy (major industries are RCA, Allison, Western Electric, Ford, Chrysler, and Bridgeport Brass; see Leary, 1973:216). More than half the labor force is in white-collar occupations, reflecting the substantial service sector and accounting for a slightly more affluent population than the average SMSA.

Politically, Indianapolis is fairly representative of a fundamentally conservative and Republican state. Democratic mayors between 1951 and 1967 were succeeded by two Republican mayors (Richard Lugar and William Hudnut), the first of whom was later elected to the United States Senate. Similarly, two Democratic governors were followed by a two-term Republican, Otis Bowen. Control of the state legislature seesawed recently between the two parties. In national elections, with the exception of the Johnson landslide in 1964, no Democrat has carried Indiana since Franklin Roosevelt. Indiana has a long tradition of resisting federal government aid, with the result that the state consistently ranks near the bottom in terms of per capita grants received from Washington. An historical perspective on the curious Hoosier political mixture is found in the Ku Klux Klan control of the State House in the 1920s, the 1958 founding of the John Birch Society in an Indianapolis living room, and the reelection in the 1960s and 1970s of the liberal Birch Bayh to the Senate (Leary, 1973).

Indianapolis local government was reorganized in 1969 by a legislative act that consolidated the City of Indianapolis and Marion County, creating what is colloquially referred to as "Unigov." (Four small municipalities were excluded from the merger.) The city is thus the largest unified local government in the country, one of nine successful consolidations in twenty-eight attempts in the nation since 1945 (Ostrom and Neubert, 1973). The formal government structure is basically a strong mayor-council one. The mayor, elected to a four-year term, appoints the heads of six major executive departments and the majority of members of all governing boards. A twenty-nine member city-county council is composed of four at-large members and twenty-five elected from single-member geographic districts. The council has exclusive power over general ordinance making for the county, while the mayor has item-veto authority subject to a two-thirds veto vote by the council. Apart from the consolidation, this city government form is found in about half of the central cities of the 1970 SMSAs (Dye and MacManus, 1976).

Some survey data is available to compare voluntary association memberships in Indianapolis with the nation. In 1967 an Indianapolis Area Project found that 57 percent of the adult population belonged to one or more voluntary associations (excluding churches), very close to the 59 percent in a 1967 National Opinion Research Center national sample. In 1977 an NORC national study found that 62 percent of respondents belonged to at least one voluntary association. This classification, however, embraces all types of organizations, the majority of which probably are not social influence associations. Narrowing the range to embrace only service-civic clubs, political organizations, and charitable groups, the Indianapolis sample shows 15 percent in these categories and the two national samples 14 and 16 percent respectively. Thus, in gross terms the Indianapolis general population approximates the national norm for joining voluntary associations.

This brief overview of the city and state in which our research was conducted implies that, despite some unique aspects, Indianapolis is fairly typical of other urban settings. Findings about social influence associations based on this study should hold for a large number of comparable cities, though only careful replications of the present study in other environments can confirm or disprove that conjecture.

Defining the Sample

Designing a study of membership commitment in social influence associations involves a series of compromises and trade-offs. An intensive case study of a single organization, using multiple methods of participant observation and survey interviews, would surely produce an in-depth portrait of vastly richer dimension than any other approach. Case studies such as those by Sills (1957) and Lipset, Trow, and Coleman (1956) advanced our understanding of the way voluntary associations ensure their members' loyalty. But the case study runs an enormous risk of capitalizing upon idiosyncrasies, particularly historical fluctuations at the time of observation. Separating the general from the unique becomes especially troublesome in the absence of comparable organizations upon which to construct a baseline from which deviations can be charted. Efforts to unravel the effects of organizational structure founder when only one organization with a unique structure is available for analysis.

A sample survey of the general population of a community or society has the virtue of permitting maximum generalization about people's behavior in and toward their organizations. Because respondents are drawn into the study in proportion to their frequency in the population, conclusions about rates and proportions would be highly reliable. But the survey of individuals is unable to perform meaningful analyses of organizational effects. A sizable portion of the adult population does not belong to any voluntary association, and many more do not belong to social influence associations. Further, few respondents in a survey of acceptable size share membership in the same organization, thus rendering impossible the comparative analysis of organizational attributes aggregated from individuals.

Another approach would be to draw a large sample of voluntary associations from a listed population and to interview key informants such as officials about their organization. This strategy, often used in studies of formal work organizations such as business corporations and the government agencies, means that informants could not give accurate responses about many of the organizational variables with which we are concerned. Evidence on the mass membership's attitudes and many of their behaviors can only be collected from the members themselves.

The compromise we chose was to sample a small set of social influence associations and within each organization to select a sample of members. The details of the sampling procedure are contained in Appendix B and will not be recapitulated here except in broad outline. The two-stage sampling process required us to enumerate a defined population of social influence associations in the Indianapolis area (Marion County), sample a set of organizations that would maximize variation in organizational purposes and structures, and draw a sufficient number of members from various formal roles within each organization to reach meaningful conclusions about authority and participation in each organization.

The definition of social influence associations, spelled out in Appendix B, serves mainly to eliminate certain types of voluntary associations from the population. These excluded groups are trade unions, business associations, professional societies, and "sociable" voluntary associations. The organizations remaining seek as a primary goal neither to advance the economic gains of members nor to gratify members' affiliative needs. This study does not pretend to analyze all types of voluntary associations, only "social influence" associations—those voluntary groups with instrumental objectives of affecting social conditions by influencing other societal institutions.

Within each organization participating in the study, stratified random samples of respondents were drawn for interviews. Details of this design are found in Appendix B. While organizational leaders comprise only about 15 percent of all members, our design ensured that about one-third of the completed interviews would be with leaders and two-thirds with members and/or volunteers. All presidents and executive directors, where such existed, were interviewed.

A total of 820 interviews were completed in thirty-two organizations, an average of 25.6 per organization, with a range from 11 to 49. In the chapters ahead, the unit of analysis will be not the individual member and that member's characteristics, but the thirty-two associations. Organizational characteristics may be global (e.g., size, budget) or rates of membership attributes aggregated from individual reports (e.g., alienation, meeting attendance). Hypotheses tested therefore refer to behavior of organizations rather than to behavior of persons in organizations. Organizational anonymity and respondent confidentiality were promised and are safeguarded in this volume by pseudonyms whenever we refer to a specific organization.

The Sample Associations

In many of the forthcoming analyses we are interested in overall averages, trends, and relationships among variable attributes of organizations and of their members. From time to time illustrations from specific associations will underscore important points. Deviant cases, exceptions, and statistical outliers can each in their own way illuminate general situations. To facilitate reader comprehension of individual associations, as well as to put empirical flesh on theoretical bones, thirty-two thumbnail sketches of the organizations follow. This catalog can serve as a handy reference guide for establishing a context for understanding some interesting and/or puzzling relationships reported later in this volume. In giving these thumbnail sketches, as well as later factual information about specific organizations, we have been careful not to reveal detailed information that would enable an astute reader to guess an association's true identity.

Legal-Justice Associations

1. Legal-Beagles, Inc. (LBI). This state-wide association is affiliated with a national body. Members living in Indianapolis do not have a local chapter although locals exist in other cities; instead, the state officers act for the Indianapolis membership. Major goal of the organization is to litigate court cases bearing on legal matters in which its members have an interest of a nonpersonal nature.

2. Reform of Repressive Laws (RRL). A state-wide association

affiliated with a national organization, this organization's main purpose centers on the legislative repeal of laws its members find noxious.

3. Better Housing Now (BHN). A state-wide association that has no national body, BHN aims primarily to change housing laws in Indiana to provide greater tenant rights.

4. Kids in Trouble (KIT). The Indianapolis chapter is affiliated with a state-wide organization that has no national body. The local organization was created the year before our study, although many members belonged to the state organization for several years. KIT attracts mainly legal-system and social-work professionals interested in the legal rights of children.

5. Rights for Prisoners (RFP). A commission begun by a coalition of religious organizations and now affiliated with a state-wide ecumenical body. Its main purpose is to gain more equitable treatment for prisoners and ex-offenders.

6. Pro-Life Coalition (PLC). One of several antiabortion groups, PLC is controlled by a religious organization. Its members specialize in giving direct assistance to women with problem pregnancies.

7. Freedom from Fear (FFF). Freedom from Fear is a locally organized group that seeks more favorable treatment for victims of violent crimes.

Health–Mental Health Associations

8. Organized Blind Persons (OBP). A local chapter of one of several associations for blind persons, OBP is chartered by a national group. It aims to improve the legal status of blind persons as well as to provide a setting for social activities.

9. Health Professionals Coalition (HPC). This organization is a state-wide association chartered by a national group. It tries to enlist members from the general public as well as professionals. Through education and legislative activity, HPC seeks to enhance and safeguard the status of professionals.

10. Advocates for the Handicapped (AFH). A state-wide commission of both individuals and organizational representatives, it

tries to coordinate legislative activities for funding and program development.

11. Health Outreach Program (HOP). This local unit is chartered by a state-wide organization that is affiliated with a national body. HOP provides extensive health services to its clientele, using both professional and volunteer labor; it also engages in legislative influence activities.

12. Society for Disease Elimination (SDE). A state chapter chartered by a national, SDE is typical of a large number of "disease-oriented" associations which combine public education, fund-raising, research, and some legislative activity to increase efforts to detect, treat, and cure a specific debilitating disease.

13. Organization for Retarded Persons (ORP). Affiliated with a national group, this state body of local chapter representatives advocates better programs and treatment for its clientele.

14. Organized Deaf Persons (ODP). Also affiliated with a national organization, this state-wide body has an individual membership that both engages in legislative and executive-agency influence and serves as a social group.

Civic Action Associations

15. Women's Rights Organization (WRO). A chartered local chapter with state and national parent organizations, WRO emphasizes a wide range of issues important to women.

16. Nature Lovers' Society (NLS). The local chapter is chartered by regional and national organizations. The organization's interests include conservation as well as social activities for members.

17. Ethnic Protection Society (EPS). A state body chartered by a national, it is mainly a watchdog commission to ensure more favorable treatment of minorities in Indiana.

18. Civic Advancement League (CAL). This local unit of volunteers coordinates and assists other service agencies to carry out their activities.

19. Senior Citizens Society (SCS). One of several chapters in the state embracing agencies and interested individuals in sev-

eral counties. Coordination of activities and improvement of services to the elderly are its main objectives.

20. Disaster Relief Society (DRS). The local chapter is chartered by a national body. DRS aids victims of natural and man-made disasters.

21. Civil Rights Organization (CRO). The local unit is chartered by regional and national parent organizations. It emphasizes a wide range of problems encountered by blacks, and also delivers counselling and employment-training services to individuals.

22. Coalition of Women Activists (CWA). The local chapter is chartered by a state and national body. It works on a wide range of issues affecting women.

23. Women's Political Alliance (WPA). The local chapter is affiliated with a state and national body. The organization tries to influence issues revolving around women's status in society.

24. Wilderness Preservation Organization (WPO). The state chapter is chartered by regional and national bodies. It concentrates on legislation affecting conservation practices and offers members outdoor recreational activities.

Neighborhood and Community

25. Shady Grove (SG). This association in a low-income transient black area faces several problems—crime, physical deterioration, and lack of financial support for a community-center program.

26. Elm Lawn (EL). This organization is in a white middle-class neighborhood with a history of zoning conflicts with the city.

27. River Green (RG). This association in an upper-class residential neighborhood (houses in $100,000 range) has relatively few current community problems.

28. Poplar Drive (PD). PD is another association in an upper-class residential community with a relatively quiescent situation.

29. Downtown (DT). This association of community leaders in a racially mixed working- and lower-class inner-city community

confronts problems of service delivery, adult education, and youth delinquency. It is a Community Action Against Poverty (CAAP) affiliate.

30. Locust Hills (LH). This organization in a working- and lower-middle-class inner-city black community with some remaining white families addresses undesirable situations in two city parks, and similar problems.

31. Uptown (UT). This umbrella group of neighborhood associations has both group and individual members from a large white working-class community. Problems include physical deterioration and lack of amenities.

32. Westend (WE). An umbrella group of block associations, Westend has both group and individual members from mainly white working-class areas. This organization is an action unit of a multiservice center. Problems include service delivery and physical deterioration.

Association Characteristics

On the whole, our sampling design selected a diverse set of social influence associations according to their substantive goals. The groups run the gamut of social controversies of the middle 1970s: women, disabled persons, ethnic minorities, abortion, environmental concerns, delinquents, prisoners' rights, crime victims, drug laws, the aged, neighborhood control, and so forth. One obvious shortcoming of the sample is the relative paucity of organizations favoring conservative or right-wing solutions to social problems. This imbalance may reflect a greater tendency for liberal groups to be active and well publicized at the local level, but it also reflects a higher refusal rate among conservative groups (such as the John Birch Society and the American Legion) asked to participate in the study. Even so, the individual respondents are approximately evenly distributed among Democrats and Republicans and across a self-identified liberal-conservative scale. Several groups were active in current controversies, such as the attempt to ratify the Equal Rights Amendment in the Indiana legislature and efforts to attain more equitable treatment for the disabled.

That the sampling procedure selected social influence associations is borne out by the respondents' own impressions of their organizations. The first question in the interview was to state in their own words what their organization was all about. Almost all the responses identified social influence features. More than a third mentioned either political or legislative advocacy and action, 10 percent cited public educational-informational efforts, and another 15 percent pointed to improvement of situations without stating specific actions involved. Twenty-two percent said the organization's purpose was to provide direct services to individuals (which was in fact true of several organizations), which may be construed as departing from a general social influence orientation. Virtually no members, however, mentioned either attainment of personal economic benefits or sociable goals as the main objective of their organization. Clearly, from the point of view of both leaders and ordinary members, these organizations qualify as social influence associations.

A major assumption of the present study is that voluntary organizations depend largely upon their members to generate resources necessary for organizational maintenance and goal attainment. Later in this book, *resources* will be broadly defined to include material and nonmaterial facilities such as participation and tolerance of leader decision. Confining attention here only to financial resources, considerable variation occurs in income sources among the thirty-two associations. In Table 2.1 organizations are classified by the total size of their annual budgets and the mean proportions derived from four sources. In general, the larger the budget, the more likely the organization is to rely upon sources other than members. Three groups had no current income. Most organizations with budgets below $2,000 per year were able to raise all or most of their income from dues, contributions, or fund-raiser events such as parties. Contracts and grants from city or federal agencies or the direct sale of products or services to clientele accounted for nearly half the income of medium-budget associations, although five of these ten organizations

Table 2.1. Sources of Financial Support for 32 Associations

Size of budget	Average proportion derived from				Total (N)
	Dues, fund raisers	Contracts, services	United Way or CAAP	Other	
$50,000–500,000	24%	43%	28%	5%	100% (7)
$2,000–50,000	49%	40%	6%	5%	100% (10)
$2,000 or less	87%	13%	0%	0%	100% (12)
No income	0	0	0	0	100% (3)

produced 90 percent or more of their budget from dues and contributions. But among the seven affluent associations, only two raised a majority of their funds from members (Ethnic Protection Society) or from a door-to-door campaign (Society for Disease Elimination). The other five associations (Health Outreach Program, Civic Advancement League, Civil Rights Organization, Senior Citizens Society, Downtown Neighborhood Association) received the bulk of their money from contracts and grants or as designate-associations in either the United Way or Community Action Against Poverty. These large voluntary associations typically employed professional staff as well as volunteers to deliver multiple services to target clientele such as the aged, the mentally disturbed, the physically handicapped, the unemployed, the uneducated, neglected or abused children, and low-income tenants.

Our initial assumption that voluntary associations acquire their resources mainly from members is not true for financial support among about a quarter of the sample associations. In these instances we are perhaps observing the transformation of an association into a semibureaucratic, professionalized formal organization. However, even the very affluent organizations still retain a substantial voluntary membership component in accord with the formal definition for inclusion in the sample. Although members provide only a fraction of the financial resources, they may still contribute other important resources—time, participation, responsiveness to mobilization. Even indirectly, the voluntary participants can help their association obtain money from third parties. Many government agencies, foundations, and central fund drives insist upon hard evidence that an organization has community support before they will authorize contracts and grants to the group. A sizable, committed voluntary membership is a vital nonmaterial asset that an association can cite to attract further financial resources.

Social influence associations typically operate under normative constraints of an ideology of membership control, and there is abundant evidence that the associations in our sample at least pay lip service to this norm. Several aspects of the written constitutions and the responses of principal officers suggest that almost all the organizations studied facilitate some degree of membership control.

The meetings of the chief policy-making bodies (board of directors or set of officers) are open to the general membership in thirty-one of the thirty-two organizations. One organization, the Pro-Life Coalition, has no policy-making unit; the leaders of its parent organization—a religious organization—set its policies against abortion and birth control. In most associations, policy-making meetings are frequent enough to allow members several contacts throughout the year. In twenty-six organizations the policy-making body meets at least four times a year (and half of the sample associations have at least ten meetings per year). Newsletters keep members informed of pending actions and past decisions. Nineteen associations mail newsletters at least quarterly (monthly in twelve groups), and only three have no regular newsletter or other publication.

In twenty-six organizations the general membership elects the chief policy-making body. And more than half the organizations have special provisions to prohibit the perpetuation of board control. For example:

Nine organizations provide that the majority of the nominating committee must come from the general membership and/or provide for additional nominations from the floor.

Six organizations limit board members' terms to two years or less.
Three organizations provide for membership recall of board members and officers.

The most dramatic example is the provision in the Organized Deaf Persons that the board dies during the biennial convention so that the delegates (any member who attends is a delegate) are the sole policy-making body during that time.

We asked our principal-officer informants whether there were any organizational decisions that could not be challenged by the membership. Responses indicated that members of all thirty-one organizations with local policy-making bodies could challenge any decision made by those bodies. Two officers indicated, however, that certain policies central to the purpose of their organization could not be challenged, and three other officers indicated that the local membership could not challenge national decisions.

When asked whether members had opportunities to influence major policy decisions, thirty principal-officer informants voiced their belief that nonofficers had a genuine opportunity to influence major policy decisions. Twenty-six thought that speaking one's mind to the board or at a regular meeting was an effective way to influence policy. Three additional informants felt that expressing an opinion to officers or staff would be most effective. Another stated that nonofficers could join or even head committees that influence major policy.

Thus, an overwhelming majority of the sample associations take precautions to allow ordinary members input into major policy decisions. Provision of such opportunities is not, of course, synonymous with their use in daily operations. Associations undoubtedly vary considerably in the extent to which the normative ideal of membership control is realized in actual decision making. Norms never translate into action in a simple equation. Furthermore, some norms encourage members to refrain from control attempts when those attempts derive from interests that are not shared by the collectivity or will stand in the way of the attainment of the organization's goals. Nonetheless, we have documented that the vast majority of sample social influence associations at least nominally assent to the idea that the membership should have the ultimate say in what actions the organization undertakes. Later in the book we will look at the members' assessment of their opportunities for participating in decisions.

Respondent Characteristics

Research on the social characteristics of members of all types of voluntary associations has repeatedly documented the disproportionate concentration of people of high socioeconomic status in these organizations (Wright and Hyman, 1958; Hausknecht, 1962; Hyman and Wright, 1971; Verba and Nie, 1972:200–204). The respondents in our sample social influence associations are no exception. Comparison of the sample with a national sample survey collected in the same year (the 1977 General Social Survey of the National Opinion Research Center [NORC]) shows this upward bias in social class.

Members of our sample social influence associations are overwhelmingly in nonmanual occupations: more than 85 percent work or have worked in professional, managerial, or clerical and sales jobs. Nationally, only 48 percent of the adult population have nonmanual occupations. The mean occupational prestige score (NORC) for the association respondents is 50, a standard deviation above the national average of 30. In our social influence association sample, the mean years of formal education is 15 and the mean family income is $25,600, markedly higher than the national norms of 12.2 years of schooling and $15,400 annual (1977) family income. Taken together, the characteristics of the social influence associations strongly suggest a dominant upper-middleclass membership to this type of voluntary organization.

Other social background attributes of the Indianapolis respondents reflect smaller departures from distributions found in the local population. Most respondents are white; the 20 percent who are black belong mainly to civil rights and certain neighborhood associations. Women outnumber men in the sample by 58 to 42 percent, in part from the presence of several associations whose membership is virtually all female. Protestants (62 percent of sample) are present in proportion to national levels (66 percent), but Catholics are underrepresented by 16 percent and Jews over-represented by 8 percent (nationally Catholics are 24 percent and Jews 2 percent; Indianapolis, however, has relatively few ethnic groups from Catholic countries compared to other large Mid-western cities). Jewish overrepresentation in our sample occurs because of that group's higher social status and generally greater political activity. Most sample respondents are currently married (70 percent compared to 66 percent nationally), and a majority have children living at home. The median age of the association members (48 years) is older than that of the adult population of the country (43 years). On the whole, then, the sample respon-dents exhibit an upper-socioeconomic class profile typical of other voluntary association joiners, but on other attributes they do not depart substantially from the demographic distributions of the general adult population.

A Note on Data Analysis

The theory of political action by voluntary associations is de-veloped and tested at the level of organizations. The hypotheses concern covariation between properties of organizations, not the attributes of individual members of social influence associations. While organizational concepts are the relevant explanatory vari-ables, several are represented indirectly by aggregating members' characteristics. For example, *decentralization* is the proportion of the membership participating in making important decisions, based on self-reports by all respondents interviewed in an asso-ciation. Decentralization is a property of the association, not of in-dividual persons, and will be analyzed in relation to other organi-zational phenomena, such as the level of normative social control (that is, commitment) and goal attainment. At the level of the indi-vidual, participation in decision making may be an important be-havior explainable by combinations of individual variables (e.g., education, outside time obligations) and organizational variables (e.g., frequency of meetings, committee structure). But our theory deliberately ignores processes operating at the individual level, since to include such cross-level analyses would further complicate the research task. (See the article by Lincoln and Zeitz, 1980, for a cogent discussion of using data on organizations aggregated from the reports of individual participants.) While the problem of individual member motivation and behavior in social influence associations is worthy of attention in its own right, a full treatment must await a separate study.

The sample size, thirty-two associations, fundamentally constrains the analyses that can be performed to test the theoretical hypotheses. The limited data points prevent us from inspecting relationships between variables in cross-tabulation format. Even with dichotomous measures, simultaneously cross-tabulating more than three variables would result in so many empty cells that meaningful patterns would be impossible to detect. Instead, we rely upon linear statistics—bivariate correlations and multiple regression equations—that allow us to determine whether two empirical variables covary systematically as predicted by the theory, even after holding constant variation induced by other factors.

Even with the linear model, however, simultaneously controlling many independent variables is unjustified. One rule of thumb is to have at least ten cases per independent variable. Although we often will violate this conventional wisdom, we seldom include more than a half dozen independent variables. Another complication that occurs when additional variables are added is that the standard errors of all the regression coefficients increase. Larger confidence intervals increase the probability of rejecting variables as statistically insignificant that really do affect the dependent variable.

Therefore, the data limit us to considering only a handful of independent variables at one time. In deciding which ones to include, we rely mainly upon theoretical considerations to specify the selection of variables to explain variation in organizational behavior.

With so few cases to begin with, we are also unable to explore possible contingent or conditional relationships that might prove to be exceptions to the theoretical expectation. For example, neighborhood associations and nonterritorial groups may differ in the extent to which two variables such as resources and goal attainment vary together. But with only a handful of neighborhood groups, trying to isolate such interesting specifications on the basic theoretical propositions become impossible. Only a much larger sample will permit exploration of such differences among social influence associations.

In testing the theory, we follow an incremental strategy, beginning with zero-order correlations between pairs of indicators of theoretical concepts. If the empirical evidence supports a theoretical hypothesis, we next introduce other variables into a multiple regression equation, both to observe what contribution such additional measures make and also to determine whether the original relationship changes when these other factors are statistically held constant. This procedure is especially insightful in tracing direct and indirect effects between variables implied in the theoretical causal scheme. In working with a type of organization and a set of measures that have seldom been analyzed before, a cautious, incremental strategy seems preferable to immediately analyzing complex and sophisticated relationships among many indicators.

Finally, the tables and discussions to follow frequently refer to the statistical significance of relationships. With so few data points, correlations and regression coefficients must be sizable to attain significance under the usual assumptions of simple random sampling, let alone the more complex stratified design used in this study. Since the actual sampling distribution for our design is unknown, we use significance tests for simple random samples primarily to decide the importance of relationships in the data. Correlations with a probability equal to or less than .05 of coming from a sampling distribution with a population value of zero are noted. For multiple regression coefficients, a more liberal .10 probability is noted.

Chapter Three

The Incentive Approach
to Social Control

The Nature Lovers' Society, one of two major national conservation groups, boasts a large mass membership. The Indianapolis chapter numbers more than a thousand members, yet only a few dozen ever attend the monthly meetings. The national organization conducts extensive conservation activities: lobbying Congress, fighting court cases, building wildlife refuges, conducting wilderness tours, and trying to enhance nature conservancy attitudes in the general population. Yet when members of the Indianapolis NLS were asked why they had joined the organization in the first place, only a minority cited these goal-oriented activities.

The overwhelming majority of NLS members said they joined to receive the magazine published monthly by the national organization. The magazine is full of wildlife articles, award-winning photographs, and updates on conservation controversies. Several respondents said that they received subscriptions as gifts, and some did not realize that they had thereby been automatically enrolled as dues-paying members in the Indianapolis chapter (the national organization gives a percentage of the annual dues to local units to support their activities). The NLS has obviously hit upon a successful formula to boost membership by offering an attractive material inducement, although, as we shall see, members' commitments often extend no further than the annual subscription renewal.

The Nature Lovers' Society stands out in our sample as a social influence association that relies heavily for membership resource contributions on an exchange of material incentives. Most associations lack adequate material resources to offer material rewards of comparable magnitude or value and must therefore structure a different set of inducements. This chapter explores the hypothesis relating organizational incentives and the social influence association membership's commitment.

Incentive theory is a logical beginning, since the concept of organizational inducements is rooted in individuals' earliest decisions to affiliate with a collectivity and to maintain membership. The combination of individual motives for joining and of organizational incentive offerings constitutes a person-organization system with major implications for a group's ability to generate high levels of membership commitment.

The central theoretical hypothesis to be examined in this chapter is:

1. The greater the incentives offered by the association, the stronger the membership's commitment.

Among the various types of incentives available, purposive incentives will be most important for social influence associations. To understand why we believe this will be so, we must delve into the history of incentive theory.

Incentive Theory

Formal organizations face the perennial problem of motivating their participants to apply their energies effectively toward achieving the collectivity's goals. A huge literature (see Work in America Institute, 1978; and Dachler and Wilpert, 1978, for recent overviews) treats various aspects of maximizing worker performance in production organizations. Research on the relative effectiveness of wage and salary schedules, working conditions, job enrichment programs, status perquisites, and the like can all be viewed as attempts to understand how organizational arrangements of work and its rewards can enhance employee performance. March and Simon (1958:84) succinctly stated a guiding principle behind such research: "Each participant will continue his participation in the organization only so long as the inducements offered him are as great or greater (measured in terms of *his* values and in terms of alternatives open to him) than the contributions he is asked to make." In formal work organizations, financial compensation is usually the basic incentive used by the organization to obtain employees' labor time. Utilitarian motives are thought to predominate in workers' decisions to participate in the organization. Only the top policy makers need to be concerned about the specific ends toward which work efforts are directed, since financial incentives normally create a "zone of indifference" among the lower-level participants (Barnard, 1938: Chapter XII).

In contrast to production organizations, voluntary associations find member participation extremely problematic because they cannot rely on utilitarian incentives and pecuniary motives. Unable to exchange money for activity, voluntary associations often rely on other types of incentives. A common complaint by leaders of churches, social clubs, and political organizations is the episodic and unreliable involvement of the mass membership. Still, social influence associations differ markedly among themselves in their ability to mobilize their members to contribute time, labor, money, effort, and psychological support toward collective action.

Incentive theory applied to organizations has a strong theoretical root in exchange theory as formulated by sociologists such as Homans (1961) and Blau (1964). Because several expositions of exchange theory are available (Ekeh, 1974; Heath, 1976), we will sketch only its main features before indicating the theory's relevance to organizational incentives. Sociological versions of exchange theory have philosophical origins in utilitarian microeconomics, with a generous dash of psychological conditioning theory in some versions (Emerson, 1972a; 1972b). While Homans sought to reduce all social behavior to a small set of psychological principles, Blau was more sensitive to emergent properties of collectivities. Thus, for our purposes, the Blau version is most useful for developing an analytical model of exchange between members and social influence associations.

Unlike the motivations of actors in economic exchange theory (see Downs, 1957, and Olson, 1965, for applications of economically derived choice theory to noneconomic situations), in which the values of goods and services are designated by prices in a monetary system, social exchange rests upon unspecified obligations between exchanging parties. A relationship of trust must emerge between social exchangers—the belief that benefits will ultimately be reciprocated in the future even though the obligations cannot be rigorously priced like economic commodities—if the relationship is to be sustained. Social exchange thus sets up a situation where feelings of "personal obligation, gratitude, and trust" develop between parties in social exchange (Blau, 1964: 94–95).

In collectivities with common goals, such as social influence associations, "the individual who makes contributions to their attainment obligates all members to accept him as their superior in return for advantages they all derive from his efforts" (Blau, 1964:198). Organizational leaders structure and control the set of incentive offerings used to induce members to relinquish their personal resources to the organization (i.e., to the organization leaders or agents). The advantages members derive from the leaders' efforts are the successful exercise of power in bargaining with other centers of institutional power in the society. The successful achievement of social influence through external power in its turn increases the leaders' advantage in internal exchanges with members, thus further enhancing the leaders' power relative to that of members (Blau, 1964:223, 321).

An individual must decide whether and in what amounts to commit personally controlled resources to a collectivity. The amount depends on the anticipated mix of collective and personal objectives to be obtained, compared to the mixture obtainable elsewhere for the same resource investment. Organizational behavior can affect these subjective estimates, or utilities, by offering rewards (incentives) or threatening deprivations (sanctions) in return for participation. By offering sufficient incentives, an organization can overcome members' tendencies to commit resources to other activities where they can obtain greater net "profit" for their resource "investments." Most voluntary associations do not have enough control over their boundaries to make coercive sanctions meaningful incentives for members. Hence, only positive incentives are effective for voluntary associations, and most voluntary groups lack substantial material resources to provide highly valued financial incentives that can be readily transferred to external situations.

Therefore, the main classes of positive incentives available to most voluntary associations are those with low transferability: intrinsic satisfaction from associating with other members; intrinsic satisfaction from the tasks the group performs; and satisfaction from the goals the organization strives to attain (Zald and Jacobs, 1978). Given the great intangibility of such incentive offerings and the difficulty of determining whether they are being adequately supplied in return for participation, both organizations (personified by their leaders) and members may experience great uncertainty about their exchange relationship, each feeling they may be contributing more than they are receiving. The tendency at equilibrium is for voluntary associations to operate at suboptimal levels of resource acquisition from members.

A second source of resource shortfall comes from the "public good" nature of many social influence association goals. Some organizational incentives are directly delivered to individuals who contribute toward their production (a wildlife sanctuary restricted to members); others may be available to all members of a class regardless of their participation in its production (removal of all criminal penalties for marijuana smoking); other benefits may be secured only for third parties (improved treatment facilities for the mentally ill). A classic theoretical analysis by Mancur Olson (1965) suggested that collectivities that offer only public goods (those not exclusive to contributors) inevitably suffer from a "free rider" problem. Since the costs of production are likely to exceed most members' personal benefits, no incentive exists for most members to bear the costs of production; hence, suboptimal (or no) amounts of the good will be produced. Olson argued that unless coercion or selective incentives (private goods) were also supplied to members, collective objectives would seldom be obtained. One exception might be in small groups where a few rich patrons could supply the collective good because of their personal satisfaction (this argument has been strongly criticized as unrealistic; see Riker and Ordeshook, 1972:72–77; Frohlich, Oppenheimer, and Young, 1971:145–150). Applied to social influence associations, many of whose primary formal goals involve public goods, Olson's analysis suggests the importance of material incentives or intrinsic task and sociability activities as selective incentives for binding members to the association. Alternatively, members may gain compensating utility from their contributions either by identification with the direct beneficiaries or through "the sense of moral or altruistic self worth that comes through the assuagement of internalized values" (Zald and Jacobs, 1978:422).

The foregoing analysis indicates the potential impact of any type of organizational incentive on the normative social control beliefs of social influence association memberships. Several schemes for classifying incentive types have been proposed (Etzioni, 1975; Warriner and Prather, 1965; Zald and Jacobs, 1978), but the direct stimulus for our analysis was Peter B. Clark and James Q. Wilson's seminal paper (1961; see also Wilson, 1962 and 1973). The core of the Clark-Wilson incentive theory lies in its discrimination among three types of incentives that organizations may offer participants in return for contributions and the assertion that executives alter the incentive system so that the organization can persist despite environmental changes affecting supplies of incentive-yielding resources. Briefly:

1. *Material incentives* are tangible rewards that have monetary value or can be translated into monetary terms. Wages and salaries offered in utilitarian organizations are the most obvious example.
2. *Solidary incentives* are intangible benefits derived "in the main from the act of associating and include such rewards as socializing, congeniality, the sense of group membership and identification, status resulting from membership, fun, conviviality, the maintenance of social distinctions, and so forth."
3. Unlike the other two types, *purposive incentives* are inextricably tied to the organization's ultimate objectives and goals. Like solidary ties they are intangible, but they involve suprapersonal ends: "the demand for the enactment of certain laws or the adoption of certain practices (which do *not* benefit the members in any direct or tangible way)" (Clark and Wilson, 1961:135).

Clark and Wilson acknowledged that an organization might appeal to various motives of potential participants through a mix of incentives. No real organization relies exclusively on one type of incentive to attract and hold participants, although one incentive

may predominate. Similarly, participants in an organization seldom join and participate from only one motive. Thus, one important theoretical and empirical task is to determine how organizational incentives and participant motives vary together.

Previous Research

The Clark-Wilson incentive theory was developed largely to
aid understanding of organizational rather than individual behavior. To our knowledge, however, no previous studies have used
quantitative data from a sample of organizations for comparative
analysis of the effect of incentives on members. Most applications
have been discursive and anecdotal, as in Salisbury's (1969) interpretation of the American agricultural movement as an exchange
of material, solidary, or expressive benefits between members and
the entrepreneur/organizers of farm interest groups. Wilson's
(1973) book-length expansion of incentive theory used extensive
case studies to illustrate how political parties, labor unions, business associations, and civil rights organizations try to develop sufficient incentives to attract and hold members. Persuasive as his
examples are, the theory has yet to receive a rigorous empirical
examination.

Another set of articles, however, examined member motivations to participate in terms of the incentives involved. Warner
and Heffernan (1967) found that the more that benefits (such as
insurance, fellowship, information, or purchasing of supplies and
services) in three Wisconsin farm organizations were viewed as
contingent upon members' participation, the higher was a farm-
er's involvement. Several studies dealt with motivations of political party workers. Conway and Feigert (1968) showed that ideological or purposive rewards were the principal attraction for
Democratic and Republican precinct chairmen in two counties,
but that when asked what they would miss most if they gave up
their posts, they cited personal or social rewards most often. A
study of activists in the Canadian Liberal party (Clarke et al.,
1978) disclosed that purposive motives predominate in initiating
party activity but that social solidary motives increased in impor-

tance as reasons for sustaining activity. However, in a multiple regression of activity level, none of the three Clark-Wilson motives was statistically significant (partisan motives and length of office holding were the most important predictors).

These and other studies (e.g., Burgess and Conway, 1973) measured members' perceptions of the benefits to be gained from participation but did not measure the actual incentives available from the organization. With only three or four organizations and individual members taken as the unit of analysis, these studies could only focus on the member motivation side of incentive theory. But such research ignores the central idea of incentive theory—that an organization's provision of benefits is systematically related to other aspects of organizational behavior.

Measuring Incentives and Motives

To measure organizational incentive systems, we used information acquired through a two-hour, semistructured interview with a key informant, usually the president or executive director of each association. During one segment of the interview, informants were asked to indicate what benefits they felt attracted members to join and participate in the organization. Interviewers probed for solidary and material benefits as well as for the purposive attractions that were usually spontaneously volunteered.

The flavor and diversity of the incentive offerings can best be captured in a few examples.

One neighborhood organization leader said, "We enjoy getting together, having a good time, getting drunk together." Prizes were awarded annually for the best-kept lawn, and frequent picnics and parties were held. Another neighborhood group leader said that little sociability was involved and that no group activities occurred beyond an annual business meeting. The Health Professionals Coalition also held no social activities, but it did provide an extensive array of material incentives, including scholarships for continuing education, tutorial services, and frequent workshops and seminars for members.

The Legal-Beagles exhibited another profile, deemphasizing

both solidary and material rewards but offering "particular issues to attract members," a systematic monitoring of legal developments in the state, public speakers, an information newsletter, and numerous mass media efforts to inform the public of its purposes. The Women's Rights Organization combined high levels of all three types of benefits:

> We have consciousness-raising groups and social fund-raisers. There's a lot of tight bonding among our members. We support a drop-in center where women can find out about services. Frequent workshops are held at the state and local level on women's problems, and publications are available from the chapter, the state and the national organization. The cause of eliminating sexism is a major attraction which brings in new members. We routinely monitor local television programs for evidence of sexism and urge broadcasters to give more women important roles in the media.

To measure the incentive offerings made by the thirty-two social influence associations, four coders independently read the entire transcript of each informant interview. Rather than relying only on the query specifically intended to elicit the complete range of incentives, they extracted all mentions of solidary, material, and purposive benefits, using a coding scheme based on definitions of each incentive type derived from Clark and Wilson's typology. In many instances an organizational staff need not intend to reward (Zald and Jacobs, 1978), yet a real incentive may appeal to some portion of the membership. Appendix C.1 describes the method for constructing the three incentive indices.

To measure motivations to join organizations in terms of the attractiveness of various types of incentives, interviewers read a list of twelve reasons different people give for joining organizations and asked respondents how important each reason was in their decision to join. Items were designed to capture solidary, purposive, and material as well as other types of demands that members might recall as attracting them to the association. These items and the factor analysis results that produced three motivation scales are discussed in Appendix C.2. On these three reasons for joining scales, each association's score was the mean of its members' scaled scores. Thus, each social influence association was measured on three incentive scales and three corresponding motives-for-joining scales. Information on motives was inadvertently omitted from the short mail-back questionnaire sent to ORP members, so analyses using these variables are based on thirty-one associations.

Purposive Incentives Predominate

From the nature of the sample, we expected that purposive incentives would predominate. We cannot directly compare scores across the three incentive scales since the relative weights of items are not meaningful across scales (e.g., an organization scoring 3 on solidary and 5 on purposive incentives is not necessarily more purposive than solidary). However, upon breaking the rank orders on the three incentive scales into trichotomies and classifying associations as pure types if they fell into the upper third on only one scale, we found that fourteen associations were primarily purposive, three mainly solidary, three mainly material, and the other twelve mixed (usually including purposive with one other type of incentive).

In Chapter Two, we reported that a majority of respondents had classified their associations as dealing primarily in purposive goals or personal services, while almost none mentioned personal economic benefits or sociability objectives as "what this organization is all about."

The average importance accorded to the items in the three scales of reasons for joining is evidence that the members perceived purposes as the main attraction of these organizations. Purposive reasons were accorded an average rating of 2.47 (nearly a third of the respondents rated all three items as "very important"), while the mean rating of the three solidary items was 1.83 and that for the two material items only 1.52. Thus, the associations in our sample rely mainly upon purposive incentives and attract a membership that seeks primarily purposive rewards.

Covariation of Incentives

Purposive incentives are not significantly correlated either with material incentive offerings (r = .20) or with solidary incentives (r = −.04). (For simple random samples of thirty-two units, correlations must exceed .30 to be significant at the .05 probability level.) But solidary and material incentives are slightly positively related (r = .31). These correlations imply that large amounts of one type of incentive are not offered in conjunction with large amounts of another type, with the possible exception of material and solidary rewards.

Congruence between Incentives and Motives

According to Clark and Wilson, organizational incentive offerings should align with member demands for certain types of benefits by mutual adjustment over time. This relationship is examined in Table 3.1 by correlating the three incentive scales with organizational means on each of the three reasons for joining scales. If the hypothesis is correct, the largest positive correlations should occur between a given type of incentive and its corresponding membership motivation score. This pattern emerges very clearly for the solidary and purposive incentive scales. The material incentive scale correlates insignificantly with aggregate material motives, although the covariation lies in the predicted positive direction. Purposive incentives are unrelated to the two other reasons for joining. The presence of solidary incentives also accompanies higher levels of material motives (r = .58), but material incentives do not correlate with solidary motives (r = −.08). Solidary benefits may satisfy material interests of members, but the reverse is apparently not true.

Although purposive motives correlate significantly with purposive incentives (r = .44), their congruence is not exceptionally great. Part of this discrepancy may occur because members' purposive motivations often originate in factors outside the organization's control, such as personal altruism or religious and humanistic values. Clark and Wilson, in fact, suggested that organizational leaders tend to underplay the importance of purposes as means of getting members to join and become active in an organization. In social influence associations, the purposive elements may be so pervasive and taken for granted that all informants tend to pay lip service to their importance without distinguishing differences in

Table 3.1. Correlations between Organizational Incentive Scores and Mean Organization Scores on Reasons Members Joined

Reasons for joining	Organizational incentives			Mean	Standard deviation
	Purposive incentives	Solidary incentives	Material incentives		
Purposive motives	.44***	−.18	−.04	7.42	0.68
Solidary motives	.09	.73***	−.08	5.49	0.86
Material motives	− .13	.58***	.09	3.03	0.53
Mean	2.72	1.72	2.03		
Standard deviation	1.17	1.14	0.82		

***p ≤ .01 one tailed.

the prevalence of these incentives. Thus, our method of measuring purposive incentives may be insensitive to subtle differences that are more apparent to members who are seeking the intangible benefits of affiliating with a cause-oriented organization.

Since our data come from a single cross-section sample, we cannot determine the process by which organizational incentives and member demands align in this manner. Following Clark and Wilson, however, we speculate that the adjustment of supply and demand occurs continuously at both the organizational and the individual level. Organizational executives create and modify bundles of incentives that they know are attractive to potential supporters. Potential members, acquainted with the organization through a variety of information channels, are aware of the general benefits that will be available to them. To some degree, recruitment involves member self-selection. Faced with several alternatives, a person may decide to join one organization and not others because it promises to fulfill that individual's idiosyncratic demands for varying mixes of rewards. Misperception may also lie behind the failure of incentives to perfectly match motivations: members may mistakenly believe that an association offers material, solidary, or purposive benefits that in fact it does not. Presumably, such mismatches in the short run result in disappointed members either dropping out of the association or adjusting their expectations to meet the true incentives. In the longer run, given a

large and persistent group of members who desire certain benefits, the organization may modify its incentive offerings to satisfy
these demands. Unfortunately, the cross-sectional data at hand are
inadequate to examine these hypotheses.

At the aggregate organizational level, the combinations of individual motivations produce quite distinctive membership profiles, just as the incentive offerings distribute across organizations
in distinct patterns. For example, 84 percent of the Nature Lovers'
Society members score above the median value on material reasons for joining. As noted earlier, this association's chief attraction
for members seems to be its monthly magazine. In contrast, only
15 percent of the NLS members scored above the median value on
purposive reasons for joining, despite the national leadership's
emphasis on conservation issues. Thus, the NLS has the most ma-
terially oriented and least purposive membership among our
thirty-two associations. In stark contrast, the Pro-Life Coalition offers only its antiabortion cause as incentive to its members, and
100 percent of the members scored above the median on purposive motives; only 12 percent scored higher than the median on
material motivations. In a third example, the River Green Neighborhood Association basically offers no incentives of any kind
to its members. Its membership scored well below the median on
all three types of reasons for joining, and 44 percent of the group,
the highest of the sample, could cite no reason as important for
joining.

Measuring Commitment

Before examining the evidence concerning the first hypothesis,
we must describe how we measured the membership's aggregate
levels of commitment. These scales will be used in this chapter
and the two following chapters as dependent variables and in
later chapters as independent measures. As discussed in Chapter
One, social control in voluntary associations requires members to
develop beliefs oriented toward the interests of the collectivity
rather than toward personal interests. Coercive and material bases
of social control are largely absent or ineffectual in promoting mu-

tual self-regulation in this type of organization. In order to translate the concept of membership commitment into questionnaire items that could be answered by individual members, we combed the sparse literature for a variety of psychological and attitudinal measures of positive and negative orientation toward the group and other members.

Our selection of indicators was strongly influenced by a symbolic interaction perspective on member's relations with their organization. Social actors continually construct and interpret their social world, creating social selves that assume an objective character for both the actor and the actor's significant others. Members of social influence associations presumably objectify the organization as an entity with which they interact. This process is evident even in casual conversation with members, who frequently express their feelings toward the group in strong emotional tones.

In objectifying the organization, members also form a portion of their social self in relation to the group as an Other. When we say a member "identifies" strongly or weakly with an organization, we essentially describe the degree to which a member has incorporated aspects of the group into his or her social self. The extent of such identification is presumably amenable to measurement by presenting members with various statements about their cognitive, emotional, and evaluative attitudes toward the organization.

Identity theory, which springs from symbolic interaction roots, emphasizes the complexity of the social self. Multiple identities exist in a more or less hierarchic fashion, and the probability of enactment varies with situational cues and the relative importance of competing identities (Stryker, 1977). The respondent's identity, which embraces organizational membership, is organized in relation to other identities—family, work, religion, leisure, and so on. The centrality, or salience, of the member identity is an important indicator of a respondent's orientation to the organization. "Salience is presumably a function of commitment measured by the 'costs' entailed in giving up relations to particular others premised on a given identity" (Stryker, 1977:151). The more salient the member identity, the more important the organization will appear relative to other roles in the respondent's repertoire.

Gouldner (1960) found that a major dimension of control in her study of members of the League of Women Voters was the extent to which organizational introjection occurred. By *introjection* she meant a subsuming of organizational goals and values as though they were the member's personal values and goals. Dubin (1956, 1975) showed that the extent to which employees find their organization's goals central to their major life interests affects their job satisfaction. Here again we see the importance of the organization's salience as a measure of participant commitment to the collectivity.

Symbolic interaction also stresses the importance of perceptions of social others for the formation of one's own self. Seeing ourselves reflected in the responses of others, we learn to modify and adjust our behavior to ease the path of interaction. Applied to social influence associations, perceptions of how other members behave in their role should have a formative effect on the respondent's member identity. Of course, such reports about how others conform to the member role may mix elements of selective perceptions and misperceptions with accurate interpretation. The chief purpose in querying respondents about how other members behave, however, is not to develop reliable information on this behavior (which can be more accurately gauged by aggregating self-reports). Rather, we want a reflection of the respondent's own feelings about the commitment shown by a significant group of social others in the organization. If acquisition of a member identity is truly a social learning process, the more salient a respondent's organizational identity is, the more likely is a perception that other members have strong commitment and vice versa.

With these considerations in mind we selected from past studies or improvised sixteen statements to measure the level of commitment among members. We attempted to cover perceptions of other members' commitment, the salience of the member identity in the larger social self, and the general importance of the organization and the member's role in it. In seeking to measure the degree to which individual members were oriented toward the collectivity's interests, we considered that a person who put organizational objectives and interests ahead of personal ones (and viewed others as similarly oriented) reflected a high level of normative social control by the organization. By inference, the higher the aggregate level of commitment among the membership, the stronger the association's social control system.

The exact wording of the sixteen items is in Appendix C.3, along with a description of the factor analysis that produced four scales capturing distinct aspects of organizational commitment among individual members. Respondents' scores on these scales—goal salience, loyalty, personal salience, and member perception—were then subjected to a second-order factor analysis that revealed them loading on a single general factor. Thus, an overall scale, the commitment index, combined standardized values on the four scale scores in a manner described in Appendix C.3. Later chapters analyze the separate scales, but at various times we shall use the overall index as a convenient summary for the aggregate member commitment in relation to other variables.

Incentive and Commitment

Having described the measurement of organizational incentives, motives for joining, and aggregate membership commitment, we now proceed to the empirical test of the theoretical hypothesis. Incentives, particularly purposive incentives, should covary positively with the average level of commitment in an association. This expectation comes from the fundamentally purposive nature of the sample. Because incentive systems include both organizationally provided incentives and membership motives in seeking incentives, we will also investigate the covariation between the motives for joining and the membership commitment.

The multicollinearity (see Table 3.1) between incentive scales and motivation indices prevented simultaneous use of all six measures as predictors of the five membership commitment scales. Instead, two sets of multiple regression equations are presented—one using the three incentive scales as independent variables, the other using the three motivation scales as predictors. Each equation also includes the natural logarithm of organization size as a control for spurious effects.

Organization size, that is, the number of members in each local

Table 3.2. Standardized Coefficients from Regression of Membership Commitment Scales on Size and on Incentives and Motives

Dependent variables Membership commitment scales	Independent variables				
	Purposive	Solidary	Material	Size	R²
A. Incentive measures					
Goal salience	.39**	.29*	.01	−.12	.275*
Loyalty	.39**	.28	−.01	−.14	.282*
Personal salience	.29*	.37**	.07	−.26	.308*
Member perception	.33*	.21	−.06	−.19	.231
Commitment index	.38**	.32*	−.01	−.20	.324*
B. Motivation measures					
Goal salience	.44**	.32	.07	.06	.326**
Loyalty	.53***	.31	.04	.08	.397***
Personal salience	.54***	.21	.39*	−.15	.520***
Member perception	.49**	.07	.27	−.12	.292**
Commitment index	.52***	.32	.13	−.01	.444***

* p ≤ .10.
** p ≤ .05.
*** p ≤ .01.

unit under study, can be anticipated to have an inverse relationship with membership commitment. Large memberships present difficulties of physical coordination and communication for any association trying to socialize its members to a common normative orientation. In large organizations a typical member's fractional resource contribution is relatively small and may lead to the free rider problem noted by Olson (1965). In smaller groups, mutual interdependence is more visible, and members are probably subject to greater mutual social control, which should generate higher aggregate levels of commitment. Extant empirical research on the size-participation relationship almost universally confirms an inverse relationship (for example: Talacchi, 1960; Faunce, 1962; Warner and Hilander, 1964; Indik, 1965; Marcus, 1966; Wilken, 1971).

In multiple regression analysis, the contributions of a predictor variable to explaining variation in a dependent measure, net of the effects of other predictors, is most readily gauged by the relative size of the standardized regression coefficients. (For readers unfamiliar with regression analysis, a brief exposition of procedures and interpretations is found in Appendix D). These coefficients, or betas, are shown in Table 3.2 along with the coefficients of determination (multiple R^2), which shows the total proportion of variation in the dependent variable accounted for by the linear combination of all the predictors.

The results generally support our first hypothesis. When the incentive scales are used as predictors (panel A), purposive incentives are all positively and significantly related to membership commitment levels. Solidary incentives attain statistically significant standardized coefficients in only three of the five equations. Only in the personal salience equation does the solidary incentive scale seem to be more important than the purposive incentives in explaining variation among organizations. The magnitudes of the beta coefficients imply that a difference of one standard deviation between associations in the amount of purposive incentives offered will lead to a difference of .29 to .39 standard deviations in the level of commitment.

Material incentives have no important effect in any equation. Logged size, as expected, has a negative relationship to the aggregate level of commitment net of the incentives, but none of these coefficients achieves statistical significance. The insignificance of size as a predictor of membership commitment justifies our dropping it from further analyses of these variables. The multiple R^2 shows that the four independent variables explain between about a quarter to slightly less than a third of the variation in the commitment variables.

Turning to the analyses using the motivation measures (panel B), we find reinforcement for the expectation that purposive factors play the major role in developing favorable membership orientation towards the collectivity. Aggregated solidary reasons for joining do not reach statistical significance, and material motives have a significant beta in only one instance (personal salience). But the purposive motivation betas are substantial, accounting for approximately a half-standard deviation difference in average membership commitment level between organizations whose memberships differ from each other by a standard deviation on purposive motivation. As before, group size does not affect social control score once other variables are held constant. The equations using motivations as predictors have greater R^2s than the comparable equation using incentives as predictors.

Taken together, these equations confirm that it is important for social influence associations to attract members responsive to and strongly motivated by the organization's purposive goals. Such members are substantially more likely to express favorable normative sentiments toward the collectivity, toward the place of the organization in their personal lives, and toward other members. But the significance of solidary incentives suggests that interpersonal relationships are also important in socializing members toward high levels of commitment. Only material incentives and motivations appear weak and ineffectual in producing organizational support, possibly because of the low value of the material goods available through this type of association.

In sum, the evidence presented in this chapter is consistent with the theoretical hypothesis derived from the incentive approach to social control in voluntary associations. Greater quantities of purposive incentives covary positively with higher membership levels of commitment to the organization. The same pattern emerges when the motivation indicators are used. As anticipated from the type of organization we studied, material incentives and motives and solidary motives did not contribute independently to variation in the five commitment scales, although solidary incentives did attain significance in a few equations. Social influence organizations with control systems built around purposive incentives therefore appear to be more effective in developing self-regulatory beliefs among members than do systems depending on other types of incentives.

Chapter Four

The Decision Participation
Approach to Social Control

The Sunday afternoon calm of a park in southwest Chicago was
shattered when twenty-two young men wearing Nazi uniforms
piled out of a white police van, set up loudspeakers behind a
cordon of helmeted policemen, and began an hour-long harangue
on "white power." More than a thousand onlookers—white and
black—jeered and chanted anti-Nazi slogans, at times drowning
out the invectives screamed by red-faced Frank Collin, the would-
be storm troopers' leader. When the Nazis marched back into the
van for the return trip to their headquarters, they left behind a lit-
tered park and a shaken American Civil Liberties Union (ACLU).

For the better part of the previous year the Illinois chapter of
the ACLU had played a leading role in a First Amendment drama.
When the Chicago Park District in effect barred the Nazis from
marching in Marquette Park by requiring a $350,000 liability bond
posted in advance, Collin switched tactics and sought a permit to
demonstrate in the suburban village of Skokie. The target could
not have been better chosen to generate emotion and publicity:
Skokie's population was heavily Jewish, including many sur-
vivors of the Holocaust. The village board responded by requiring
a high insurance bond and passing an ordinance banning any
group seeking to defame religious or ethnic groups. When the
Skokie village board filed suit to stop the Nazis, Collin phoned the
Illinois ACLU's chief legal advisor, David Goldberger, and asked
for defense counsel on the grounds of a violation of the First
Amendment.

70   Normal ACLU procedure calls for a staff decision on the merits

of individual cases seeking the organization's assistance. But Goldberger, in consultation with Executive Director David Hamlin, decided the circumstances surrounding this case warranted clearance with the full Illinois ACLU board of directors. Two weeks earlier, anticipating that the ACLU would be asked to defend him, the board had viewed a police film of Collin's arrest during an earlier attempt to speak in Marquette Park. No decision had been made at that meeting, although several board members expressed unease after viewing the storm troopers in full regalia. When the Skokie case burst unannounced in the board's face, the board had at least some familiarity with the contenders. It unanimously (with one abstention) authorized the staff to litigate against the Skokie ordinances and clear the way for the Nazis to rally there. Perhaps the ACLU only partially anticipated the enormous negative consequences the decision would have upon many supporters of the ACLU, both in Illinois and across the nation.

Legal maneuverings stretched over the next fourteen months before federal district court rulings invalidated both the Skokie and Chicago Park District rulings banning demonstrations. With legal victory in hand, Collin cancelled the potentially violent Skokie rally and settled for the police-guarded rally in Marquette Park, saying that had been his goal all along. In the interim, the Illinois ACLU lost two thousand of its eight thousand members, at least twelve hundred of whom Hamlin estimated resigned because of the Skokie affair. The national ACLU in the same period lost twenty to thirty thousand members. Ironically, a special appeal for funds by the Illinois chapter seemed likely to more than make up for the half-million-dollar budgetary deficit that the membership losses created, so that the organization seemed likely to end the year of the Nazi episode in as sound a financial condition as the year before.

This incident dramatizes the perils of unpopular policy decisions that can rack a social influence association if it attempts to pursue goals unacceptable to a substantial portion of its membership. This specific episode did not involve widespread consultation between the ACLU staff and officers and the rank-and-file members, but, contrary to routine, the staff met twice at great length with the board of directors to secure its approval of its action. While the policy was decided by relatively few people acting on short notice under time pressure, it drove many people away from affiliation and strengthened the commitment of many others. In this chapter we shall take a close look at the consequences of typical decision-making processes for the normative social control of our sample social influence associations.

Decisions, Decisions

The essence of organizational decision making is to select goals or policies toward which organizational resources will be applied. Parsons (1969:318) succinctly captured this relationship:

Committing a collectivity to attain a goal implies . . . a commitment to relatively specific measures designed to effect the desired goal state. Hence, it involves the mobilization of resources at the collectivity's disposal, through authorized agencies. Thus, commitment to the attainment of a goal implies resource commitments which, under the pressure of conditions, themselves require further decision-making processes.

We interpret Parsons to mean that an organization's decision-making processes largely determine the resources that can be mobilized and applied to implement specific goals. From our basic theoretical perspective, certain decision-making procedures facilitate membership commitment, which in turn enhances an association's ability to acquire resources useful in pursuing collective decisions. In particular, decision making that generates widespread membership involvement increases the level of aggregate commitment within the association. Our second hypothesis expresses this relationship:

2. The greater the opportunities for participation in decision making, the stronger the membership's commitment.

Three concepts—organizational complexity, decision participation, and total influence—constitute the core of the decision-making approach to normative social control, the second theoretical perspective underlying our analysis.

"Organizational democracy" is a perdurable theme in the literature on voluntary associations. Concern with member access to the decision-making mechanisms of an organization parallels the problem of popular control of government at the societal level. The classic theoretical statement on organizational decision making remains Robert Michels' 1949, *Political Parties*, an inquiry into the origins of the oligarchical tendencies inherent in nominally democratic associations. *Political Parties* was the lodestar for many later efforts to uncover the conditions under which a self-interested elite would wrest control of the organizational polity from the larger membership. Michels' famous "iron law" of oligarchy is also an ironic law—the paradox that socialist political parties dedicated to achieving democracy at the societal level inevitably become the private preserves of their officers, who use organizational power and authority to pursue personal ends at variance with the best interests of the mass following.

Michels' analysis suggested a number of social conditions that strengthen leaders' hands relative to members'. Leaders' advantages are built upon control of resources sufficient to determine organizational decisions: superior knowledge of organizational affairs; control over formal means of communication; practical experience in organizational politics; higher general education and sophistication than members; and the greater amounts of time and attention that can be invested in the daily guidance of the organization. Michels' argument that organizational decisions reflect the interests of leaders rests on the assumption that leaders, because they occupy a more privileged position in the organization, inevitably develop preferences for policies at odds with the desires of the members (for example, placing survival of the organization and defense of leaders' status ahead of goals benefiting members). Entrenched as a self-perpetuating oligarchy, leaders need not fear the efforts of an apathetic membership to evict them from power, and hence become increasingly unresponsive to members' preferences for policies that do not also satisfy the interests of the leaders. If the theft of the organization is discovered, members lack effective means for reasserting control.

Michels' gloomy conclusions about the inevitable drift of democratic organizations toward elitism stimulated many later theorists to investigate social conditions conducive to keeping organizational decision making responsive to members and clients.

Lipset, Trow, and Coleman's (1956) massive study of the International Typographical Union (ITU) sought to expose the internal politics of an organization in which democracy flourished despite Michels' predictions. The bedrock of the ITU's failure to develop a closed elite was its institutionalized two-party system, a rarity among American trade unions. Many conditions supported the persistence of this formal democratic structure, including close social ties within an occupational community; numerous secondary voluntary associations; widespread leadership skills; small status differences between leaders and members; and a normative climate legitimizing organizational factions and opposition. These and other social factors combined to stimulate political interest and activity among the mass membership and severely limit the tendency for bureaucratization to seal off the incumbent union leadership from the members. While frequently misread as a rejection of Michels' argument, the ITU study in fact is a counterinstance that underscores the tendency for elite monopoly power to emerge in most organizations:

This study has not "disproved" Michels' theory; rather, in a sense, it has given additional empirical support to his analysis of the connection between oligarchy as a political form and the overwhelming power held by the incumbent officers of most private organizations, by demonstrating that where an effective and organized opposition does exist, it does so only because the incumbent administration does not hold a monopoly over the resources of politics [Lipset, Trow, and Coleman, 1956:464].

For our investigation, the important insight in Michels and Lipset is not the social conditions that facilitate oligarchy, but the impact of the decision-making process upon members' commitment to the organization. It may be inferred from their writings that oligarchy and membership orientation vary inversely. The relationship is undoubtedly complex and dynamic, with the decision-making process and member social control mutually affecting each other. One probable source of oligarchy is member apathy, that is, feelings of powerlessness to influence the outcomes of organizational decisions. When apathy is widespread, a self-interested minority should have an easier time gaining and keeping control over the decision-making machinery without rousing member opposition. Once in place, an oligarchy that makes decisions in secret

and distorts or conceals them from the membership further rein-
forces member passivity and disinterest in organizational affairs.
If, as Michels' iron law argues, an entrenched leadership tends to
enact its particular policy preferences while disregarding members' interests, the effects of oligarchy should combine with member apathy to erode favorable normative attitudes of the membership toward the organization. If, as also seems likely, organizational
structures in an oligarchy prevent dissatisfied members from seeking changes in unpopular decisions, such members should become
further alienated to the point of withdrawal (unless exit is not a
feasible alternative, as in some unions). This vicious cycle, in
which constricting access to decisions and deteriorating member
beliefs feed on each other, implies that highly centralized associations will contain largely passive and apathetic memberships.

On the other hand, an active membership interested in the
organization is the lifeblood that sustains a viable democratic
decision-making process (Lipset, Trow, and Coleman, 1956:45).
When members are highly efficacious, that is, feel able to affect
organizational policy decisions, they are likely to exhibit very
positive commitment to the organization. Efficacy is fostered in
great measure by the openness of the decision-making process to
member influence. In turn, a highly active, highly controlled
membership is an effective vaccine against the establishment of
an oligarchy, since members can be more easily mobilized by opposing factions on each side of major controversies (this point is
stressed by McMahon and Camilleri, 1975). Stogdill (1967) wrote
that greater participation in the formulation of goals and policies
of an organization leads to greater subsequent support for them,
perhaps in the form of greater resource contributions toward their
attainment.

Furthermore, in organizations with a democratic polity, members who are dissatisfied with particular collective decisions may
remain loyal because they were able to present their case and gain
a meaningful hearing. A democratic decision-making process
thus fosters control even when members "lose" on specific issues,
whereas members dissatisfied with the decisions produced under
oligarchy will lapse into apathy and withdraw their resource
commitments.

The empirical research literature on actual participation in decision making in formal work organizations confirms that oligarchic or centralized organizations obtain less commitment from their members. A. Gouldner (1954) found that in a gypsum plant, subordinates whose work activity was controlled by bureaucratic superiors had the highest levels of expressed alienation from the organization. Aiken and Hage (1966) and Hage and Aiken (1967), investigating sixteen welfare agencies, found that professionals in the more centralized agencies (centralization being measured by participation in program and personnel decisions) had the highest levels of alienation from their work and from expressive relationships with coworkers. An experiment that increased clerical employees' participation in decisions involving their work activities resulted in higher levels of satisfaction with the organization, even though sense of accomplishment and satisfaction with personal job position were reduced (Morse and Reimer, 1956). Similarly, studies of schoolteachers have consistently shown that when teachers are given greater input into school policy decisions, identification with the organization is higher than that of teachers who are deprived of such opportunities (Hodgkins and Herriott, 1970; Carpenter, 1971; Alutto and Belasco, 1972).

The relevance of these studies to voluntary associations, where decision making nominally lodges in the membership at large, has yet to be demonstrated. We were unable to locate any comparative study of voluntary associations that presented empirical evidence on members' participation in the decision-making process. Our study is probably the first to collect an extensive amount of information on actual decentralization and to relate it to the level of membership commitment. Social influence associations vary considerably in the degree to which members actually participate in decision making, and we will investigate whether this variation predicts variation in the mean level of member commitment.

Another aspect of decentralized decision making with potential impact on commitment is the formal structural arrangement of decision-making units. Our term for formal aspects of decentralization is *organizational complexity*. In work organizations, *complexity* usually refers to task specialization in the division of labor as distinct from structural differentiation along vertical (supervisory) and horizontal (departmental) lines (Dewar and Hage, 1978). Social influence associations, however, seldom involve complicated production technologies and job descriptions that require great structural differentiation. Hence, our use of the term *complexity* will simply indicate the number of distinct formal decision-making units in an association (e.g., officers, board of directors, standing committees, professional staff).

The relationship between complexity and membership commitment levels is similar to that involving decentralization of actual decision making: the more complex the decision-making division of labor, the greater the organization's ability to generate high levels of social control. Greater complexity in work organizations reduces the centralization of decision making, pulling larger numbers of persons into the decision-making process (Collins, 1975:334). Complexity, by providing more entry points into the decision process, enables more members to make their preferences known and thus to influence the final outcome. While empirical evidence in voluntary associations is sparse, Warner's (1964) study of 191 rural Wisconsin voluntary groups found the highest rates of member participation occurred where a complex division of labor increased the proportion of members holding official positions.

Our view of the relationship between complexity and organizational self-regulation clashes with some other perspectives. Although a professional executive director and staff may formally represent yet another entry point for member control over decisions (by offering a highly visible and potentially accessible target for members to direct views), such professionals may also discourage membership participation. Zald and his colleagues indicate that professionalized social movement organizations, particularly when supported by a technical knowledge base, tend to reduce the involvement of board and ordinary members in the daily affairs of the organization (Zald, 1969; McCarthy and Zald, 1973). The more ideologically committed the professional is to the means he uses, the harder it is for an organization to change (Zald and Denton, 1963). Thus, a complex "amateur" social influence association may be more responsive, and hence better able to

obtain higher levels of mutual social control, than its professionalized counterpart.

The internal democracy theme echoes through studies of organizational control patterns, particularly those conducted by Arnold Tannenbaum and his colleagues. *Control* is "any process in
which a person or group of persons or organization of persons determines, that is, intentionally affects the behavior of another person, group, or organization" (Tannenbaum, 1968:5). Thus, control
is internal influence directed toward goal attainment, rather than
an aspect of the formal organizational complexity. The control
concept is especially useful for voluntary associations without organizationally defined powers and responsibilities (e.g., job descriptions) (Hougland, 1976:11).

Tannenbaum's approach to the control process emphasized the
nonfixed nature of influence, particularly within normative associations designed to promote the shared values and interests
of members. The total amount of influence in an association can
be expanded through "(1) structural conditions expediting interaction and influence among members and (2) motivational conditions implying increased interest by members in exercising
control and a greater amenability by members to be controlled"
(Tannenbaum, 1968:14–15). By expanding into its environment,
an organization may acquire more opportunities for making decisions, thus increasing the number of chances to exercise control.
At all levels of the organization, increased opportunities for control over decisions may enhance members' interest in exercising
control and their willingness to be controlled, further expanding
the total amount of influence available to the collectivity.

In "laissez-faire" organizations (Marcus and Marcus, 1965), a
leader exercises little control over subordinates and is largely in-
different to their wishes. In a high total-control, or "polyarchic,"
organization, superiors interact often with, welcome opinions
from, and solicit advice and attempts at influence from rank-and-
file members. Suggestions from subordinates influence leaders'
behavior. In turn, leaders' efforts to influence subordinates' behavior meet with favorable responses. A high amount of effort
to solve problems can increase the benefits received by one group
of members without decreasing the benefits for another. Thus, a

high total amount of control is synonymous with a tightly knit social structure, "a substantial system of interaction and influence
among members and between members and leaders" (Likert,
1961).

A distinct but related aspect of the control process is the distribution of control over decisions among participants, particularly differences in influence across hierarchical levels within an
organization. This distribution is, in effect, a measure of decentralization closely related to the decision participation concept.

Control process research by Tannenbaum and others investigated the consequences of total influence and influence distribution for organizational effectiveness and member satisfaction. The
basic measure asks respondents to rate the amount of influence in
organizational affairs by various positions in the hierarchy (e.g.,
managers, supervisors, workers). The aggregate across all levels is
the total influence; differences between the highest and lowest
echelons measures the distribution, or *slope*, of control. For a variety of businesses and unions, the total amount of control was
positively related to organizational effectiveness and to member
morale and loyalty (Tannenbaum and Kahn, 1958; Smith and
Brown, 1964; Warner and Rogers, 1971; Hougland, 1976; Pennings, 1975). The implications of the slope of control were less
consistent, with some studies finding the predicted negative effect
(Tannenbaum, 1962; Tannenbaum and Smith, 1964; Bowers,
1964) and others no relationship (Smith and Ari, 1964; Warner and
Rogers, 1971; Tannenbaum, 1968:73–89).

Especially relevant to the present analysis of social influence
associations is the League of Women Voters' study by Tannenbaum and others. For 112 local chapters, both effectiveness (as
rated by judges from the national office) and member satisfaction
were significantly related to higher total control and to a positive
influence slope; that is, members were relatively more influential
than the president (Tannenbaum, 1962; Tannenbaum and Smith,
1964; Smith and Brown, 1964). But for most organizations, Tannenbaum deemphasized the importance of the distribution of
control in favor of total influence: "Within 'normal' ranges, variation in power differentials (differences in power between persons
of different rank) are *not* likely to be associated with criteria of

performance. . . . [The] preoccupation by researchers with 'power equalization' may be misplaced in that this preoccupation has detracted from a consideration of the *total amount* of power as a possible explanation of organizational functioning" (Tannenbaum, 1968:309–310). Research findings on 58 mainline Protestant congregations implied that the League of Women Voters' results might be atypical even among voluntary associations (Hougland, 1976:Chapter 5). Total influence affected member satisfaction in the expected direction, but the slope of influence had weak and inconsistent relationships with satisfaction.

The empirical evidence on organizational control thus suggests that total influence should strongly increase organizational performance, including membership commitment. Despite the League of Women Voters results, expectations are less clear about the effect of influence slope. Most social influence associations support a democratic ideology of membership control over collective goals. Where large inequities in control exist between leaders and members, withdrawal of participation and support may follow.

We have identified three aspects of associational decision making. Scattered theoretical and empirical evidence implied that each may affect members' commitment, and hence organizational control. Decentralization of decision making, organizational complexity, and total amount of influence each facilitate the emergence of normative social control in organizations and therefore can be expected to increase an association's ability to obtain resources from its membership. The next section describes the operationalization of these decision-making concepts in our sample.

Measuring Decision Making

There are several ways to conceptualize the decision-making process. Measures of formal structure emphasize the opportunities for participation in issue resolution. Measures of actual participation reflect the breadth of membership involvement in making policy stands for the collectivity. Appendix C.4 describes in detail the operationalizations of the various decision-making measures we summarize here.

The formal complexity of decision-making bodies is the first indicator of potential membership input into decision making. Most voluntary associations are less complex than work organizations with elaborate departmentalization, task formalization, span of control, and similar structures.

The main variation in formal structures among social influence associations occurs in the number of distinct internal units with designated responsibilities for arriving at binding decisions for the collectivity. Simple structure associations have relatively few titled positions; more complex associations may involve an elaborate division of labor for selecting issues, screening alternatives, and adopting final stands. For example, Better Housing Now has five officers who can decide policy for the entire membership. The Health Outreach Program is structured as a relatively elaborate bureaucracy, with a thirty-person board of directors, five officers, a seven-person executive committee empowered to conduct business between board meetings, thirteen standing committees charged with responsibilities in a wide variety of program areas, and a full-time paid executive director who supervises more than sixteen full-time staff people. The number of units as well as number of persons formally involved in many decisions is much larger in the HOP than in BHN.

The categories of formal complexity, as shown in Appendix C.4, are simple structure; elaborate structure; professionalized structure; and board only. Simple-structure associations tend to be small, autonomous neighborhood groups and professionalized organizations tend to be local chapters of nationally known associations, but no one type is exclusively represented by a single formal structure. Some neighborhood groups are professionalized, and various health, legal, and community organizations have at least three of the basic formal structures. The formal complexity variable is rank-ordered by increasing complexity. Our explicit assumption is that the greater the number of formal decision-making units present in an association, the more opportunity individual members have to make their preferences on issues known and thus influence the final outcome. To the extent that decentralized decision-making processes enhance mutual self-regulation in a social influence association, we expect commitment to be lowest in organizations with simple decision-making structures and highest in those consisting solely of a board structure. Elaborate and professionalized structures should exhibit intermediate levels or aggregate membership commitment.

Our second approach to measuring decision making was to determine the actual participation rates in making policy decisions. A typical decision by a social influence association requires the collectivity to take a stand for or against a specific social situation; often other institutions, such as government, must enact the preferred outcome. A small proportion of issues are mainly "in-house" matters, such as raising dues or launching a recruiting campaign.

Decision participation, as described in Appendix C.4, allows each respondent to determine which issue has the greatest personal salience. Thus, in an organization where many issues appeal to different members' interests, decision making will be decentralized if many members are involved in making these decisions. In another organization, only one issue may interest most members, and the degree of decentralization depends upon the proportion participating in that decision. Thus, the decision participation measure does not depend on the number of issues confronting the organization, but only on the extent of awareness and involvement of members. Obviously, if few members can even think of an important issue, actual decision participation must be considered centralized.

Third, to operationalize the concepts of total amount of influence and slope of control, we literally followed the "control graph" technique developed by Tannenbaum. As described in Appendix C.4, this method presents each respondent with the major hierarchical positions in the association and asks for a five-point rating of the influence that role position has in determining policies and actions of the organization. The rating across all relevant positions is the total amount of influence (adjusting for differences between associations with two or three hierarchical levels). The difference in ratings between the president/chairperson and the membership as a whole is the slope of control measure.

In conjunction with analyses of decision-making effects on the commitment measures, we will briefly inspect two variables closely related to decision-making processes: average attendance and vertical communication. The proportion of the membership attending regularly scheduled meetings does not precisely measure involvement in decisions, since input can also occur in special committees and informally by telephone or in face-to-face conversation. If only a small proportion attend meetings, however, extensive membership involvement in decision making seems unlikely. Hence, we expect average attendance to vary positively with the level of organizational commitment among the membership.

An association's vertical communication rate, as described in Appendix C.4, is the mean frequency of communication across strata on "organization matters." While again not specifically measuring participation in decision making, vertical communication is also expected to vary significantly with membership commitment. Communication systems are especially crucial in hierarchical and elaborately differentiated organizations where various subunits must continually coordinate their outputs and inputs. Voluntary associations, most of whose members are only tenuously involved, use communications less for participation coordination and more for normative social control objectives.

Etzioni's organizational compliance theory leans heavily upon expressive communication in normative organizations as a process for creating the member consensus and cohesion essential to effective organizational performance (1975:244). Voluntary associations need relatively little instrumental (task-oriented) communication because the skills and knowledge required of most members to conduct the association's business are fairly elementary. But effective communication of expressive (norm-oriented) communication is facilitated by an "intensive flow" of downward communication from leaders to lower participants, as well as by horizontal communication networks to bind members together. Upward communication may be less frequent, although more prevalent in normative organizations with representative polities. But even in democratic organizations, downward communication is expected to exceed upward flow rates (Etzioni, 1975:244). Regardless of the direction, an absence of normative communication would lead to deterioration of organizational effectiveness.

Mulford, Klonglan, and Warren (1972) conducted an empirical analysis of Etzioni's hypothesis using role performances of civil defense directors and personnel (some paid and some volunteer). Communication, measured by frequency and medium used, was significantly related to effective role performance, even after controlling for level of socialization (job training). A subsequent paper (Klonglan, Mulford, and Tweed, 1974; reported in Etzioni, 1975:399–403) posited that organizational consensus intervened between communication and socialization as antecedent variables and effectiveness as a dependent variable. A path model supported these expectations, although the magnitude of the consensus impact on effectiveness was small and the direct effect of communication on effectiveness remained sizable. To the extent that effectiveness reflects the beliefs of organizational members, the Etzioni hypothesis and the Mulford, Klonglan, and Warren findings indicate that certain communication patterns in voluntary associations stimulate members' commitment more than others.

Decision Making and Commitment

The test of Hypothesis 2 takes the form of inspecting zero-order correlations and multiple regressions of the five membership commitment scales upon the various decision-making indicators. Table 4.1 presents the correlations. The four dummy variables for organizational complexity variable must be considered as a set. Each correlation contrasts the effects of one category with all the others. For example, the −.55 correlation between goal salience and simple structure indicates that associations lacking many formal units for access to decision making are substantially less likely than all the others to have memberships to whom goals are highly salient. But the +.34 correlation of goal salience with elaborate-structure shows that these associations have memberships to whom the goals are very important. The professionalized and board-only associations' correlations suggest intermediate goal salience levels. This general pattern—simple structure associations with the least normatively oriented membership, elaborate struc-

Table 4.1. Correlations between Membership Commitment and Decision-making Variables

Decision-making variables	Membership commitment scales				
	Goal salience	Loyalty	Personal salience	Member perception	Commitment index
Organizational complexity					
Simple	−.55***	−.40**	−.41**	−.34**	−.46***
Elaborate	.34**	.31**	.32**	.23	.34**
Professional	−.03	−.13	−.08	−.13	−.12
Board only	.21	.21	.14	.24	.22
Decision participation	.46***	.54***	.40**	.26	.51***
Total influence	.41**	.60***	.47***	.54***	.58***
Average attendance	.51***	.56***	.58***	.54***	.57***
Vertical communication	.64***	.67***	.73***	.55***	.71***
Influence slope	.23	.20	.11	.15	.20

** $p \leq .05$.
*** $p \leq .01$.

ture associations with the most normatively oriented—persists across all five membership commitment measures. Whether the effect of organizational complexity remains once other association differences in decision making are held constant will be determined shortly in the multiple regression analyses.

Both decision participation and total influence variables perform as predicted by Hypothesis 2. Organizations with widespread decision making (i.e., decentralized associations) have significantly higher levels of membership commitment to the association (except for the member perception indicator) than do centralized associations. Likewise, where a high total amount of influence over policies is available to the association, the membership is strongly oriented toward the association. High membership control over decisions produces high membership belief in mutual self-regulation of the association. However, the influence slope indicator did not produce significant correlations with any of the five membership commitment indicators. The absence of covariation is contrary to expectations from the decision-making approach. Since the other three independent variables perform as predicted by Hypothesis 2, the problem seems to lie with this par-

Table 4.2. Standardized Coefficients from Regression of Membership Commitment Scales on Decision-making Variables

	Decision-making variables					
Membership commitment scales	Elaborate structure	Professional structure	Board only	Total influence	Decision participation	R^2
Goal salience	.72***	.65***	.50***	.28*	.38**	.624***
Loyalty	.57***	.43***	.32**	.48***	.35**	.662***
Personal salience	.59***	.48**	.30	.42**	.24	.487***
Member perception	.48**	.35*	.29	.54***	.02	.432***
Commitment index	.65***	.53***	.37**	.48***	.33**	.688***

* p ≤ .10.
** p ≤ .05.
*** p ≤ .01.

ticular measure of organizational control rather than with the theoretical proposition. Therefore, we eliminate the influence slope variable from further empirical analyses, concentrating on the joint effect of the other three measures of decision making.

Before turning to that analysis, we present a final bit of evidence in favor of Hypothesis 2. As noted, both average meeting attendance and vertical communication rates are probably closely related to the decision-making process in social influence associations. Therefore, these two variables should correlate positively with the commitment measures. And, as the bottom two lines in Table 4.1 show, that is exactly what happens. But, since both attendance and communication may reflect other aspects of organizational behavior besides decision making, these indicators will not be used further. Instead, we concentrate on the joint effects of the more precise decision-making measures. The purpose of this analysis is to determine whether each of these variables makes a unique contribution to explaining variation in the average level of member commitment after holding constant the effects of the other two decision-making indicators.

In the multiple regression analyses, three decision-making measures with significant correlations—organizational complexity, decision participation, and total influence—were used simultaneously as predictors of each of the member commitment scales. Because complexity is a set of dummy (dichotomous) variables, to include all four in the same equation would create a linear dependency making estimates of each category's effects impossible. The standard procedure is to omit one dummy category from the equation, interpreting the beta coefficients of the remaining categories as deviations from the omitted category (Kerlinger and Pedhazur, 1973:105–109). In the equations reported in Table 4.2, the category "simple structure" was omitted so that the betas for elaborate, professional, and board-only associations show how much higher those associations' memberships are in average level of commitment to the organization, holding constant any difference in total influence and decision participation across the four types of organizational complexity.

Even taking such differences into account, the simple structure associations clearly have less normatively oriented memberships than the other three types. In each equation, the effect of elaborate structure is greater than that of professional structure, which in turn is greater than that of board-only structure. However, these three coefficients are not significantly different from each other, leading to the conclusion that the main effect of organizational complexity on membership commitment scales lies in the contrast between simple structure associations and the other three formal structures.

Since professionalized associations' memberships are not substantially less normatively oriented than the "amateur" elaborate structure associations, we conclude that little evidence exists here to support Zald and his colleagues' contention that professionalized voluntary associations tend to depress the level of membership social control. Instead, these findings imply that a professionalized formal structure promotes greater membership commitment levels, presumably by offering more access points through which members can affect organizational policy.

Total influence and decision participation remain important even after holding each other and complexity constant. Total influence especially retains robust regression coefficients in all five equations, although decision participation fails to remain significant in two equations (personal salience and member perception). Some differences in relative effects may be noted. For example, decision participation is more important in the goal salience equation, while total influence has a larger beta in the loyalty equation. (These differences support the separation of the constituent items into two scales despite their common factor loadings as described in Appendix C.3). The great importance of decision participation for goal salience is understandable, since direct involvement in making policy decisions is likely to raise members' consciousness of fundamental association values and objectives.

In contrast, equations for personal salience and member perception found actual decision involvement less important than the total influence available to the association. This finding suggests that decentralization is not the relevant decision-making factor for certain types of commitment. Instead, an association's ability to generate high levels of mutual influence from all strata—in Likert's words a "tightly-knit structure"—appears to convince most members that the association is an important part of their personal lives and that other members are positively oriented toward the association's welfare. This effect occurs independently of decision participation. Such apparent divergences between total influence and decision participation across specific types of membership commitment should not obscure the fundamental finding that widespread decision-making opportunities generally produce higher levels of mutual self-regulation. All three measures combined explain between two-fifths and two-thirds of the variance in mean levels of association commitment levels.

In sum, the empirical evidence in this chapter strongly substantiates the hypothesis drawn from the decision-making approach. Organizational control structures and social control beliefs covary strongly. Only the influence slope measure failed to correlate significantly with the dependent variables, leading us to conclude that the measure lacks validity as an indicator of decision-making distribution. Organizational complexity, while it may also reflect other aspects of organizational structure besides opportunity for decision making, disclosed a strong difference between simple structure and more complex organizations in average level of membership commitment. But no evidence was found that professionalized associations obtain less membership self-regulation than do similarly complex but "amateur" associations. In line with Tannenbaum's research, total amount of influence predicted greater membership enthusiasm and dedication. Decision participation, as an index of decentralization, is perhaps the best single indicator of the decision-making approach, since it directly measures the extent of membership involvement in making decisions on important issues. Its strongest relationships occurred with those commitment indicators most likely to reflect exposure to goals and objectives of the association. Taken together, the analyses of various decision-making indicators for data on the social influence associations provide strong confirmation of the decision-making approach.

Yet an intriguing question remains: Is the decision-making approach effective in generating membership commitment that will not readily evaporate in a stormy controversy? Let us return to the case of free speech for American Nazis. Would the ACLU have ex-

perienced the same loss of members and money if their procedures had required greater rank-and-file involvement in reaching
the decision? Would the decision have been the same? There is no
easy way to answer these questions. The legitimate-leadership approach to organizational control at least places them in another
light, however. In Chapter Five, we will develop this third approach to normative social control in social influence associations, then compare the effects of all three control perspectives on
membership commitment.

The Legitimate Leadership Approach to Social Control

In the bicentennial year, Civil Rights Organization's leaders faced a controversy when the celebration committee recommended a former convict to play a historical character revered by CRO's membership. Since a major concern of CRO is jobs for minorities and the poor, among both of whom the conviction rate is high, hiring an ex-offender for such a visible role would be congruent with CRO's values. Yet there were great risks involved. The hiring could upset not only members but the larger community, especially the United Way—a major source of funds.

Despite the potential controversy, the leaders did not poll members on the question or take the issue to a membership meeting. The decision to hire the recommended actor was made by the board alone in a context where the organization's goals could be given major consideration and individuals' fears could be relegated to the background. The members accepted the leaders' decision, and the program was successful. CRO's formal structure empowered the leaders to make such decisions, and members felt an obligation to accept them. Thus, CRO's leaders were exercising legitimate leadership. In this chapter we will develop a theory of legitimate leadership rooted in the work of Weber and other organizational theorists and apply the theory to social control within our sample. The following hypothesis shows how this understanding fits into our general theory of voluntary association behavior:

3. The greater the leaders' legitimacy, the stronger the membership's commitment.

We conceive leaders' legitimacy in voluntary organizations to be composed of two basic elements: the formal legitimacy structure and the membership's belief in leadership legitimacy. Both elements are expected to covary positively with the strength of the membership's aggregate commitment.

In an organization with a strong formal legitimacy structure, a supralocal unit (such as a regional or national body) retains for itself considerable rights to control the local chapters. We contend that such arrangements permit local leaders to exercise considerable leverage in implementing policies either derived from the supralocal level or from general organizational values rather than from policy preferences expressed by local rank-and-file members.

Under the decision participation approach described in the previous chapter, such strong formal legitimacy structures should be inherently alienating. Removal of local control over certain policies should result in a reduced belief among members that the organization is serving their interests. Thus, when an association is dominated by a strong formal legitimacy structure, the level of membership commitment should diminish. An alternative view stressed in this chapter suggests that a strong formal legitimacy structure may instead bolster the local membership's social control orientation. Supralocal domination can provide local chapters with a number of benefits. By backing up local leaders' decisions, a strong supralocal body allows local leaders to act swiftly and decisively on short notice, without the necessity to delay action in order to consult the rank and file. Furthermore, the supralocal body can act as a role model for effective operations, provide skilled and experienced management training, facilitate linkages with other nonlocal organizations, and create a national reputation that is an asset for the local chapter's efforts. These potential benefits from a strong formal legitimacy structure may therefore lead not to diminished membership commitment but to enhanced support.

Membership belief in legitimacy, the second element of leaders' legitimacy, is the attribution of propriety to the local leadership to act for the association as a whole to further the collective interests. In associations where members attribute high legitimacy to the leaders, they view policy making by the leaders as appropriate and accept leaders' decisions without becoming demoralized. Thus, where membership belief in legitimacy is high, the level of aggregate member commitment should also be high. The link between formal legitimacy structure and membership belief in legitimacy is straightforward: organizations with strong formal legitimacy structures attempt to inculcate their members with the belief that local leaders have the right to support from the rank and file.

Theoretical Origins

Peabody asserted that "what clearly distinguishes authority from coercion, force, and power on the one hand, and leadership, persuasion, and influence on the other hand, is *legitimacy*" (1968:474). In other words, authority is rightful power; authoritative leaders run the organization with the consent of members, who acknowledge the leaders' right to rule the organization. We will use the terms *formal legitimacy* and *belief in legitimacy* instead of *authority* because the latter is too often restricted to leaders who have one specific kind of legitimacy—rational-legal, or formal, legitimacy. A major tenet of our theory of legitimacy is that formal legitimacy, though an important asset to an organization, requires belief in legitimacy to maintain high organizational morale. We refer to the combination of formal legitimacy and belief in legitimacy as *legitimate leadership*.

If they accept their leaders' claim to legitimacy, organization members will feel an obligation to go along with leaders' proposals for organizational actions (Simon, Smithburg, and Thompson, 1970). Voluntary acceptance of leaders' policies can be critical to an organization's success. Hierarchical structures can contribute toward goal attainment for a number of reasons. As Michels pointed out, one of the most important reasons is the ability to "strike while the iron is hot." For example, had CRO's officials needed to poll members or call a membership meeting to decide on the selection of an actor, they might have missed the opportunity to hire him or delayed so long that the program could not be properly rehearsed. Often, external issues in the community need rapid assessment and immediate response if the organization is to have any community influence on that issue.

Also, as Meyer and Rowan (1977) argued, a hierarchical structure is often necessary to secure community resources. Meyer and Rowan argued that much of organizational structure is designed not to carry out the organization's activities efficiently but to secure from the community and the surrounding institutions trust that will be beneficial in securing resources (financial resources, interorganizational cooperation) from outside the organization (1977:352). Yet, as Likert (1961) argued, there is a major drawback to centralized power. When people do not participate in making decisions yet must abide by them or see their resources expended to implement them, they tend to become demoralized. That is why Likert proposed the decision participation approach, which he felt would increase morale and result in increased member contributions of resources (e.g., effort, money).

On the question of morale (included in our conception of social control as self-regulation), the theory of legitimacy suggests that belief in legitimacy is a functional alternative to decision participation. Formal legitimacy structures, in which higher-level units of the organization have the power to determine policies of lower-level units, can produce high commitment levels if lower-level members have been socialized or persuaded to believe that the structure is the proper one for the organization. These structures counteract the tendency that Likert noted for individuals to resent carrying out somebody else's orders. The roots of this theory are found in Weber, whose classic statement on legitimacy discusses three types of authority (legitimate domination) based on three corresponding types of legitimacy.

> There are three pure types of legitimate domination. The validity of the claims to legitimacy may be based on:
> 1. Rational grounds—resting on a belief in the legality of enacted rules and the right of those elevated to authority under such rules to issue commands (legal authority).
> 2. Traditional grounds—resting on an established belief in the sanctity of immemorial traditions and the legitimacy of those exercising authority under them (traditional authority); or finally,
> 3. Charismatic grounds—resting on devotion to the exceptional sanctity,

heroism, or exemplary character of an individual person, and of the normative patterns or order revealed or ordained by him (charismatic authority) (1968:215).

One additional type of authority is implied in Weber's discussion of authority: value-rational authority (Willer, 1967; Satow, 1975; Wood, 1981). A claim to legitimacy based on value-rational grounds rests on "a conscious belief in the value for its own sake of some ethical, aesthetic, religious, or other form of behavior, independently of its prospects of success" (Weber, 1968:24). It is distinguished by a "clearly self-conscious formulation of the ultimate values governing the action and the consistently planned orientation of its detailed course to these values" (1968:25). Examples include "the actions of persons who, regardless of possible cost to themselves, act to put into practice their convictions of what seems to them to be required by duty, honor, the pursuit of beauty, a religious call, personal loyalty, or the importance of some 'cause' no matter in what it consists. Value-rational action always involves 'commands' or 'demands' which, in the actor's opinion, are binding on him" (1968:25).

Value-rational authority is especially appropriate to social influence organizations because such organizations typically try to influence public policy in conformance with organizational values. Furthermore, contemporary society is marked by an erosion of legal and traditional forms of authority; this erosion is manifested in less respect for superiors, lawsuits against those in authority (e.g., employers, school boards, governmental agencies), and the inability to enforce sanctions against those who defy authority (for example, an injunction based on the Taft-Hartley Act failed to return striking coal miners to work during the 1978 strike). Erosion of authority stems in part from high levels of education increasing the competence of those subject to authority to judge issues for themselves, and from mass media exposure of incompetent, self-seeking, and/or corrupt authorities at all levels. In this climate, legitimacy may be established through appeals to deeply ingrained collective values that clearly link those values with the actions or directives for which legitimacy is claimed. Hence, value-rational authority stresses legitimacy based on the content of directives rather than the legitimacy of the procedure by which the directives were enacted.

Satow (1975) contended that an independent type of organization evolves from the value-rational basis of legitimacy. A primary trait of this new structure is that members who possess a strong ideology are segmented from those who do not. According to Satow, churches (and other organizations in which professionals play a central role) are of this type. She pointed out that during the socially active 1960s, outspoken religious professionals were on college campuses or in denominational offices where they were not directly vulnerable to members who opposed their pronouncements. Satow argued that such segmented structures would be the logical solution where groups of persons within an organization are committed to preserving the ideology.

However, Wood's (1981) study of fifty-eight churches in Indianapolis suggested that value-rational authority is most important where segmentation is no longer possible; this study highlights the potential importance of value-rational authority for voluntary organizations, where leaders are especially vulnerable to members. Rank-and-file members' resources are needed; the use of those resources is visible; therefore, leaders allocating those resources to controversial actions are vulnerable. In this context the ideologue must try to convert others or to resuscitate the ideology within them. Wood found that the leaders of those churches able to pursue controversial social-action policies first framed policies to reflect fundamental values of the church, such as Biblically-based concepts depicting the church as the servant of a just and compassionate God. They then evoked those values as a basis for claiming legitimacy for the controversial policies. The basic process was to bring to consciousness the members' belief in those general values (thus raising the rank of those values within members' value hierarchies), then to encourage members to see these general values in the specific policies.

A Fundamental Issue

A fundamental issue arises from the discussion of authority types—an issue that Weber did not clearly resolve. Weber did not expect leaders in any structure of dominance (e.g., a state, a bureaucracy, an organization) to rule for long by coercion. In order to assure voluntary compliance, leaders would attempt "to establish and to cultivate the belief in . . . legitimacy" (1968:213). But is that belief established within those who are to comply voluntarily or within those higher in the structure or outside the structure who have power to back up leaders' directives with force? Value-rational legitimacy suggests the former, but rational-legal legitimacy at least in part suggests the latter. At least in employer-employee relations, there is a large zone of acceptance by subordinates of commands from superiors because all participants have been socialized to the rules of the hierarchical game (Simon, Smithburg, and Thompson, 1970). But when commands fall outside this zone, the superior can call on higher authorities to force compliance or to enforce the ouster of the subordinate, and so has the last word.

Stinchcombe blurred the distinction between those persons backing up commands and those obeying commands: "A power is legitimate to the degree that, by virtue of the doctrines and norms by which it is justified, the power-holder can call upon sufficient other centers of power, as reserves in case of need, to make his power effective. Some of these reserves may, or may not, be the popularity of a man's powers in public opinion or *the acceptance of a doctrine of legitimacy of his powers among subordinates* (1968:162).

Dornbusch and Scott (1977), however, made a helpful distinction between authorized power and endorsed power—both of which are legitimate power, i.e., authority. An actor's power is authorized "to the extent that beliefs held by groups superior" to that actor legitimate his or her power. An actor's power is endorsed to the extent that beliefs held by groups subordinate to that actor legitimate the actor's control over them. "These two dimensions are conceptually independent in that authorized power may or may not be endorsed and endorsed power may or may not be authorized" (1977:41). Legitimate power is normatively regulated power. The norms of those superior to the power wielder and/or of his subordinates regulate the power wielder's actions as well as the subordinates' actions. In their extensive empirical research on a wide range of organizations, Dornbusch and Scott emphasized authorized power, treating it as backed-up power, much as Stinch-combe did. However, they expected that in practice authorized power would be endorsed.

These theorists were concerned primarily with getting subordi-nates to perform tasks. The central concern of Dornbusch and Scott, for example, was the relationship between evaluation of task performance and the stability of authority systems. They were aware that an organization containing volunteers has a less stable authority system than one containing employees, but their theory only encompassed organizations whose volunteers are en-gaged in specific task performances. By contrast, an exclusive focus on a theory of voluntary organizations requires us to give special attention to belief in legitimacy (endorsed power), ne-glected by both Stinchcombe and Dornbusch and Scott.

Belief in legitimacy is a psychological dimension of legitimacy. Our legitimacy research and theory is based largely on the prem-ise that what many voluntary organizations need from most of their members most of the time is not task performance but the rather passive contribution of resources (e.g., financial support, use of name) that allows the specialized leadership to carry out the goal-oriented tasks of the organization. Thus, the understand-ing of voluntary organizations is enhanced by preserving the dis-tinction between members' compliance based on a felt obligation and that based on knowledge of the coercive potential of outside centers of power.

Formal legitimacy is anchored in an organization's formal structure (e.g., the constitution and bylaws). The strongest organi-zational polities give leaders the right to set policies and to en-force them with strong sanctions (e.g., expulsion of members, withdrawal of the charter of local units). Furthermore, so long as leaders stay within boundaries set by the formal structure, there are nests of power (Stinchcombe, 1968)—higher levels of the or-ganization, the civil courts, the police—that can be called on to enforce those sanctions. The rash of court cases in the 1960s by which church denominations restrained local congregations from leaving the polity is a case in point (Wood, 1972). Formal legit-imacy is congruent with Dornbusch and Scott's authorized power.

Bierstedt (1954) would restrict the term *authority* to formal legitimacy, since the sine qua non of authority is that it can require obedience. Stinchcombe (1968) argued convincingly that Weber's concrete analyses of power systems emphasize formal legitimacy.

Weber did not expect those with formal legitimacy to rely heavily on coercion. Rather, he expected that organizations with formal legitimacy would instill in their members a belief in legitimacy that would produce a sense of obligation to cooperate voluntarily with leaders' efforts to achieve collective goals, even when members disagreed with some aspects of those efforts. Simon, Smithburg, and Thompson stressed this link between legitimacy and voluntary compliance when they called legitimacy "a psychological matter." "A legal or any other system of authority is legitimate only to the extent that those persons to whom it is directed feel that they ought to or must accept it" (1970:86). Studies of churches have shown, for example, that congregations with high belief in legitimacy are better able to pursue controversial goals (Wood, 1975; 1981).

Little empirical research bears directly on the theoretical problem of the differential impact of formal legitimacy and belief in legitimacy on organizational morale and effectiveness. In one relevant study, Peabody (1968) drew on several social scientists, including Weber, to present a composite typology of the bases of authority. Peabody described two types of formal authority—authority of position and authority of legitimacy—and two types of functional authority—authority of competence and authority of person. The latter types are not important for our present focus, but the first two types roughly correspond to what we have called respectively *formal legitimacy* and *belief in legitimacy*. Peabody's measures, however, did not clearly differentiate these concepts. In the measurement of authority, some responses seem to reflect belief in legitimacy ("Authority to me is something you're bound to obey. It's something I respect") while others seem closer to formal legitimacy ("A lot of authority is in the manual—it's the law").

Peabody applied his typology to a police department, a welfare office, and an elementary school. Responses to the question "What does authority mean to you?" were classified according to the typology. Forty-five percent of all the responses were classified as indicating authority of position, 22 percent authority of legitimacy, 17 percent authority of competence, and 14 percent authority of person. There were some important differences across organizations, although authority of position received the most responses within each organization. Authority of person appeared far more important in the police department than in the other organizations; authority of competence was far more important in the elementary school than in the other organizations.

Hammond, Salinas, and Sloane (1978) studied clergy conceptions of authority, using a typology based on distinctions between office and person and the rational and the sacred. One of their types, rational-legal authority (rational authority of office), corresponds conceptually to our formal legitimacy, though the measure is, at best, an approximation of the concept. In interviews with ministers, the researchers read sketches of hypothetical clergymen's conceptions of their authority. The respondents were asked to rate how well each description fit their own conception of authority. Of the 250 respondents, 167 were classifiable according to three authority types. Twenty-eight percent were classified rational-legal, 28 percent pragmatic, and 45 percent charismatic. Hammond, Salinas, and Sloane found that ministers describing themselves as having rational-legal authority were more likely than others to be involved in community groups; to be involved in the local council of churches or ministerial associations; and to say that their congregation was somewhat more liberal than its surrounding community.

Formal Legitimacy and Belief in Legitimacy Combined

We turn now to the relationship between formal legitimacy and belief in legitimacy. As we have noted, Weber expected those organizations with formal legitimacy to attempt also to generate belief in legitimacy. Dornbusch and Scott agreed with this expectation:

Power in formal organizations may be both authorized and endorsed. There will be many instances within organizations where the authorized power of officials is reinforced by the norms held by those subordinate to such power. In fact, it may safely be asserted, as Weber (1947:325) does, that virtually every organization attempts to "establish and to cultivate the belief in its 'legitimacy'" [1977:61].

Peabody (1968), too, held that authority of position and authority of legitimacy are "inextricably fused in reality."

Upon finding close relationships among authority, effective control, and legitimacy in a social welfare agency, Miller and Fry discussed possible causal linkages among these variables: "Weber implies that authority is reflected in effective control *if* the organizational system itself and the individuals occupying positions of authority are legitimated (indicating the sequence: AUTHORITY ⟶ LEGITIMACY ⟶ CONTROL)" (1973:317–318). According to Miller and Fry, their data suggested another causal sequence: "Authority is more likely to be legitimated where it has been translated into effective control (implying the alternative sequence: AUTHORITY ⟶ CONTROL ⟶ LEGITIMACY" (1973:317–318). Their measure of legitimacy as prestige departs markedly from Weber's discussion of the concept, however.

In a sample of twelve local churches, Wood (1975) explored the relation between formal legitimacy and belief in legitimacy and a dependent variable (organizational transcendence) tapping the churches' persistence in racial justice policies that were controversial among the members. He used path analysis to explore the possibility that "against the backdrop of strong formal control, norms of legitimization develop that cause members voluntarily to restrain their protests against dissonant policy, and allow organizational leaders to formulate policy not predictable from members' attitudes." His logic for assigning causal direction from formal legitimacy to belief in legitimacy rather than vice versa was that while historically belief in legitimacy

may have preceded the formal structure in some of these organizations, or the structure and the belief in its legitimacy may have developed simultaneously (see Blau, 1964) the formal polities were certainly established *before* current members (e.g., our respondents), began attributing legitimacy. The direction of the arrow between formal legitimacy and [belief in legitimacy] may, nonetheless, be a better representation of the present relationship between these types of legitimacy than of the natural history of their development (Wood, 1975:207).

Results of Wood's research showed that much of formal legitimacy's effect on the dependent variable was mediated through belief in legitimacy, though the direct path was also significant. In a later study of fifty-eight churches, Wood tested a more complex model incorporating Weber's emphasis on the crucial role of the administrative staff. This model suggests that denominations with strong polities instill in their ministers a belief in legitimacy and that the ministers in turn instill such a belief in their members. This logic is consistent with our knowledge of leaders' stronger adherence to group norms. In this model formal legitimacy causes the minister's belief in legitimacy, which in turn causes members' belief in legitimacy. One further link—tolerance of dissonant policy—was posited between members' belief in legitimacy and the dependent variable (transcendence). Belief in legitimacy allows collective policies to transcend members' individual attitudes because it causes members not to protest but rather to tolerate policies with which they disagree. Data from the fifty-eight churches showed that all of the effect of formal legitimacy on transcendence was mediated by this causal chain.

Several theorists have discussed the alienating effects of formal legitimacy. Participation theorists especially have argued that organizations basing control on formal legitimacy rather than on participation in decision making are destined to have low morale (Likert, 1961; Tannenbaum, 1968). But our view is that if formal legitimacy is accompanied by strong belief in legitimacy, a narrow hierarchical distribution of control need not alienate members. Coupling belief in legitimacy with formal legitimacy not only reduces alienation but provides an alternative control structure that may be more effective than a participatory structure when collective goals of the organization conflict with other goals of individual members or collective goals can be more easily achieved if leaders are not constrained by the necessity of members' participation in decision making.

In social influence organizations, the second condition probably exists more often than the first. Associations that often face fast-breaking issues, especially if the organizations are large or geographically dispersed, are more likely to face situations in which members' participation in decision making hampers leaders' efforts. Organizations dealing with controversial public issues are the best examples. In our sample such issues arose most often in Legal-Beagles, Inc., the Ethnic Protection Society, Civil Rights Organization, and the Women's Rights Organization. The case of Civil Rights Organization with which we began this chapter illustrates a potential conflict between an organization goal (influencing public attitudes about jobs for minorities) and individuals' concerns ("Will our hero be dishonored if an ex-convict portrays him?").

In general, however, social influence organizations do not appear to experience nearly so much dissension over policies as do churches that become involved in social influence issues. When we asked our sample respondents how frequently they "disagreed with the stands taken by" their organization "on important issues," 64 percent responded that they "rarely" or "never" disagreed, 21 percent said that they disagreed "sometimes," and fewer than three percent said that they disagreed "often" or "always." This relatively low rate of disagreement may reflect the fact that the social influence goals of these organizations are fairly clear to members before they join. Members know what they are getting into. And in most of these organizations, policy-dissatisfied members probably do not feel the social pressure to remain in the organization comparable to that felt by dissatisfied church members.

Measuring Legitimacy

A leader with formal legitimacy is placed by some rational method (usually constitutionally prescribed) in a hierarchical structure of power. The levels of power above can back up as well as limit the leader's power in relation to those below him or her in the power structure. In this study we measured formal legitimacy in terms of the relation of the local organization to a higher level of organization. Based on content analysis of the transcripts of interviews with principal officers, each organization was scored on three dichotomous items: whether a national (or other supralocal level of organization) sets strong limits and obligations on the local (e.g., funding control, criteria for eligibility to hold office); whether the national can impose an issue position on the local organization; and whether the national can veto a decision reached by the local. Civil Rights Organization, for example, was subject to control by its national organization in all three ways. The three items formed a Guttman scale (see Appendix C.5 for complete details). Our rationale for this particular measure is that in such structures, local leaders can use supralocal authorities as leverage in shaping local policies. (This rationale's plausibility was evident in earlier studies of churches facing desegregation [Wood, 1967; 1975]. Several ministers in hierarchical denominations stated that they and some of their lay leaders were happy when their denomination ordered them to desegregate. Now the matter of implementing desegregation was no longer a personal confrontation of local leaders with members; leaders were seen as representatives of the larger church, carrying out its orders.)

The wide variation in formal legitimacy in social influence associations can be grasped by a few examples. In the Wilderness Protection Organization, the national board sets national policy. Local chapters cannot be involved in lawsuits or legal hearings without prior approval from the national level. The Nature Lovers' Society, however, allows great local autonomy; the national is unable to impose its positions on the local chapter. Bylaws of the Women's Rights Organization allow the national to revoke a local charter. The state Health Outreach Program disaffiliated a chapter in a northern Indiana county; the national Organization of Blind Persons reorganized its Washington, D.C., chapter. But Legal Beagles, Inc., when told not to pursue a court case by the national, "told them where to get off," according to the Indiana president, and won the case. The local chapters of the Women's Political Alliance objected to the state unit's attempts to dictate local policy stands and succeeded in reducing the state role to one of liaison and coordination between the local and national bodies.

The essence of belief in legitimacy is a sense of obligation to cooperate voluntarily with leaders' efforts to achieve collective goals. The key item in our belief-in-legitimacy scale expressed this meaning directly: "Even when I disagree, I feel an obligation to support policies set by this organization's leaders." We understood, of course, that those agreeing with this statement might represent a wide range of bases of belief in legitimacy. For example, some members might believe strongly that they must support policies arrived at in accordance with the rules, even when they disagree with the policies and when there are no sanctions against them for nonsupport (a rational-legal belief in legitimacy). Others may feel obliged to follow leaders because they are convinced that such support is an important way to implement the values they hold (a value-rational belief in legitimacy).

To discover the bases of members' beliefs in legitimacy, we immediately followed the preceding item with the probe, "Why do you say that?" The explanations given by respondents who agreed with the item (those who felt an obligation to support policies) can be grouped into five categories of belief in legitimacy. (1) Twenty-one percent expressed a belief in the competence of their leaders (e.g., "The leaders are more knowledgeable"). (2) Seventeen percent expressed a sense of obligation to the collectivity (e.g., "To preserve the unity of the organization"). (3) Sixteen percent expressed a rational-legal belief in legitimacy ("It's part of the leader's job to make decisions"). (4) Ten percent expressed a value-rational belief in legitimacy (e.g., "To enable the organization to accomplish its goals"). (5) Ten percent explained their belief in legitimacy on the basis of trust in their leaders (e.g., "Leaders have the best interests of the organization in mind"). Clearly, then, this key item in our scale covers a wide spectrum of bases for legitimacy.

The two other items in the belief-in-legitimacy scale each tapped one of these separate dimensions: (1) leader trust ("This organization's leaders can be trusted to make the best decisions possible"); (2) rational-legal ("Although I may not like a decision made by the leaders, I would not question their authority to make decisions for the organization"). The reliability coefficient (alpha) for the three-item belief-in-legitimacy scale is .46.

An insight into formal legitimacy and belief in legitimacy

emerges from these variables' relationship with perceived leadership characteristics. A three-item scale measured membership perceptions that their associations had an elite leadership. (Items are: "This organization is pretty much run by a few members looking out for their personal interests"; "This organization is run by the same people year after year"; and "This organization is as close to a working democracy as one could be," reverse scored). The elite leadership variable correlated inversely and significantly both with formal legitimacy (r = −.32) and with belief in legitimacy (r = −.44). Apparently members concede the leaders' legitimacy to make decisions binding on the entire group because the members perceive that the leaders have more than just their own personal interests in mind when making such decisions.

Legitimacy, Control, and Resources

Zero-order correlations between the two legitimacy measures and all five membership commitment scales support Hypothesis 3 (Table 5.1). Formal legitimacy and belief in legitimacy have significant positive correlations with every commitment scale. The stronger covariation with belief in legitimacy than with formal legitimacy recalls our expectation that formal legitimacy may require belief in legitimacy to counteract its alienating tendencies. Hence, we expected that belief in legitimacy would medi-

Table 5.1. Zero-Order Correlations between Legitimacy and Membership Commitment

Membership commitment scales	Formal legitimacy	Belief in legitimacy
Goal salience	.42*	.47*
Loyalty	.30*	.52*
Personal salience	.43*	.59*
Member perception	.39*	.60*
Commitment index	.37*	.56*

*p ≤ .05.

Table 5.2. Standardized Coefficients from Regression of Membership Commitment Scales on Formal Legitimacy and Belief in Legitimacy

Membership commitment scales	Independent variables		R^2
	Formal legitimacy	Belief in legitimacy	
Goal salience	.34**	.36**	.316***
Loyalty	.21	.45**	.297***
Personal salience	.33**	.48***	.436***
Member perception	.23	.54***	.414***
Commitment index	.26	.47***	.369***

** $p \leq .05$.

*** $p \leq .01$.

ate much of the effect of formal legitimacy on the membership commitment. This logic is examined in regression analyses reported in Table 5.2.

When the commitment variables were regressed on both belief in legitimacy and formal legitimacy, three of the five coefficients for formal legitimacy failed to reach statistical significance, but the effect of belief in legitimacy remained significant in all five equations. Since formal legitimacy and belief in legitimacy covary positively ($r = +.30$), an indirect effect of formal legitimacy on membership commitment exists in all the equations. That is, a stronger formal legitimacy structure increases the membership's belief in leaders' legitimacy, which in turn raises the level of membership social control orientations. The existence of positive effects from formal legitimacy in every equation (significant for goal salience and personal salience) is contrary to the expectation of the decision-making approach, which argues that removal of policy control from the local chapters will tend to alienate the local membership. Instead, these results lend support to our alternative view that a strong formal legitimacy structure both directly increases favorable membership commitment and indirectly raises such beliefs by acting first to increase attributions of legitimacy to local leaders.

Three Control Approaches Compared

In this chapter and the two preceding, we examined three distinct theoretical approaches to the social control of voluntary associations. Treating organizational control structures as independent variables and membership commitment levels as dependent variables, we established empirical evidence consistent with the incentive, the decision making, and the legitimate leadership approaches. In each analysis, one or more variables representing a particular type of control structure covaried significantly with the various aggregate membership commitment levels.

These analyses were conducted in parallel. Before investigating resource acquisition and goal attainment in the next three chapters, we will compare the simultaneous impact of the three types of organizational control structures on membership commitment. Our theory does not specify a causal ordering among the three types of control structures, so we shall not attempt to determine direct and indirect effects. Instead, we regress each of the five membership commitment variables upon three variables representing the three theoretical approaches. The relative size of the standardized regression coefficients will indicate the general importance of a variable, holding constant the effects of the other variables.

The purposive incentive scale is clearly the main variable from the incentive approach. From the legitimate leadership approach, the association's formal legitimacy is used. From the decision-making approach, several measures are available. However, organizational complexity is highly intercorrelated with formal legitimacy (simple structure associations tend not to have supralocal associations with strong legitimate control). This multicollinearity prevents both from being entered into the same equation. Instead, analyses with decision participation as the indicator of decentralized decision making will be presented, and results with total influence as the indicator will also be described.

Table 5.3 displays the standardized coefficients for the multiple regression of each membership commitment scale on the purposive incentives, decision participation, and formal legitimacy vari-

Table 5.3. Standardized Coefficients from Regression of Membership Commitment on Three Organizational Control Structures

Membership commitment scales	Organizational control structures			
	Purposive incentives	Decision participation	Formal legitimacy	R^2
Goal salience	.27*	.49***	.38**	.494**
Loyalty	.32**	.56***	.24	.509**
Personal salience	.16	.43***	.41**	.401**
Member perception	.24	.29*	.33*	.290**
Commitment index	.29*	.53***	.32**	.512***

*p ≤ .10.
**p ≤ .05.
***p ≤ .01.

ables. The relative importance of these three variables differs according to the particular dependent variables, although decision participation generally has the largest coefficient. In equations where formal legitimacy is significant, the beta for purposive incentives tends to be smaller. In the loyalty equation, however, purposive incentives have a sizable significant effect, but that for formal legitimacy is insignificant. In analyses where decision participation was replaced by total influence, the results are much clearer: purposive incentives drop to insignificance in each equation, while formal legitimacy has only slightly less impact than does total influence.

Taken together, these analyses suggest that the decision-making approach to social control is the most important of the three in explaining social control orientations, with formal legitimacy somewhat less important, and purposive incentives having perhaps only a marginal effect on membership commitment when the other variables are taken into account. A conservative conclusion is that each mechanism for creating normative social control in social influence associations tends to complement the other. Associations trying to develop high levels of membership enthusiasm and dedication to the organization should try to foster all three conditions conducive to more effective organizational self-regulation: an emphasis on the purposive benefits from affiliation, widespread opportunities for membership participation in making important decisions, and ties with supralocal units that exercise formally legitimate restraints on local policy. The additive effects of these three organizational control devices found in Table 5.3 suggest that each control structure contributes uniquely to variation in aggregate levels of membership commitment.

In sum, we established the empirical validity of the theoretical linkage between organizational control structures and membership commitment levels. Together these concepts make up the social control system of social influence associations.

Chapter Six

Social Control and Resource Mobilization

In the year after the data for this study were collected, two of the social influence associations experienced significant improvements in their financial situations. The Shady Grove Neighborhood Association received a substantial grant from a local foundation to staff and run programs for its inner-city clientele. The Society for Disease Elimination, which had relied heavily on door-to-door and mail solicitations, was approved for United Way support, thereby gaining access to the wider financial sources of that group. In both cases, the associations' social control systems provide possible clues to the attraction of outside resources.

Shady Grove's formal structure was a simple "amateur" set of officers and members, but its decision participation was extensive and its membership commitment among the highest of any neighborhood organization. This control system may have appealed to the local foundation as a sound investment for social change. Although the SDE's large membership exhibited relatively low levels of decision participation and membership commitment, it had a formal organizational structure that might appeal to United Way analysts: a professional staff with extensive experience in fund raising and program development in health service areas.

In this chapter we will consider evidence from the complete set of associations to determine whether social control systems—membership commitment and organizational control structures—enable associations to secure various kinds of resources. The basic theoretical hypothesis concerns the link between membership commitment and resource mobilization:

4. The stronger the membership's commitment, the more resources acquired by the association.

In the next section we will develop arguments from a resource
mobilization perspective to explain why voluntary associations
with more dedicated and enthusiastic memberships should be
able to raise more useful resources—financial and nonfinancial—
both from their members and from outside parties. Since we previously found empirical support for the hypothesis that organizational control structures covary with membership commitment,
we will also examine the direct and indirect effect of such control
structures on resource mobilization. Incentive structures, decision-making patterns, and legitimacy not only affect resources by
raising aggregate membership commitment levels, they may also
help to secure necessary resources directly.

Resource Mobilization

All organizations require continuous input of resources to
maintain themselves and to achieve external goals. For social influence associations, tangible resources may come from the membership and from outside parties. In either instance, the process
by which the association gains control over resources that it previously did not control may be called "resource mobilization":
"By definition, it entails a decline in the assets controlled by subunits, the supraunit of which the unit is a member, or external
units, unless the assets whose control the unit gained are newly
produced ones. . . . The change in capacity to control and to use
assets is what is significant" (Etzioni, 1968:388–389).

In addition to utilitarian resources, Etzioni also classified assets
as coercive (use of force, a largely irrelevant action for voluntary
associations) and normative (loyalty, dedication). However, we are
persuaded by Tilly's (1978:69) argument that "loyalty and obligation are not so much resources as they are conditions affecting the
likelihood that resources will be delivered when called for. . . .
We can then represent loyalties, obligations, commitments and so
forth as determinants of the probability that each resource nomi-

nally under group control will be available." Gamson (1975:140) took a similar view in asserting that "established groups must maintain the loyalty and commitment of those from whom they draw their resources; challenging groups must create this loyalty." Both authors essentially treat the strength of membership commitment as antecedent to the extraction of membership resources.

In our model, the membership's commitment is a precondition for producing utilitarian resources of the type described above. That is, unless an organization can achieve a high degree of favorable regard from its members, it will be unlikely to persuade them to relinquish control over personal resources—especially time and labor power—to the organization's use in collective actions. Where membership commitment is low, appeals for contributions in money or in kind are likely to fall on deaf ears.

Specific dimensions of membership commitment can be expected to relate similarly to members' resource commitments. The more central the organization is to members' life interests, the greater their responsiveness to perceived needs of the collectivity. Appeals for participation and financial contributions will be more successful when loyalty is strongly ingrained. Perceptions that the other members are strongly attached to the organization should strengthen individual members' resolve to do their share to see that the organization performs well. The greater the visibility and importance assigned to collective objectives, the more effort and time the membership should be willing to spend toward their achievement.

Coleman (1973b) developed a formal theoretical model of person-group relations that helps illuminate the expected relationship between membership commitment and resource commitments. In modern organizations, members yield usage rights—their direct control over property and other resources—to the collectivity in the expectation that this "loss of power" will be compensated by increased benefits from affiliation (high wages in work organizations, desired public policies in social influence associations, for example). As the collectivity gains power through increased size, the individuals within lose their ability to direct the organization's application of their alienated resources.

The loss-of-power phenomenon in voluntary organizations was noticed nearly a generation ago by C. Wright Mills:

Voluntary associations have become larger to the extent that they have become effective; and to just that extent they have become inaccessible to the individual who would shape by discussion the policies of the organization to which he belongs. Accordingly, along with older institutions, these voluntary associations have lost their grip on the individual. As more people are drawn into the political arena, these associations become mass in scale; and as the power of the individual becomes more dependent upon such mass associations, they are less accessible to the individual's influence [1956:307].

At the individual level, loss of control over events may be experienced as psychological stress. One solution to the loss of power may be to reduce involvement in areas where control over corporate actors is low—to withdraw from collective action and to withhold resources from the collectivity, instead investing them in activities one can more readily control, such as family, recreation, and consumption. (Other alternatives include trying to increase control over corporate actors, for example, by forming coalitions with other members.) This sensed loss of power may lie behind the reluctance of many social influence members to commit more than nominal levels of resources to the association.

From the association's viewpoint, the need to obtain resources from the membership requires that the membership's aggregate sense of power loss be reduced, to avoid the exit option (Hirschman, 1970). Organizational control systems that generate high membership commitment inoculate their memberships against alienation over power loss. Therefore, we expect that high levels of membership commitment will be accompanied by greater acquisition of membership resources, while organizations capable of only low aggregate rates of membership commitment will produce meager investments of resources from their memberships.

Our assumption that stronger membership commitment should produce higher resource contributions is in stark contradiction to Olson's (1965) interpretation of collective action. He argued that in the absence of coercion or selective incentives most members of organizations seeking collective goods will not feel compelled to contribute resources to produce such goals. A rational cost-benefit analysis, he argued, would convince a member that if the goal can be achieved without his or her contribution, he or she should withhold that contribution, thereby gaining the maximum benefit without paying any costs. Of course, all other members, as rational beings, make the same analysis, and as a result no contributions to the collective action will occur and the public good will not be achieved.

Olson's formal model is based on economic postulates of individual rationality and perfectly competitive markets. His theory implicitly assumes that members of an organization develop no loyalties or long-term commitments to the group. An association is merely a marketplace for individuals to attempt to maximize personal gain through collective action. In contrast, our sociological theory of organizational behavior assumes that individual members will form long-term commitments. Associations intentionally operate to socialize their members to take the organization's interests into account when deciding to contribute personal resources. (See Cook and Emerson, 1978, for a formal model of social exchange and power that points out this difference between economic and sociological exchange theories). When organizations successfully establish such commitment among their memberships, contributions of resources to the organization will be expected.

Voluntary associations can overcome the tendency for members to "take a free ride" by inculcating strong levels of membership commitment that predispose the membership to respond with resources when the association calls upon them to do so. At the individual level of behavior (which we do not analyze in this volume), the intense emotional, affectual commitment can presumably override the rational calculative analysis stressed in Olson's explanation. The one point at which both approaches to resource-generation may touch is Olson's exemption of "small" groups from the cost-benefit contingency. Where individuals' actions are highly visible to other members, as in small groups, peer-pressure processes may nullify the tendency to withhold contributions in the hope of maximizing personal gain from collective action. We saw earlier, however, that organizational size has only a slight and insignificant negative relationship to the level of membership commitment, suggesting that, at least among associations varying in size up to a few thousand, size is an inconsequential factor in promoting attachment to the organization. Nevertheless, we will investigate whether size affects the production of resource contributions independently of membership commitment.

Our hypothesis on social influence associations argues that the level of loyalty, dedication, and enthusiasm exhibited by an association's membership is an important factor in external agents' decisions to provide resources, particularly financial contributions. Outside contributions may be viewed as a form of investment in an association's effort to achieve specified objectives. (Of course, external investors are likely to be found only among persons and organizations sympathetic to the goals of the social influence association. In the next two chapters we will explore the relative advantages an association gains by forming coalitions with wealthier partners in its organizational environment.) A potential investor—whether United Way, a private foundation, or a federal agency—will generally want some assurance that the contribution will increase the likelihood of the association's objectives being attained. An important bit of evidence in making decisions on investment possibilities, once compatibility with the sponsor's goals is ascertained, is the characteristic aggregate level of affective membership commitment. An association with a visible public image as a cohesive, dedicated group will probably be a more attractive investment than an organization plagued with apathy and disunion. A high degree of mutual self-regulation will typically be read as a sign of a well-functioning organization, one that "has its act together" and is competent to use the resources provided by the external sponsor effectively. As a United Way official commented about the Organization for Retarded Persons, "They've really come a long way in just a few years, and that's one of the reasons we've substantially increased our assistance to them." Hence, we anticipate finding a positive relationship between aggregate membership commitment and externally provided resources.

In addition to any effect on resources mediated by membership commitment, organizational control structures may directly affect the acquisition of resources. We noted that potential investors will seek assurance of the soundness of their investments and that strong commitment levels in an association would be relevant evidence. Stressing the importance of matching organizational structures to the expectations of relevant elements in the environment, Meyer and Rowan advance the proposition: "Organizations that incorporate societally legitimated rationalized elements in their formal structures maximize their legitimacy and increase their resources and survival capabilities" (1977:352). As we interpret this proposition, each of our control structures (incentives, decision making, legitimacy) may be viewed as a rationalized structure that, in a given context, will function to maximize resources. Investors' concerns will determine the relevance of particular structures as evidence of a sound investment. Some investors are concerned primarily with efficiency, others with accountability; still other investors may have ideological concerns that outweigh either efficiency or accountability (e.g., whether the structure provides "maximum feasible participation" of appropriate persons—see Moynihan, 1969).

The preceding review of theoretical literature developed the rationale behind the expected link between organizational control systems (both control structures and membership commitment) and resource acquisition. Curiously, an intensive combing of the research literature failed to turn up any empirical studies of this relationship in voluntary organizations. However, in the research literature on work organizations, a number of studies, especially from the human relations perspective, argued for a direct relationship between employee morale (e.g., job satisfaction) and job performance (e.g., productivity, absenteeism). More recent work has stressed the complexity and contingency of the relationship and includes the possibility that productivity influences morale. See Schwab and Cummings (1970) for an excellent review of the literature. From Marx to Blauner (1964) there has been extensive concern with the alienating effect on workers of their loss of control over the production process and the consequences of alienation for the quantity and quality of their efforts. We could find no parallel to this concern in the writings on voluntary association behavior. Thus, our analysis provides the first attempt to link the social control process to members' resource contributions.

Measuring Resources

Resources useful to social influence associations take a variety of forms. For the empirical analyses, we discuss measures under three discrete categories: member resource contributions of participation, time, and money; disposition to maintain involvement under adverse conditions; total organizational financial resources from members and outside parties.

Member Resource Contributions

An association's membership provides many sustaining resources, including material (money, goods), energy (time, labor effort), knowledge (expertise, experience), and symbolic media (legitimation, obedience, mobilization responsiveness). The types of resource contributions useful to an association vary across situations. Some resources must be channeled into internal maintenance tasks: keeping in touch with members, creating consensus on issues and strategies, bolstering flagging spirits. Other resources can be directly applied to influence attempts: hiring professional lobbyists, directing a publicity campaign, marching in a picket line. Associations cannot always know in advance which forms of resources will prove most effective in achieving specific external influence objectives. Thus the association's internal economy (Zald, 1970a; 1970b) must generate a variety of resource contributions from members to ensure that the association will have adequate resources to meet its requirements for maintenance and goal attainment. Some resources may be more general than others and more readily convertible into other forms of resources useful in given situations (Clark, 1968a). Money is the most obvious of this type.

The first question that must be raised is whether participation in voluntary associations is a unitary phenomenon or whether it exhibits distinct analytic and empirical dimensions. If organizational participation is unitary, each respondent can be located at some point along a latent dimension. The probability that he or she engages in specific activities will be determined by that position. A unitary participation dimension would presumably range from no involvement to hyperactivity, with increasing participation in a larger number of organizational actions as one approached the upper end of the scale. Activities—whether licking stamps, attending meetings, or circulating petitions—will thus be essentially interchangeable indicators of the latent variable, and the measurement task will resolve itself into a simple cumulative count of a representative set of such actions. The more actions a member undertakes, the greater the organizational participation manifested.

In contrast to the unitary participation hypothesis, organizational involvement may be fragmented among analytically distinct dimensions—a specific mode of participation to serve different purposes. Actions prompted by one dimension would not be substitutable for actions along another dimension. If multiple dimensions were independent from each other, a respondent who shows high participation in one type of organizational activity may not participate at all on another type. The measurement problem in a multidimensional participatory framework would be more complicated than in a unitary dimension, but it would also be more realistic. The multidimensional hypothesis in part reflects differences in the individual motives, aims, resources, and opportunities that attract people to the organizational arena. In part, also, multidimensional participation reflects organizational differences in opportunities and requirements for membership involvement.

To guide our speculations on the possible dimensions of organizational participation, we are fortunate to have Verba and Nie's (1972) seminal study of political participation as an exemplar. They conceptualized the citizenry as divided not simply into more or less active citizens, but into "many types of activists engaging in different acts, with different motives, and different consequences" (1972:45). The particular dimensions they selected for analysis were arrayed according to general problems associated with participation: the type of influence exerted over government leaders; the scope of the outcome sought; the amount of conflict in which such acts involve a participant; and the amount of initiative required to engage in the activity. Combined in different ways, these distinctions suggested alternative rather than complementary channels by which citizens could attempt to influence the selection of government personnel and/or their actions.

One of Verba and Nie's modes of participation, cooperative activity, reflects primarily the type of activity with which we are concerned here. Citizen cooperation in formal and informal groups is aimed more at outcomes of a collective nature than at individual benefit. Conflict is usually intermediate between electoral situations and citizen-initiated contacts. "Groups act for what they perceive as a benefit for their group or for the community as a whole, and in neither case are they likely to be directly opposed by other citizens pushing an opposite policy" (1972:53). Because Verba and Nie's measurement of voluntary association activity was primarily at the global level and not focused on the internal dynamics of the organizations, they did not inquire into the possible multidimensional nature of cooperative activity itself. Our analysis in a sense extends their inquiry to a much finer-grained analysis. Both conceptually and empirically, we have been strongly influenced by the example set forth in Verba and Nie's now classic study.

Early in the interview, our respondents were asked many questions about their behavioral involvement in their association. They answered the bulk of these items either yes or no to indicate whether they had performed any of the specified tasks during the previous year; three measures asked the extent of participation in meetings and outside of formal meetings, and the amount of money donated. The exact items and their distributions across all respondents may be found in Appendix C.6.

Results of an exploratory oblique-rotated factor analysis similar to that done to identify the dimensions of membership commitment produced four distinct member resource contribution scales—internal activity, leadership, infra-resources, and external activity. A secondary factor analysis of these standardized scale scores also resulted in a single summary resource contribution index that will be used whenever an overall pattern of resource contributions is required.

Tolerance

Membership activism is not the only type of resource useful to an association pursuing social influence goals. Often an organization must act swiftly and decisively on issues that arise so abruptly that mass membership mobilization is both infeasible and unnecessary. Instead, leaders need the membership's backing in order to act authoritatively. Wood (1975, 1981) showed the importance of tolerance for churches seeking to implement social action policies that transcended members' attitudes toward public issues. Perrow (1968) pointed to the same phenomenon in his discussion of "names" as an important resource for voluntary associations. Voluntary associations relying on names and money have the greatest freedom to develop "derived goals," including those that go beyond members' views.

An incident involving two social influence associations illustrates the importance of tolerance for organizational action. The city of Indianapolis decided one Christmas to erect a nativity scene on public property. Within hours the local directors of the National Conference of Christians and Jews and the American Civil Liberties Union objected on constitutional grounds of church-state separation and hinted at legal action. The city backed down. While the association leaders undoubtedly suspected that many of their members did not object to the scene, the directors were confident that the members would tolerate their actions in order to uphold a fundamental organizational principle. Such reservoirs of support enabled the chapter leaders to claim united organizational strength when they confronted city officials with their policy demands. Organizations lacking tolerant memberships may be less able to influence public policies.

Our measure of membership tolerance is members' probable responses to a hypothetical situation where their association continued to make decisions that were unsatisfactory to them. Exact item wording appears in Appendix C.7. In associations scoring low on membership tolerance, a larger proportion would choose to leave the group if they were dissatisfied with organizational decisions on key issues. Highly tolerant memberships say they would more often remain in the organization and either go along with the decision or try to get it reversed. We view this item as representing an organization membership's willingness to persist in the association under personally unfavorable or unsatisfactory conditions. Associations with widespread tolerance thus have an important resource that allows leaders greater freedom of decision and action. Associations with memberships more prone to withdraw in adversity constrain the leaders and reduce their effectiveness in dealing with external institutions.

Total Budget

The third category of resources is the total amount of money available for organizational operations in a year. As we saw in Chapter Two, for the majority of sample associations the membership provides most of the operating funds. But a few organizations receive substantial funds from outside parties, primarily foundations and government agencies. By combining revenues from all sources, we obtain a total budget measure. Note that this resource indicator differs from the infra-resource scale described under member resource contributions. Infra-resources includes per capita contributions of money, as well as unspecified time.

But total budget is a measure of all available revenues, and as such may be a better indicator of the association's capacity to affect public policies. Because total budgets are skewed by the presence of a handful of associations with large expenditures, we also transform the distribution by taking the natural logarithm of the budget (logbudget).

Resources and Membership Commitments

The test of Hypothesis 4 begins with an examination of the correlations between the five measures of aggregate membership commitment and the three types of resources, reported in Table 6.1. With few exceptions, all correlations are positive and significant. Some are especially strong, for example, the +.70 correlation between the commitment index and the membership resource contribution index, showing that almost half the interorganizational variance is held in common. Member perception has the least covariation with the membership resources measures. The other indicators—goal salience, loyalty, and personal salience—which reflect the members' reports of their own orientations toward the association, better predict the average rate of various membership contributions. Among resource indicators, external activity correlates least highly with all five social control belief measures. We will return to this finding in Chapter Seven. But the general conclusion is that the higher the aggregate membership commitment, the greater the rate at which members contribute personal resources to the association.

Included in the last column of Table 6.1 are correlations of resources with organizational size, measured as the log of the number of members in the local chapter. In Chapter Two we investigated whether size was related to membership commitment levels and discovered that it was not. But the research literature discussed in that chapter had found consistent inverse relationships between size and participation. The correlations in Table 6.1 confirm that pattern for these social influence associations. In subsequent analyses we will include size in multiple regression equations involving resources. Here we simply note that holding size constant does not significantly diminish the partial correlations between membership resource contributions and membership commitment.

Thus, we conclude that Hypothesis 4 is strongly supported when membership resources are the dependent variable.

Turning to tolerance, we again find the anticipated positive relationship between this resource and membership commitment. Personal salience has an especially high correlation, implying that when members consider the organization central in their life interests, they will be willing to stick by it rather than leave if the association makes unsatisfactory policy decisions. In contrast,

Table 6.1. Correlations of Resources with Membership Commitment and Size

Resource measure	Membership commitment scales					Size (log)
	Goal salience	Loyalty	Personal salience	Member perception	Commitment index	
Member commitments						
Internal activity	.59***	.60***	.69***	.47***	.65***	−.38**
Leadership	.48***	.54***	.46***	.30**	.52***	−.39**
Infra-resources	.57***	.66***	.64***	.46***	.66***	−.49**
External activity	.33**	.37**	.31**	.26	.37**	−.23
Resource contribution index	.63***	.68***	.67***	.47***	.70***	−.46**
Tolerance	.24	.30**	.61***	.40**	.35**	.08
Budget	.22	.26	.10	.14	.20	.20
Logbudget	.47***	.47***	.38***	.46***	.46***	.19

** p ≤ .05.
*** p ≤ .01.

goal salience has an insignificant correlation with tolerance, suggesting that when the goal rather than the organization is particularly important memberships may be less willing to stick by the malperforming organization. Exit in search of other organizations capable of achieving the same objectives may be a preferred option. In general, tolerance is greatest when membership commitment to the association is high. Thus, these relationships further confirm Hypothesis 4. These findings could also have been anticipated from Hirschman's (1970) discussion of loyalty to deteriorating organizations. Where membership attachment is initially strong, deterioration in organizational performance is more likely to be responded to by voice (attempts to change the organizational policy) than by immediate exit.

Finally, the relationship between total budget and membership commitment depends upon the functional form of the measure. Actual dollar amounts have insignificant correlations, but the natural log transformation (logbudget) is significantly positive with all five commitment indicators. Therefore, in further analyses we will rely exclusively on the logbudget figure to represent the total financial resources mobilized by the social influence associations. In sum, all three types of resources have the positive relationship to membership commitment hypothesized by the theory.

We observe that these findings are in agreement with the "loss of power" analysis. The commitment scales are inversely related to an index of alienation from the association. This alienation scale includes items such as "I don't have much say about what this organization does" and "As a member I play an important part in my organization" (reversed scoring). The loss-of-power or loss-of-control argument is that alienated members will tend to withdraw their resource contributions from the collectivity. And, indeed, we find that high levels of alienation correlate inversely with the membership resource commitment variables (for example, $r = -.81$ between alienation and the resource commitment index). Presumably the strength of membership commitment mobilizes resources to some extent by reducing members' sense of alienation resulting from their loss of control over these resources.

Resources and Control Structures

We now turn to the question of whether the second component of social control systems—organizational control structures—affects resource mobilization in social influence associations. In the theoretical scheme outlined in Chapter One, we assumed that control structures preceded the formation of aggregate membership commitment. Therefore, we must assess the impact of control structures on resources after holding constant the effect of membership commitment. We are especially interested in two possible outcomes.

1. The relationship between control structures and resource mobilization may be entirely indirect; that is, control structures may generate high levels of membership commitment, which in turn mobilize resources. This simple causal chain is depicted in Figure 6.1A.

2. Alternatively, membership commitment may fail to completely mediate the effects of control structures on resources. As shown in Figure 6.1B, some of the covariation of control structures and resources is direct.

Which outcome is most consistent with the evidence will be determined by a path analysis that includes both membership

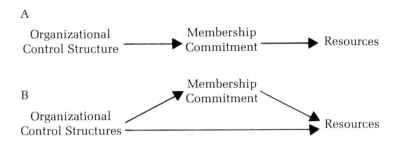

Figure 6.1. Alternative Causal Models of Resources

commitment beliefs and organizational control structures as independent variables predicting the three types of resources. Logsize will also be held constant. Appendix D provides a brief exposition of path analysis for readers unfamiliar with the technique. Since Chapters Three to Five established the connection between control structures and normative control orientations, our interest here focuses on the existence of direct impact of control structure on resources, after holding both size and the summary commitment index constant. If the regression coefficients for control structure variables fail to attain statistical significance in the multiple regression equations, we will conclude that the mediating model (Figure 6.1A) is appropriate, provided the commitment index continues to exert a positive effect on resource mobilization. However, if the betas for control structures are significant in the multiple regression equations, the model of direct and indirect effects (Figure 6.1B) is appropriate. Interpretation of the model will depend on the particular magnitude and sign of the coefficients.

Our strategy for assessing the causal relationship is to add only one variable representing an organizational control structure to a regression equation including size and the membership commitment index. As in the comparison of the three control approaches at the end of Chapter Five, we select one indicator of each approach: purposive incentives, decision participation, and formal legitimacy. The three sets of three regression equations are presented in Table 6.2. To conserve space, analyses using all five indicators of membership resource contributions are not presented. Only the results for the summary index are displayed, although these findings are comparable to those with the specific scales.

The membership commitment index remains significant in every equation except that for tolerance when formal legitimacy is entered. Thus, the effect of membership commitment levels on resource mobilization observed in the correlations is robust even after holding various control structures and organizational size constant. Size has significant, if opposite, effects on membership resource contributions and total logbudget. The larger the organization, the lower the rate at which members provide personal resources. But larger organizations attract greater total financial con-

Table 6.2. Standardized Coefficients from Regression of Resource Measures on Membership Commitment Index and Organizational Control Structures

Resource measure	Commitment index	Size (log)	Independent variables Purposive incentives	Decision participation	Formal legitimacy	R²
Resource contribution	.68***	-.30**	-.13			.586***
Resource contribution	.46***	-.22*		.36***		.664***
Resource contribution	.62***	-.30**			.00	.573***
Tolerance	.33*	.18	.14			.165
Tolerance	.43**	.16		-.08		.155
Tolerance	.23	.12			.41**	.294***
Logbudget	.36**	.33**	.43***			.463***
Logbudget	.72***	.24		-.39**		.412***
Logbudget	.39**	.27*			.38**	.434***

* p ≤ .10.
** p ≤ .05.
*** p ≤ .01.

tributions from members and outside parties. Only for tolerance does organizational size have no impact.

Among the three types of control structures, the occurrence of direct effects is quite mixed. Neither purposive incentives nor formal legitimacy directly affects membership resource contributions, but decision participation has a substantial direct positive effect that also reduces somewhat the magnitude of the betas for size and the commitment index. Thus, decentralized decision making appears to generate high rates of membership resource mobilization both directly and indirectly by bolstering normative social control orientations.

With tolerance as a dependent variable, neither decision participation nor purposive incentives directly affect such resources. However, formal legitimacy has such a substantial effect on tolerance that it reduces to insignificance the impact of the membership commitment index. Identical results would occur if belief in legitimacy were substituted for the formal legitimacy variable. Formal legitimacy thus appears to be an important control device for developing memberships less likely to withdraw from the associations if dissension over policy decisions arises. The strong norms of due process and orderliness that accompany high formal legitimacy and high belief in legitimacy may be invoked by leaders to encourage members to remain in the association in the face of provocations that might drive many members out of organizations lacking such control structures.

Finally, the three equations for logbudget each have significant direct effects from the antecedent control structure variables. Purposive incentives and formal legitimacy both have positive betas, implying that larger financial resources can be mobilized from members and outside parties by organizations that stress purposes and have supralocal units with strong authority over local chapters. But the direct effect of decision participation on logbudget is significantly inverse. In Chapter Four we found that decentralized decision making raised the level of membership commitment, which in turn increased the total amount of financial resources, as shown in the equation in Table 6.2. Thus, the indirect effect of decision participation is positive, while its direct effect is negative. These contrary effects are almost completely offsetting, so that the observed zero-order correlation between decision participation and logbudget is only $-.10$.

This unanticipated divergence in the direct and indirect effects of decentralization on logbudget demands a substantive interpretation. The positive indirect effect is explainable in terms developed earlier in this chapter: decision participation encourages high levels of membership orientation toward the association, which in turn elicits larger financial contributions. But the negative direct effect implies that, holding membership commitment levels constant, decentralization impedes the mobilization of larger financial contributions. The reason may lie in the perceptions and expectations of outside funding sources for social influence associations.

When potential donors—foundations, government agencies, and individual constituents—consider possible recipients for contributions, they may be more concerned with organizational accountability in using the funds than with the extent of member participation. Indeed, associations that strongly emphasize decentralized decision making might be viewed by outside funders as risky investments. Such contributors may prefer to deal with associations where direct control over policy decisions is concentrated in fewer hands. If this is the case, we would expect that, after holding the aggregate membership commitment levels constant, associations with widespread decision participation would be less likely to attract large outside funds, exactly the negative direct effect observed in Table 6.2.

If this interpretation is correct, we should observe a strong effect of organizational formal structure on logbudget, with professionalized associations attracting higher levels of funds, particularly from outside parties, than associations lacking professional status. Professional structures may be seen by outside contributors as more legitimate claimants on resources than would "amateur" associations.

Meyer and Rowan (1977) developed the rationale underlying this legitimating function of formal organizational structure. They argued that the formal structures of most postindustrial organizations "dramatically reflect the myths of their institutional environments instead of the demands of their work activities" (341). The creation of a highly rationalized formal structure, as exemplified by the professionalized social influence associations, may be dictated less by intrinsic task requirements than "by the views of important contributors, by knowledge legitimated through the educational system, by social prestige, by the laws, and by the definitions of negligence and prudence used by the courts" (343). Meyer and Rowan suggested that organizational conformity to prevailing myths about appropriate formal structure can yield advantages in obtaining legitimacy and resources from the external environment, and hence in organizational survival and growth.

External funding agencies may prefer to deal with professionalized social influence associations under the assumption that such organizations have a maturity, competence, and fiscal integrity lacking in nonprofessional associations. Therefore, a professionalized association is better situated to obtain grants and program funds from foundations, the United Way, and the federal government. Members and other individual constituents may be more willing to contribute to the coffers if the formal structure has full-time staff looking after collective affairs.

To the Meyer and Rowan argument we may add another explanation for expecting a relationship between professionalization and the procurement of external funding. A primary function of a social influence professional is to act as the fiduciary, or agent, of the collectivity. To seek out potential coalition partners and persuade them of the merits of supporting the association's programs and policies is a central task of the executive director. Indeed, the wages and salaries of staff members, particularly those engaged in direct service delivery to clients, may be wholly dependent upon a continual flow of grants and contracts from foundations and government agencies. Thus, not only the greater cultural legitimacy but the mundane hustling for advantage in the modern grants economy leads directly to the larger external budgets enjoyed by professionalized social influence associations.

If the foregoing arguments are correct, we would expect that formal organizational structure accounts for the negative direct effect of decision participation on logbudget found in Table 6.2.

Table 6.3. Standardized Coefficients from Regression of Logbudget on Formal Structure, Decision Participation, and Membership Commitment Index

				Independent variables			
Resource measure	Commitment index	Size (log)	Decision participation	Elaborate structure	Professional structure	Board only	R^2
Logbudget	.56***	.13	−.19	.06	.58***	.33*	.656**
External funds (log)	.25	−.21	.05	−.11	.64***	.01	.416***

* p ≤ .10.
** p ≤ .05.
*** p ≤ .01.

Specifically, if professionalization of the association is held constant, the negative impact of decision participation on logbudget should be greatly reduced. This hypothesis is examined by entering the three categoric variables for organizational complexity into the equation in Table 6.2. The results appear in Table 6.3. The coefficient for decision participation, while still negative, is no longer significant. The substantial beta for professional structure shows that, as expected, these associations receive larger funds than the other types. Board-only associations may also obtain more total funds than the simple- and elaborate-structure associations. The membership commitment index remains a significant predictor of logbudget after holding formal organizational complexity constant. Apparently this net covariation arises from that portion of total logbudget that is directly contributed by the members of associations with high commitment levels. To further pinpoint the effect of formal structure on resource mobilization, we created a second budgetary measure that includes only those funds obtained from outside sources. The log of external funds has significant relationship only with professional structure. The commitment index has little impact upon external funds, suggesting that funding agencies attend mainly to formal features of the association in their funding decisions and not to the membership's dedication and enthusiasm for their organization.

In sum, the analyses presented in this chapter provide the first empirical evidence to link membership social control beliefs to resource mobilization in social influence associations. The results strongly substantiate the hypothesis that high levels of membership commitment generate high levels of resources. Even after controlling organizational size and a series of control structures postulated to precede the formation of commitment, the latter variable persists as a significant predictor of organizational variation in three types of resources—membership resource contributions, tolerance, and logbudget.

In terms of two alternative path models by which control structures might affect resources, we found mixed results. In several cases, the membership commitment scales mediated the effects of organizational control structures (e.g., of purposive incentives on member resources, and of decision participation on tolerance). In other cases, strong direct effects occurred (e.g., of formal legitimacy on tolerance, and of purposive incentives on logbudget). A curious inverse direct effect of decision participation on logbudget seems to be due to a tendency of external funding sources to provide financial resources mainly to professional associations rather than to amateur groups with widespread decision making.

Chapter Seven

Goal Attainment

Beginning in the 1960s the natural environment has been the target of a major social movement whose prime movers form a loose coalition of citizen activist groups (Caldwell, Hayes, and Mac-Whirter, 1976). Southern Indiana saw its share of controversies that pitted environmentalists against government agencies and private enterprise. Two recent cases illustrate the success and failure of social influence associations in preventing depredations against the natural environment.

In February 1977 the U.S. Forest Service supervisor for the Hoosier National Forest, which covers parts of nine southern Indiana counties, decided to proceed with plans to lease portions of the forest for oil and natural gas drilling. His decision came after four years of internal study but without public hearings or an environmental impact statement, because, said the supervisor, the issue was "not highly controversial." Immediately, several environmental groups, including the Izaak Walton League and the Hoosier Sierra Club, wrote letters to higher officials demanding a thorough environmental impact statement and hinting that legal steps might be taken to enjoin the leasing. Within three weeks the supervisor rescinded his decision and recommended making the area part of a comprehensive land-management planning process that would require public hearings and a full impact statement.

In 1973 the major state electrical utility, Public Service Indiana, announced plans for a 2,260,000-kilowatt nuclear power plant to be constructed at Marble Hill on the Ohio River. Nuclear power opponents, citing potential hazards of reactor safety, waste product storage, and construction damage, began administrative and legal challenges that succeeded only in delaying the ground breaking. When the final permit for construction was granted by

135

the Nuclear Regulatory Commission in April 1978, the Paddle-wheel Alliance turned to direct nonviolent action. The first in a promised series of sit-ins was held that fall on the construction site, resulting in thirty-one trespass arrests. The Alliance's efforts did not prevent the continuing construction of the plant, although the date for full operations has been delayed by construction problems.

These two incidents exemplify the final theoretical concept in our theory of organizational behavior—goal attainment or effectiveness. In the theoretical model, resources mobilized by an association from its membership and from outside parties should improve the probability of successful goal attainment:

5. The more resources available to an association, the more effective its social influence.

But the two incidents also reveal the importance of conditions beyond the association's boundaries. The state of public opinion, the size and resources of opponents, the legal standing of parties to a controversy, the technical complexity of an issue—these and other factors may constrain a social influence association's ability to impose its preferred solution to public policies. Such factors external to the organization—"environmental" variables—must be included with organizational attributes in a more comprehensive account of goal attainment. Thus, in addition to resources and other organizational variables previously analyzed, we shall incorporate environmental variables in our analysis of goal attainment.

An examination of goal attainment extends across this chapter and the next. After reviewing the literature on organizational effectiveness, including both internal and environmental effects, we develop two measures of effectiveness in goal attainment for our sample. In the remainder of this chapter we relate these effectiveness indicators to internal organizational attributes.

Problems of Effectiveness

There are fewer studies of organizational effectiveness—also called goal attainment—than of covariation among organizational structures or the behavior of organizational members. This disparity probably arises from the great difficulty in conceptualizing and measuring goals in complex organizations and their attainment. A recent review of seventeen proposed multivariate models of organizational effectiveness disclosed the lack of consensus about a useful, valid set of effectiveness measures. Adaptability-flexibility was the most frequently used criterion (ten studies), dropping off rapidly to productivity (six), satisfaction/morale (five), and profit and resource acquisition (three each). The author concluded that effectiveness cannot be "universally defined or measured in terms of a static set of variables as has been done elsewhere" (Steers, 1975).

Another study concluded that the major reason for the disarray in the organizational effectiveness literature is researchers' failure to take seriously the multidimensional character of organizational effectiveness.

Since the concept of organizational effectiveness differs with different constituents, different levels of analysis, different aspects of the organization, and different research or evaluation purposes, effectiveness not only possesses multiple dimensions, but it is not a unitary concept. Rather it is a construct composed of multiple domains which are therefore operationalized in different ways. Effectiveness in one domain may not necessarily relate to effectiveness in another domain. For example, maximizing the satisfaction and growth of individuals in an organization, the domain of effectiveness for Argyris (1962), Likert (1967), Cummings (1977), and others, may be negatively related to high levels of subunit output and coordination, the domain of effectiveness of Pennings and Goodman (1977) [Cameron, 1978].

This conclusion seems warranted.

Many effectiveness studies concentrate upon economic organizations, where money is thought to provide a standard unit for performance comparison across organizations. Thus profits, sales, and earnings are often used to indicate how successfully a corporation or industry pursues a presumed goal of profit maximization (Lieberson and O'Connor, 1972; Pennings, 1975; Hirsch, 1975). Some specialized organizations, such as sports teams, may provide a unique performance standard not generally applicable to a wide range of organizations (Grusky, 1963; Eitzen and Yetman, 1972). Some human service organizations, including schools and hospitals, can be evaluated in terms of their efficiency in processing clients (Rushing, 1974; Hrebiniak and Alutto, 1972). The relatively few empirical studies of voluntary associations usually rely upon "soft" or subjective effectiveness ratings by judges or even by the organization participants themselves (Tannenbaum, 1968; also Pennings, 1976; Osborn and Hunt, 1974). A comparative study of Canadian and United States interest groups used both subjective evaluations by executive directors and actual results achieved on specific issues (Presthus, 1974:169).

Analysts differ in the factors to which they attribute variation in organizational effectiveness. Price's (1968) inventory of findings from fifty research studies listed numerous variables related to organizational effectiveness. A high degree of division of labor, maximum centralization of decision making, high level of legitimacy, extensive vertical and horizontal communication, and large size were internal characteristics likely to result in greater effectiveness. External relationships involving greater autonomy of action, greater cooperation, and greater representation in other organizations also contributed to effectiveness. Price's inventory, however, deliberately excluded voluntary associations, so the relevance of his propositions for this study has not yet been demonstrated.

Authors favoring an environmental explanation of effectiveness believe that a complex external situation requires organizations to adjust their internal structure and processes to maintain and/or increase their competitive advantages. This perspective has been formalized under the rubric of the "structural-contingency" model, the notion that for a given environment and production technology a particular structure is appropriate. Those organizations with inappropriate structures will be relatively ineffective and eventually must change or perish. An alternative perspective—equifinality—suggests that the fit is much looser and that a variety of structures are compatible with adaptive success.

Empirical studies can be cited to support both sides. Environmental contingencies such as industry structure may be much more important than internal factors such as leadership in accounting for the profitability performance of production corporations (Lieberson and O'Connor, 1972; Hirsch, 1975). Interorganizational position in a market or field may account for vastly more variation in performance than do internal attributes (Aldrich, 1976a, 1976b; Osborn and Hunt, 1974). On the other hand, internal structures appear in various studies as strong predictors of organizational performance. Tannenbaum's (1968) control graph studies implied that the distribution of power among members determines how successfully both business and voluntary associations achieve their goals. Pennings' (1976) analysis of brokerage firm branches supported this result. Using indicators of worker morale, anxiety, sales production, and change in productivity, the study showed "that autonomous, decentralized, and participative organizations are more effective."

The relative impact of external environmental versus internal structure on organizational goal attainment remains unclear, particularly for voluntary associations. Furthermore, the importance of explanatory variables may depend upon the dimension of effectiveness. Cameron (1978), for example, found nine dimensions of effectiveness appropriate to colleges. Some dimensions are intrinsically related to internal structure (e.g., organizational health—indexed by benevolence, vitality, and viability in the internal processes of the institution); others are related to the environment (e.g., systems openness and community interaction—indexed by the emphasis placed on interaction with, adaptation to, and service in the external environment). Clearly, the social influence organizations' environments are important when they attempt to influence public officials and specific, contested public policies. Available evidence implies that whenever external conditions are difficult to calculate, collective actions will be much less effective in affecting public policies than under more stable and simple conditions. In this chapter we will focus on the relationship between associational characteristics and goal effectiveness, reserving until Chapter Eight consideration of environmental effects on goal attainment.

These associations, like all types of organizations, have other relevant effectiveness dimensions besides influencing public policies (for example, organizational health). A clue that members perceive different dimensions to be important is revealed in their responses to the first interview question: "If someone were to ask you what this organization is all about, what would you tell them?" About a third of the open-ended responses could clearly be classified as attempts to affect public policy (e.g., to influence legislation or government administrative decisions; political advocacy). Another third, however, emphasized either information to the public or specific organizational programs and services. Given the diversity of goals that members may hold for their associations, internal and external variables may differ markedly in importance according to the dimension of goal attainment examined.

Measuring Effectiveness

Two distinct measures of goal attainment were available in the data. The first, member ratings, is based on the association respondents' judgments of their organization's general performance. The second, influence reputation, is based on evaluations by a panel of knowledgeable community informants judging how much influence each organization has on public policies.

Member Ratings

Price (1972:101–106) advocated this technique (based on a study of hospital effectiveness by Georgopoulos and Mann, 1962) as being adaptable for general use across diverse organizations. Our social influence association members were asked to rate their organization on a ten-point scale "in terms of effectiveness in achieving organizational goals." Mean scores for each association were calculated; officer and member ratings correlated +.79 across associations, implying high agreement between these strata.

By referring only to unspecified general "organizational goals" as the criterion to be rated, this measure allowed respondents considerable leeway in selecting the salient dimensions to be evaluated. Such a global measure is useful for two reasons. First, while all the associations wished to influence society, the directness with which they attempted to influence public policy varied. For example, one of HOP's goals was to influence public attitudes and

policies toward the mentally ill, but the major portion of its organizational effort was directed toward providing services to the
mentally disturbed and their families. We suspect that many HOP
members would consider the association's effectiveness primarily
in terms of organizing and carrying out such service activities. Yet
it would be meaningless to ask other organizations' members specifically about service effectiveness since these groups did not directly supply services to clients. Hence, a general member rating
of "organizational goals" permits respondents to consider those
aspects of associational performance most meaningful to them.

Second, some associations define their public policy influence
objectives quite narrowly. Their goals, if attained, often do not
leave a large impression on the wider community. Therefore, the
members of some groups may be more thoroughly acquainted with
the performance of the organization than are the community informants who helped us develop the second effectiveness measure.
Some organizations tend to be active only when specific issues gal-
vanize them into action. As the president of one neighborhood
group said, "You can't have an issue all the time." Organizations
that had not recently experienced a visible issue would be less
salient to external informants. For example, the Elm Lawn Neighborhood Association removed an objectionable business from its
territory, but no great impact was felt in the larger community and
there was no sustained press coverage. In contrast, Legal-Beagles,
Inc., fights numerous controversial battles for civil rights and is
continually in the news. Thus, member ratings of effectiveness
have the additional advantage over judges' ratings of a more knowledgeable evaluation for the less-visible associations.

Influence Reputation

The inspiration for this measure comes from the community
power research tradition's "reputational method" for determining
the persons and groups felt to be relatively more powerful in making collective decisions (see Ehrlich, 1967). In contrast to the unspecified dimension of effectiveness to be rated by the members,
the influence reputation task specifically focused on the public
policy dimension of association goals.

The influence reputations of the associations in our sample were measured during a larger study of interorganizational networks in Indianapolis, part of which will be explored in the next chapter. The thirty-two associations were included in a list of seventy organizations or types of organizations that encompassed government agencies, private corporations, and additional voluntary sector groups at both the city and state level. The complete list of organizations and details of the procedure are presented in Appendix C.8. Two dozen persons knowledgeable about community affairs were asked to place each organization in a seven-point scale using this criterion:

On the basis of your experience and information, please sort each organization name into the category which best describes how much *influence* the organization has had in the past couple of years on public policies in that organization's areas of interest.

Please consider in your decisions *only* how much influence an organization has in *achieving its own objectives*, and not how widespread its influence is in the entire community. If you feel you don't know enough about a particular organization, feel free to ignore it.

To avoid the distorting effect of averaging extremely discrepant ratings, we used the median value given by informants rating each social influence association. (Keep in mind that these median values were produced not solely with regard to the thirty-two associations, but in the context of the entire set of seventy organizations.) None of the social influence associations was rated higher than 4.79 on the seven-point scale, while one association received a 1.33, close to the bottom ("little or no influence"). The bulk of the associations tended to fall between 3.00 and 4.00, the latter equivalent to "a moderate influence."

Comparing member ratings with influence reputation scores produced several interesting differences. Two neighborhood organizations rated highly by their members fell below the mean on the informants' ratings. Both associations had impressive records of concrete achievements for their neighborhoods (e.g., street lights, snow removal, street improvements, educational services). The member ratings reflected these achievements, but their low salience to most community informants caused much lower influence reputation scores. On the other hand, Kids in Trouble was rated lowest among the members' evaluations but in the middle on the informants'. This discrepancy arose from the local chapter's recent formation. The informants probably assumed the chapter would be as influential as the state body, which had been active in delinquency issues for several years. Members, however, probably focused on the local unit's lack of specific accomplishment in the city during its first year of existence.

These and other differences between members' and judges' evaluations resulted in only a +.53 correlation between the two effectiveness measures. Enough covariation occurs to support an interpretation that both tap a common underlying construct. But enough divergence exists to imply that each may capture variation along different domains of goal effectiveness. Influence reputation seems to reflect primarily an association's ability to achieve goals outside organizational boundaries. The measure's strength lies in its comparative basis and the neutrality of the informants (in the sense that few were members of organizations they rated). Member ratings seem to reflect a greater mixture of goals, allowing both internal and external objectives to be considered in the evaluations. Their strength lies in the evaluators' more intimate knowledge of the organization and its goals. Given the different criteria and judges used to construct these two goal attainment indicators, we anticipate that different organizational processes may affect their variation.

Given the large number of measures for each set of theoretical concepts, the potential multicollinearity, and the small number of organizations in the study, all independent variables cannot be included simultaneously as predictors of goal attainment. Instead, an incremental strategy examines the validity of the hypothesis. Working backward in the causal sequence, we first identify the resource variables with the strongest relationship to goal attainment. Next, one at a time, indicators of commitment are introduced to determine whether any of these variables directly affect effectiveness in goal attainment while resource contributions are held constant, and whether the latter variables diminish in size when members' commitments are included. Finally, having identified the important resource and commitment relationships with goal attainment, again one at a time, the various indicators of organizational social control structure are entered into the equations. At that stage, we shall have identified specific organizational attributes with substantial direct effects on the two social influence effectiveness measures. We conclude the chapter with an assessment of the indirect effects of prior variables operating through intervening measures to affect goal attainment.

Goal Attainment and Resources

A test of Hypothesis 5 calls for inspection of bivariate and multivariate relationships of the two goal attainment measures with the various indicators of the three types of resources—membership resource contributions, tolerance, and budget. The relevant zero-order correlations appear in Table 7.1. At the bottom, organizational size (logarithm of number of members) has no relationships to either goal attainment increase, so it will not be considered further. Not one of the membership participation scales significantly covaries with member ratings of goal attainment. Influence reputation correlates significantly only with leadership and infra-resource contributions. Curiously, the aggregate rate of attempts to influence external agents is unrelated to either goal attainment indicator. External activity is a compound of contacts with government officials on behalf of the association, letter writing to newspapers, and picketing or demonstrating during the previous year. Organizations that mobilize large numbers for such actions should be rated more successful in achieving their collective ends than groups whose membership is passive in this regard. But the lack of covariance with goal effectiveness calls into question this interpretation of membership external activity.

A clue to the meaning of external activity appears in our findings that members' commitment correlated poorly with external activity. Weak or strong commitment is not a good predictor of external influence. Possibly the time span—a single year—in which mobilization was measured is too short to accurately capture the underlying mobilization potential among all thirty-two associations. Opportunities to activate the mass membership do not arise every calendar year. Thus, external activity, as measured in this

Table 7.1. Correlations of Effectiveness Ratings with Membership Participation and Support

Resource measures	Member ratings	Influence reputation
Member contributions		
Internal activity	.17	.00
Leadership	.02	.39**
Infra-resources	.20	.47***
External activity	.20	−.05
Resource contribution index	.18	.16
Tolerance	.54***	.27
Total budget	.24	.28
Logbudget	.53***	.59***
Size (log)	.08	−.02

**p ≤ .05.
***p ≤ .01.

study, may primarily reflect happenstance bursts in response to a particular situation or crisis confronting a handful of organizations. If the study had been conducted in a different year, the associations ranking high on external activity might have been quite different.

Mobilization, as measured by external activity, depends much more upon other institutions' decision-making agendas than upon the normative social control achieved by an association. And merely to mobilize members does not guarantee success. For every effort like the Women's Rights Organization's fantastic lobbying that helped to pass the Equal Rights Amendment, there must be comparable instances like the Uptown community's failure to evict a noxious industry from its neighborhood. Table 7.1 clearly demonstrates that associations activating their members on contemporary issues during the year preceding the survey did not achieve sufficiently important or lasting results to impress either the members or the community informants who evaluated their influence reputations a year later.

The larger the proportion of members engaged in formal leadership roles, the higher the association's influence reputation. The leadership role measure may actually be a better indicator than external activity of an association's long-term potential for mobilizing its members. Leadership roles generally demand a great investment of time and energy. Thus, an association that extracts extensive member commitments for leadership functions thereby acquires more effective resources for use in the influence process than a group that must rely on flashpoint mobilization triggered by external factors.

"Infra-resources" combines three general types of membership commitments: meeting attendance, time spent outside meetings, and monetary contributions. The +.47 correlation with influence reputation supports Hypothesis 5, since organizations receiving greater volumes of such generalized resources are reputedly more influential. Because the time and money contributions are unspecified in the infra-resources items, we can only speculate how these resources translate into enduring reputations for goal-attainment success. Clearly, given the inconsequentiality of internal and external activities, the infra-resources must be applied effectively in other ways.

Tolerance of dissonant policies, which reflects memberships' dispositions to continue in the association despite unsatisfactory performance, is significantly correlated only with member ratings. A membership with high tolerance prefers to remain silent or to voice opposition rather than to exit. The positive correlation shows that associations with high policy tolerance tend to be rated more effectively by their memberships, possibly because these groups have lower turnover and less internal dissension. A tolerant membership permits an association to pursue controversial issues and to use bold tactics without fear of large-scale defections. The greater unity that a membership tolerant of dissonant policies displays to the outside world is therefore an important organizational resource for attaining organizational objectives.

The meager relationship of most membership resource contributions to goal effectiveness led us to reassess whether such "per capita" measures might be inappropriate. Expressed as rates per member, the five participation scores reflect the average intensity of involvement within the organization. Preceding analyses disclosed that such participation intensity varies mainly in response to the level of commitment of the membership. But for purposes of achieving goals that lie partly or largely beyond organizational boundaries, the total quantity of resources mobilized by the association may be a better predictor than the per capita measures. Fortunately, the total annual financial budgets for all associations were available.

The actual dollar total budget correlates positively but insignificantly with both the member ratings and the influence reputation ratings. As noted in Chapter Six, however, a handful of organizations have exceptionally large annual budgets (two exceeded $300,000 and five others had $50,000 or more). Given the extremely skewed budget distribution, the (natural) logarithmic transformation would be a more appropriate measurement. Indeed, as Table 7.1 shows, logbudget is the strongest correlate of both goal effectiveness measures of any investigated. Because an association's budget aggregates income from all sources, it is neither a conceptual nor empirical surrogate for the infra-resources average of members' time-and-money commitments. Infra-resources correlates only $-.03$ with actual dollar budget and only $+.32$ with logbudget.

The larger the total amount of financial resources an association controls, the greater its ability to influence both public policies and the other goals which concern it. The large correlations between logbudget and both effectiveness measures confirms Presthus's observation that the budget is "perhaps the most precise index of the potential political resources of interest groups . . . and provides a quantitative index of the amounts spent for political activity" (1974 : 105).

Table 7.2 reports multiple regressions of both goal attainment measures on the resource variables which have significant zero-order correlations. For member ratings, logbudget and tolerance are clearly of equal importance. Both resource measures will be used in subsequent regressions involving member ratings. The regression equations for influence reputation find logbudget with the only significant effect when infra-resources and leadership are entered simultaneously. When leadership is left out, the beta for infra-resources remains significant, however. Therefore, both log-

Table 7.2. Standardized Coefficients from Regressions of Effectiveness Ratings on Resources

| Effectiveness measures | Independent variables | | | | |
	Logbudget	Tolerance	Infra-resources	Leadership	R^2
Member ratings	.40***	.42***			.438***
Influence reputation	.49***		.22	.18	.464***
Influence reputation	.50***		.31**		.441***
Influence reputation	.54***			.28*	.432***

* p ≤ .10.
** p ≤ .05.
*** p ≤ .01.

budget and infra-resources will be used in subsequent regressions involving influence reputation.

These findings lend some support to Hypothesis 5. Greater membership resource contributions are largely unrelated to effectiveness, with the exception of infra-resources for influence reputation. The resource of tolerance of unsatisfactory decisions predicts strongly to the members' evaluations of goal attainment but not to the community judges' evaluations. This differential importance implies that the two effectiveness measures tap different dimensions of goal attainment. The member ratings respond to the members' willingness to support the organization under adverse conditions. Such responsiveness may be seen by the members as an important goal in itself. But for the community informants, such internal cohesion is a minor consideration in evaluating associations' ability to affect public policy.

Despite the poor showing of the per capita membership resource contributions, the strong covariation of both goal attainment indicators with logbudget confirms Hypothesis 5. Apparently the total financial resources available, not the rate at which members participate, enable an association to better achieve its various goals.

Goal Attainment and Members' Commitment

Moving backwards in the implied causal sequence, we next examine the relationship of membership commitment to goal attainment. Table 7.3 displays the zero-order relationships between the five indicators of membership commitment and the two effectiveness ratings. All correlations are strongly positive, consistent with the expectation that associations with highly committed memberships are more likely to attain their goals. Member perception, that is, belief that other members are strongly committed to the collectivity's interests, is an especially important consideration in the member evaluations of how successful the organization is in achieving its objectives. In contrast, the strongest correlate of influence reputation is loyalty, an assessment of the intrinsic value

Table 7.3. Correlations of Effectiveness Ratings with Commitment

Commitment	Member ratings	Influence reputation
Goal salience	.45***	.46***
Loyalty	.58***	.59***
Personal salience	.55***	.37**
Member perception	.66***	.44**
Member commitment index	.56***	.53***

** p ≤ .05.
*** p ≤ .01.

and importance of the collectivity. These differential relationships persist in the multiple regressions in Table 7.4. These equations include the two most important resource indicators, while each of the five commitment variables is entered one at a time. Due to the high intercorrelation among the commitment indicators, they cannot be simultaneously entered. This incremental procedure allows us to observe both the direct contribution of each commitment variable and its alteration of the resource variables' effects on both goal attainment measures.

Several commitment variables exert significant direct effects on member ratings, even controlling for logbudget and tolerance. In Table 7.2 we saw that logbudget and tolerance had equal direct impact on member ratings, a pattern that is slightly disturbed when commitment variables are added to the equation. Tolerance exerts a stronger effect on members' ratings than does logbudget in most of these equations. Member perception receives the largest beta, while that for logbudget falls to insignificance. These three variables combined explain more than half of the variance in member effectiveness ratings. These findings yield further insight into the effectiveness criteria used by members to evaluate their association's success. In associations with high member perception, many members perceive that other members subordinate their personal interests to the collectivity's interest. Putting the group ahead of the person is an essential component of normative social control in social influence associations. In judging whether their association is attaining its goals, respondents may consider

Table 7.4. *Standardized Coefficients from Regressions of Effectiveness Ratings on Resources and Commitment Measures*

Effectiveness measures	Independent variables								
	Logbudget	Infra-resources	Tolerance	Goal salience	Loyalty	Personal salience	Member perception	Commit-ment index	R^2
Member ratings	.30*		.40***	.21					.473***
Member ratings	.25		.36**		.35**				.533***
Member ratings	.35**		.28			.25			.475***
Member ratings	.24		.30**				.43***		.572***
Member ratings	.27*		.35**					.32**	.513***
Influence reputation	.47***	.27		.10					.447***
Influence reputation	.41***	.13			.32				.491***
Influence reputation	.50***	.32*				−.02			.441***
Influence reputation	.46***	.27*					.11		.449***
Influence reputation	.45***	.20						.19	.458***

$* p \leqslant .10.$
$** p \leqslant .05.$
$*** p \leqslant .01.$

Table 7.5. Standardized Coefficients from Regressions of Effectiveness Ratings on Resources, Commitment, and Organizational Control Structures

Effectiveness measures	Independent variables							
	Logbudget	Infra-resources	Tolerance	Member perception	Purposive incentive	Decision participation	Formal legitimacy	R²
Member ratings	.33**		.31**	.46***	−.20			.597***
Member ratings	.28*		.36**	.37**		.16		.593***
Member ratings	.35**		.40***	.45***			−.30*	.624***
Influence reputation	.38**	.23			.26			.481***
Influence reputation	.53***	.25				.18		.476***
Influence reputation	.54***	.32**					−.10	.448***

* p ≤ .10.
** p ≤ .05.
*** p ≤ .01.

as one of the fundamental collective objectives the development of a cohesive and "other-regarding" membership. In the equations for influence reputation, the commitment measures display no significant direct effects. But their presence in the equations reduces the impact of infra-resources to insignificance or marginal significance.

Members' evaluations seem to stress internal processes to a greater degree than do the community informants' evaluations. As noted before, the domains to be considered in rating effectiveness were more explicitly circumscribed for the informants than for the members. This difference seems to permit members, already more familiar with the internal dynamics of the organization, to give greater weight to factors internal to the association. Thus, tolerance, member perception, and loyalty are stronger predictors than logbudget in the member ratings equations. The influence reputation ratings, congruent with explicit instructions to the community informants to attend to the external influence goals, seem less affected by the associations' internal conditions (which would be largely unknown to most informants). Thus, tolerance of dissonant policies has no independent effect, and logbudget is much more important than commitment in affecting variation in the influence reputation scores.

Goal Attainment and Control Structures

In our theory, organizational control structures are most antecedent to goal attainment. Few significant relationships should be found when the intervening variables of members' commitment and resources are held constant. Table 7.5 presents multiple regressions of both goal effectiveness measures upon the three control structure variables we previously analyzed according to three theoretical approaches.

Also included in the member ratings equation are logbudget, tolerance, and member perception. Neither purposive incentives nor decision participation contributes a significant direct effect on member ratings with these other variables present. The effect of formal legitimacy is marginally significant, but the sign of the beta is inverse, reflecting the high collinearity between formal legitimacy, tolerance of dissonant policies, and logbudget. We conclude, therefore, that none of the control structure variables exert an important direct effect on the member ratings of organizational effectiveness. Instead, they contribute indirectly by increasing the levels of members' commitment (particularly member perceptions) and resource mobilization (which directly increase effectiveness).

In the regressions for influence reputation, both logbudget and infra-resources are included, but since no membership commitment variable was significant, none are included when examining the direct effects of organizational control structures. As with member ratings, none of the control structures has a direct effect on influence reputation. Any indirect impact must be channeled through the two resource mobilization indicators.

A Causal Model

In this section we bring together the findings on goal attainment with results from earlier chapters relating to the antecedent variables. We will make the causal ordering among these constructs explicit and develop the magnitude of the empirical linkages. Figure 7.1 shows these findings as a path diagram, with sets of variables labelled according to their theoretical position in the scheme developed in Chapter One. The diagram does not attempt to establish causal priorities among variables with the same theoretical status. For example, logbudget and tolerance of dissonant policies are both indicators of resources mobilized by the association, but no causal arrow or path coefficient is estimated between these variables. Similarly, the two goal attainment indicators are not hypothesized to be causally connected.

The path coefficients were estimated as standardized regression betas in equations using only the relationships shown in the diagrams. Examining the findings from the left side, three of the four organizational control structures have significant impact on members' commitment.

Decision participation, purposive incentives, and formal legit-

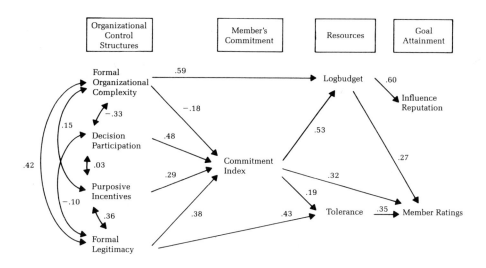

Figure 7.1. Causal Model Synthesizing Empirical Findings According to Theory

imacy all increase the aggregate rate of membership commitment as measured by the summary index. Only organizational complexity (represented here by the professional-nonprofessional dichotomy) has no important effect on members' commitment net of the other structures.

Members' commitment, in turn, has a substantial impact on total financial resources as measured by logbudget, but not upon tolerance. Instead, formal legitimacy increases the level of membership tolerance. Professionalized structure also has a substantial effect on logbudget, independent of the path from members' commitment. Proceeding forward to goal attainment, the diagram indicates distinctly different effects from resources and members' commitment. Member ratings are about equally affected by tolerance of dissonant policy, members' commitment, and logbudget. But influence reputation, as noted earlier in this chapter, receives a direct path only from logbudget. At least two notable indirect effects occur, however. The effect of professional structure on influence reputation through logbudget is (.59) (.60) = .35, while the indirect effect of commitment on influence reputation through logbudget is (.53)(.60) = .32. Similarly, formal legitimacy raises member ratings by .27 standard deviations indirectly through commitment and tolerance.

In this chapter we examined the impact of internal structures and processes upon the goal attainment of the social influence associations. We found evidence to substantiate the hypothesis that relatively resource-rich organizations would be relatively more effective in attaining their objectives. But this analysis had a narrow focus, ignoring external conditions facing the organization. An underlying theme in this research is the relative importance for organizational behavior of the internal structure versus the environmental situation within which the association must operate.

Chapter Eight

Environmental Effects

Two weeks before Thanksgiving of 1978, the Indianapolis School Board convened to decide on a third three-year term for the superintendent. For two years an often acrimonious debate had swirled around the school system's alleged failure to deal with the problems of dropouts, pushouts, and deprived black students. Much of the opposition to the superintendent, a middle-aged white man, came from social influence associations concerned with racial justice. In 1976 all seven school board commissioners had been elected on a reformist slate known by the acronym CHOICE (Citizens Helping Our Indianapolis Children's Education). The firing of the superintendent, as a representative of the bureaucratic old guard, seemed a foregone conclusion when the board met to decide on the contract renewal. One commissioner argued that "automatic renewal automatically denies Afro-Americans the opportunity to apply for this position." Before the vote, members of several organizations opposed to renewal marched to the podium and ceremoniously threw down copies of a speech distributed by the superintendent's supporters. After several hours of heated discussion, with the subject himself sitting expressionless through both commendation and condemnation, the board split 4 to 3 in favor of renewal, without even the performance evaluation demanded by the opposition.

The reasons behind the board's surprising decision were complex, but an important factor was the extensive support for the superintendent from many community groups. As one reporter put it, he had "no shortage of defenders, from the eagles of the Indianapolis establishment to fellow administrators down to parents and teachers." These groups rallied behind the superintendent in the weeks before the crucial vote, successfully persuading a majority of the board members, including one black woman, to their side. The dozen groups registered to speak prior to the meeting, following school board policy, were all prosuperintendent. No critics could speak at the meeting because none had complied with the required registration. Superior strength and tactics carried the day against the outnumbered and ill-coordinated opponents.

This incident demonstrates that social influence associations seeking community goals must operate in environments consisting of networks of organizations, some of them potential allies and others potential opponents. Successful goal attainment may often turn on crucial support from other institutions. The following two hypotheses relate aspects of the environment to the goal effectiveness of the associations:

6. The more stable and simple an association's environment, the more effective its social influence.
7. The more often the environment provides opportunities to mobilize an association's membership for social influence, the more effective the association's social influence.

After examining these two hypotheses, we will turn to the impact of the interorganizational network, a third aspect of the environment, as stated in this hypothesis:

8. The more favorable an association's position in the interorganizational network of its community, the more effective its social influence.

Uncertainty and Opportunity

In Chapter Seven we discussed various aspects of external organizational environments that might affect goal attainment. Two measures operationalizing the concepts in Hypotheses 6 and 7 are environmental uncertainty and the opportunity for mobilization provided by the eruption of a controversial issue in an organization's domain.

The uncertainty dimension of organizational environments was identified by Duncan (1972:318) as organizational decision makers' perception of "predictability with respect to the outcome of events." Environmental uncertainty combines both unstable conditions (static-dynamic features) and complexity (simple-complex features). As an association faces more unstable and complex conditions, its ability to predict and calculate appropriate responses should diminish. Associations operating in stable and simpler environments should have more rational (calculable) responses to external contingencies and hence be expected to better attain their objectives. The information to measure uncertainty in the sample associations, described in Appendix C.9, is based on organizational leaders' reports and conforms to Duncan's specifications.

The second environmental measure, issue controversy, is the recent occurrence of a situation outside the association that could conceivably require the membership's mobilization for an attempt to influence decision makers in other institutions. Most often, such events involve pending legislation or executive agency program changes. For example, in Indiana, the successful attempt to pass the Equal Rights Amendment occurred during the year this study was conducted. For associations with goals in this domain, the ERA would be considered an issue controversy. The effort by some community civil rights associations to prevent rehiring of the school superintendent, described earlier in this chapter, is another example of an issue controversy. The opportunities for social influence attempts presented by issue controversies may increase an association's goal attainment relative to organizations not facing such controversies. Although associations do not necessarily mobilize their members or exert influence whenever an issue erupts, the absence of issues may cause an association to be rated ineffectual both by members and by community judges. Uncertainty and issue controversy are virtually unrelated ($r = .05$).

The relationship of the two environmental measures to both goal effectiveness ratings, in Table 8.1, supports expectations only modestly. Greater uncertainty correlates negatively with goal effectiveness, but not significantly for either indicator. Issue controversy, as expected, correlates positively with both effectiveness ratings, but significantly only with influence reputation. This latter relationship implies that associations tend to be more success-

Table 8.1. Correlations between Environmental Indicators and Goal Effectiveness

	Goal attainment	
Environmental measures	Member ratings	Influence reputation
Uncertainty	-.20	-.28
Issue controversy	.20	.39**

**p ≤ .05.

Table 8.2. Standardized Coefficients from Regressions of Goal Effectiveness on Organizational Attributes and Environmental Indicators

	Independent variables					
Goal attainment	Logbudget	Tolerance	Commit-ment index	Uncertainty	Issue controversy	R^2
Member ratings	.26	.31**	.33*	-.16	.07	.540**
Influence reputation	.53***			-.29**	.31**	.515*

* p ≤ .10.
** p ≤ .05.
*** p ≤ .01.

ful in influencing public policies in their domains if they recently confronted a situation requiring organizational action. Associations whose environments have not presented such challenges are less likely to be rated effective.

Despite these modest correlations with goal attainment, environmental conditions may contribute significantly to goal attainment relative to the organizational characteristics identified in the previous chapter as having significant impact on goal effectiveness. For the member ratings, logbudget, tolerance, and commitment were important predictors, while for influence reputation only logbudget exerted a substantial effect. When the two environmental indicators are added to the equations, in Table 8.2, a marked contrast appears between the member ratings and the influence reputation.

In the member ratings equation, neither environmental variable reaches significance. By contrast, in the influence reputation equation the betas for both uncertainty and issue controversy are important. As with the zero-order relationships, uncertainty reduces an association's ability to influence public policies, while the occurrence of an issue controversy enhances its effectiveness. In the influence reputation equation, logbudget remains a robust predictor, but in the member ratings equation, the addition of the environmental variables reduces the logbudget beta to insignificance. This result is a good illustration of a caveat raised in Chapter Two: adding independent variables increases the standard errors of the regression coefficients, thereby increasing the likelihood of rejecting variables that in reality influence the dependent measure. We conclude that environmental conditions are not important considerations in member ratings, but that the total budget is important.

These findings strongly underscore our earlier contention that member ratings and influence reputation measure different dimensions of organizational effectiveness. The member ratings clearly respond to internal factors such as strong commitment and high tolerance, as well as to financial conditions, but they are impervious to environmental influences. In contrast, while influence reputation depends greatly on the association's financial capacity, factors outside the organization are also important determinants. Thus, Hypotheses 6 and 7 are confirmed in this latter analysis, but the relative importance of the internal organizational attributes is not greatly diminished by including measures of environmental uncertainty and issue controversy.

Interorganizational Relations

Up to this point we have treated the social influence associations as autonomous, independent units whose behavior depended mainly on their internal structures or on general conditions of the environment. Increasingly, students of organizations view such explanation as incomplete because they ignore interactions among sets of organizations that may constrain or facilitate the performance of individual organizations. In this section we shift attention to the multiple networks of relationships within which the social influence associations are embedded, seeking to identify how "the characteristics of these linkages as a whole may be used to interpret the social behavior of the [organizations] involved" (Mitchell, 1969:2). Our analyses in this section are not limited just to relationships among the social influence associations in our sample but will involve a wide range of community organizations, including governmental institutions and agencies, private corporations, and other voluntary sector groups. The goal attainment of the social influence associations cannot be understood without considering their ties to a variety of other organizations sharing the environment.

Early work on interorganizational relations (IOR) did not map the entire pattern of ties between units. Instead, this research focused either on interaction between a focal organization (or set of organizations) and its environing "organization set" (e.g., Evan, 1967, 1972), or, less often, upon connections between particular pairs (dyads) of organizations (Aldrich, 1976a, 1976b; Schmidt and Kochan, 1977). Recent methodological developments, making possible the analysis of complete network patterns, turned research efforts toward explaining entire IOR configurations (Rogers, 1974; Laumann and Pappi, 1976; Knoke and Rogers, 1979). To some extent, theoretical expectations at the network level of analysis have lagged behind methodological capabilities, so that few rigorous propositions exist to guide the present research. Fortunately, the most extensive sociological applications of network analysis occurred in community power and collective decision making, a perspective fitting well with our interests (Burt, 1976, 1977a, 1977b; Breiger and Pattison, 1978; Galaskiewicz, 1978, 1979; Galaskiewicz and Marsden, 1978; Laumann, Marsden, and Galaskiewicz, 1977). These findings offer several clues about IOR patterns that we may expect to find within a large set of community organizations. To develop insightful expectations, we adopt a resource dependency perspective on interorganizational bonds. As Laumann, Galaskiewicz, and Marsden (1978:469) pointed out, resource dependency theory is "the dominant framework proposed to explain formative processes occurring within modes of antagonistic competition and contingent cooperation," that is, when organizational actors are conceived as purposive entities pursuing goals defined narrowly in terms of organizational self-interest. This assumption is consistent with our own view that social influence associations seek to impose their preferred social values upon the polity.

The resource dependency paradigm, also called the "political economy" model (Zald, 1970a, 1970b; Benson, 1975) or the "resource mobilization" model (McCarthy and Zald, 1977), emphasizes intergroup dependencies that arise from ongoing processes of differentiation and specialization. No organization can become so self-contained that it does not need other organizations either to supply resources or to consume products (Aldrich and Pfeffer, 1976; Cook, 1977; Benson, 1975). Depending upon specific market or industry conditions, legal mandates, or informal norms, organizations will be relatively more or less advantaged in the competition for sustaining resources.

Organizational executives try to manage, or manipulate, their environments (consisting largely of other organizations) in order to reduce uncertainty, stabilize external conditions, and acquire dependable flows of resources (McNeil, 1978; Aldrich and

Pfeffer, 1976; Benson, 1975). To this end, organizations strive for the most advantageous positions in their environments, preferably ones from which they can dominate their transactions with other organizations (Benson, 1975). Dominance in a network derives from resource "essentiality" (Jacobs, 1974) an organization's willingness or ability to obtain necessary inputs or outputs from alternative suppliers and buyers. Organizations whose essential resources are controlled by one or few other organizations will find themselves in dependent, relatively powerless positions in a network. An individual organization's power is thus synonymous with its network position (Cook, 1977).

The two most basic resources are money and authority (Benson, 1975; McNeil, 1978). Organizations that control either of these resources are more likely to dominate a network, gaining power at the expense of organizations that lack these essentials. Organizations that can link, or mediate, exchange relationships both between network members and with the larger society will tend to dominate, since they control the flow of resources within the network and can mobilize forces external to the network (Benson, 1975). "A combination of network centrality and the exchange value of resources controlled defines the position of an organization in the status hierarchy which emerges as a consequence of the restricted exchange process" (Laumann, Galaskiewicz, and Marsden, 1978:471). Dominant organizations, which often play "linking pin" roles for other units (Aldrich, 1979), can use their positions as resources in retaining power, manipulating or mediating relationships among less powerful actors in their own interests.

In sum, resource dependency imperatives impel organizations either to engage in dyadic exchange relationships with other organizations or to attempt to internalize all essential resources to remain autonomous. Network structure is a largely unintended consequence of many organizations' self-interested pursuits to survive and adapt to the social order. Once a routinized pattern emerges, however, the network structure becomes a fact of social existence with which all organizations must contend. Various mechanisms of law, tradition, and cooperative ideology as well as norms of reciprocity hold the network together and limit the individual members' ability to alter their position (Galaskiewicz, 1979). Not only does an IOR network enable individual organizations to meet their resource needs, it also defines a set of structural positions within a community.

An individual organization's position in an IOR network is determined by the complete set of relationships of various kinds to and from every other organizational actor (cf. Burt, 1976). Two or more organizations jointly occupy the same network position if they have identical or similar interactions with the other network participants. Organizations occupying the same network position are said to be "structurally equivalent" to each other. Their location within the network may be described as a single abstracted position having a particular pattern of ties to other generalized network positions. Thus, the network structure as a whole is the configuration of relationships between positions. This conceptualization of networks as configurations of positions that may be jointly occupied by many organizations simplifies the investigation of relationships among the empirical organizations making up the interorganizational environment.

The resource dependency perspective dovetails nicely with the IOR network concept. An organization's capacity to command essential resources varies with its position in the full network of interorganizational relations ("positional" or "structural advantage," Cook, 1977:71–72). Network analysis implies consequences for two levels of analysis. At the micro-level, an organizational actor's network position, especially its centrality in a status/power hierarchy, can explain its adaptation success and its participation and influence in decision-making coalitions. Network position may be more important than organizational attributes or internal structure in accounting for goal attainment. (See Burk, 1978, for a similar conclusion on organizational activation on community issues.) At the macro-level of analysis, the entire configuration of network ties can explain a community's ability to respond effectively to collective problems. The activation of organizational coalitions to handle nonroutine issues may be a function of preexisting linkages among community organizations. Our interest in network analysis lies mainly at the micro-level in its contributions to an understanding of social influence association goal attainment. A macro-level analysis would take us beyond the scope of this book into the field of community decision making.

Although the network perspective holds great promise, sufficient ambiguities remain to prevent the paradigm from generating precise testable hypotheses. Assuming that a power/wealth hierarchy emerges and stabilizes in an IOR field, which particular organizations will occupy the various positions? How many central and peripheral positions will emerge? What types of exchange relationships will occur between dominant and subordinate positions? What principles will explain exchange concentration within various subsets of corporate actors (Laumann, Galaskiewicz, and Marsden, 1978)? The perspective cannot predict the mobilization and transformation of network structure over time. While acknowledging these shortcomings in the current status of resource dependency theory, we can still draw upon theoretical insights and empirical studies for suggestions about the configuration of ties among governmental, private, and voluntary community organizations.

The whole network configuration may take several distinct forms, for example, a prestige/status hierarchy, a circular "ring" of connected equals, or an unconnected set of autonomous positions. Based on past research on community power, we anticipated that a central "core" position would be found, consisting of organizations controlling the financial and political authority of the community, although a fine-grained analysis might disclose distinct positions within this core. The major political institutions and economic organizations should be found within or near the central positions of the IOR network. Core organizations can be expected to enjoy high goal effectiveness, since they control essential resources needed by noncore organizations. The core should be extensively connected by asymmetrical resource exchanges with subordinate positions, although we could not readily predict which types of resources would be exchanged with which positions.

Evidence for the existence of an economic core may be found

in two analyses of a small midwestern city's IOR network. In a smallest-space analysis of money, information, and moral support exchanges among seventy-three organizations, two variables consistently predicted location at the center (Galaskiewicz, 1979). Organizational resources (total funds) and dependency on local revenue sources had the largest partial regression coefficients. Inspection of the two-dimensional diagrams shows that banks, industries, the newspaper, radio station, mayor and city manager, and several mediating voluntary associations (United Way, Chamber of Commerce) occupied the center of the money and information networks. The moral support network center, however, was occupied by health and education organizations and civic voluntary associations.

A principal components analysis of the same data (Galaskiewicz, 1978) identified four positions roughly corresponding to Parsons' functional subsystems (Adaptive: business organizations; Goal Attainment: coordinating or government organizations; Latent Pattern Maintenance: health, education, and welfare organizations; Integrative: political and labor-professional groups). Frequencies of exchanges in the three networks between these four positions disclosed patterned dependencies. The business position generated money and the community-coordination position initiated moral support. The health-education-welfare complex was the clear consumer of both types of resources. Information exchanges tended to be reciprocated between positions, although the coordinating position was a primary consumer.

The functional specialization of organizations and the asymmetrical flow of resources between positions discovered in this study implies that noncore, or peripheral, organizations not only should be less effective in goal attainment (because of their dependency upon core organizations for essential resources) but may be differentiated into distinct positions. Organizations sharing similar substantive goals should tend to occupy similar positions in the organizational division of labor in relation both to the core and to other noncore clusters of organizations. The number of peripheral positions and the nature of their exchanges is difficult to specify given the rudimentary state of IOR theory, however.

As a general principle, we might expect that the more dissimilar a peripheral position's substantive interests, the less the interaction with other peripheral positions. And the more tightly linked a position is to the power core(s), the more effective its constituent organizations should be in obtaining their individual goals.

In effect, we suggest an "organizational sponsorship" model. Certain centrally placed organizations may form enduring ties to social influence associations whose goals are compatible with theirs. The core organization helps to buffer its clientele associations by legitimating its activities in the community, by directly financing its services, or by indirectly mediating the flow of funds from extra-community sources (such as federal programs). Often the organizational sponsor may maintain formal connections with its protégé by placing a representative on the association's governing board. The existence of a sponsorship relation will show up in a network analysis by the closer proximity of some positions to the financial and authority core of the community system.

Finally, as several network analyses have discovered (Burt, 1976; Knoke and Rogers, 1979), some of the actors will be isolated from the rest of the participants. These organizations will be the least powerful and least effective units in the system.

Blockmodel Patterns

Data on interorganizational relations were collected in the summer of 1978 in conjunction with the influence reputation ratings. We sent each leader of our thirty-two social influence associations a questionnaire consisting of thirteen different types of interactions, each followed by a checklist of the seventy community organization names used in the reputation study. We asked the informants to check all organizations with which their group had specific types of relationships during the past two years. Relationships ranged from exchange of money to generalized sentiments of moral support. Appendix C.10 gives more information, including the exact wording of the questions about the thirteen types of relationships.

The initial data were thirteen different matrices, each with the thirty-two social influence associations in the rows and the seventy community organizations (including the thirty-two associations) in the columns. Entries of 1 indicated a relationship from an association to an organization, entries of 0 indicated no relationship. The data thus represented the networks of specific ties among the thirty-two social influence associations and with the thirty-eight other government, private, and voluntary organizations. In leaving out reports from the nonsocial influence associations, the structure depends only on the interactions involving the sample associations. Since our primary interest is in explaining these associations' goal attainment, the restrictions are not problematic. By comparing interorganizational ties across different networks, we can determine which organizations are directly connected and whether the connections involve single or multiple networks. Rather than assume that any one type of tie represents the IOR network in the community, we want to use networks of all types of ties to detect structure, while still distinguishing the different patterns of specific types of ties connecting associations with organizations.

With 28,704 possible links between pairs of organizations (ignoring self-ties), interpretation of the data becomes unwieldy without some form of data reduction. We applied a clustering technique, grouping together organizations that were similar by some criterion; we thus required fewer network positions to depict structure within the data.

Traditional sociometric methods cluster actors together when they have a high tendency to interact with each other. Such clustering identifies "cliques" that have direct or indirect chains of choices from one member to another (Alba, 1973). An alternative clustering method, which we used, combines actors if they have similar patterns of relationships to the other actors in the network system. That is, actors are "structurally equivalent" if they have similar patterns of ties to all third parties across the networks being considered (Burt, 1978; Sailer, 1978). The structural equivalence approach to relational data conforms more closely than clique detection to the sociological concept of "role" in a social system (White, Boorman, and Breiger, 1976; Burt, 1976, 1977a, 1977b). Positions in the networks are defined not by mutual choices, as are cliques, but by the pattern of connections that structurally equivalent actors have with other sets of actors. Structural equivalence implies that two organizations occupying the same position are basically substitutable for each other with regard to the relational ties. Therefore, by reducing the complex multinetwork data to a smaller number of distinct positions whose member organizations are structurally equivalent, we can better observe the underlying role system that organizes the relationships among the various corporate actors in the community.

Several methods for locating structurally equivalent clusters of organizations are available. Given the nonsymmetrical nature of our data, the most accessible method was the blockmodeling technique proposed by Harrison White and his colleagues (Lorrain and White, 1971; Breiger, Boorman, and Arabie, 1975; White, Boorman, and Breiger, 1976; Boorman and White, 1976; Arabie, Boorman, and Levitt, 1978). *Blockmodeling* may be briefly described as a procedure for partitioning relational data into mutually exclusive and exhaustive sets of actors ("blocks"), either by a priori theoretical specification or by some data-based criterion. Because we lacked a strong theory that specified how community organizations should form a role system, we used the CONCOR algorithm to partition the thirteen network matrices simultaneously. This clustering method iteratively correlates pairs of columns in the thirteen stacked matrices, using the standard Pearson product-moment formula. When the algorithm converges, all actors will be assigned to one of two blocks. Proceeding sequentially, the successive bipartitions can produce any desired number of blocks. In practice, however, the analyst's decision to further divide a block should be guided by his or her insight into the trade-off between the greater realism of a more complex role structure and the greater difficulty of substantively interpreting more complex blockmodels. (See Appendix D for further exposition on blockmodeling.)

In our data, partitioning was halted after eight blocks had been identified from the 32-by-70 set of thirteen IOR matrices. Table 8.3 lists the organizations occupying each block, underlines the thirty-two social influence associations, and gives the mean influence reputation score for each block in parentheses. While the blocking process designates no intrinsic order among positions, we arranged them in a sequence that conforms to a rough influence gradient (r = +.95 between rank and mean influence reputation) while still reflecting the general sequence in which the positions split off from each other. Because of the generally monotonic influence reputation means from left to right in Table 8.3, we shall refer to blocks to the left as "higher" and blocks to the right as "lower" relative to each other.

The eight positions are labelled to reflect the fundamental functions each seems to play in the system. Blocks IA and IB are obviously the power cores of the community. The top block contains the four law-making and executive bodies of the city and state, along with two mass media organizations. Their mean influence reputation is almost a point higher than the second power position, which contains the banks, major industries, Lilly Endowment, the Chamber of Commerce, and three social control city bureaucracies (police, welfare, and zoning). Only one sample influence association falls into this power block, the Senior Citizens' Society, a regional body with responsibility for coordinating activities and program improvements for the elderly population. SCS is also the most influential in the sample; its structural location in the second power core is not surprising.

Although the blocking was performed on reports from only the thirty-two social influence associations and omitted the questionnaires returned by the other thirty-eight organizations, the depiction of the two power core positions accords well with independent evidence. In 1976, the Indianapolis *Star* published a series of articles on the "movers and shakers" in Indianapolis, profiles of the ten most influential men identified by a reputational technique similar to that used to rate our organizations. The top ten reputational power leaders were the heads of three banks, two industries, and the chamber of commerce, the newspaper publisher, the mayor, a realtor, and a partner in a major law firm. The corporate bodies represented are all located in the top two positions in Table 8.3.

Block II contains several of the public and private social ser-

Table 8.3. *Organizations in Eight Block Positions*

Power Core IA	Power Core IB	Service Bureaus II	Mixed Interest III	Health IV	Residual V	Neighbor-hoods VI	Isolates VII
Broadcasting	SCS	CAAP	AFL-CIO	SDE	Legion	OBP	RG
City Council	Banks	CAL	EPS	ODP	NLS	SG	PLC
Legislature	Chamber	Community Service	Bar Assn	AFH	DRS	PD	EL
Governor	Courts	Employment	Archdiocese	Health Systems	Birch	BHN	RRL
Mayor	Industry	Education	LBI	Hospital	KKK	RFP	HPO
Newspaper	Lilly	Legal Services	Churches	Medical Society	WPO	INDI	LH
(6.30)	Police	GIPC	Democrats	ORP	(2.37)	DT	(2.45)
	Welfare	United Way	NCCJ	Service Clubs		UT	
	Zoning	(4.61)	KIT	(4.01)		WE	
	(5.35)		Martin			WPA	
			HOP			(2.86)	
			NAACP				
			WRO				
			Republicans				
			CRO				
			FFF				
			CWA				
			(3.94)				

NOTE: Sample associations are underscored.

vice and welfare bureaucracies, including the Civic Advancement League, which provides numerous evaluation and assistance services to organizations in the social service field. The United Way, a major funder for many social service groups (including three of the sample social influence associations), and CAAP (Community Action Against Poverty) , the poverty-funding agency (which supports three other sample associations), are both located in this block, reflecting their structural similarities.

Although Block III seems at first glance to contain heterogeneous voluntary associations, a basic function appears on closer inspection. None of the organizations is residentially based and none is a government agency or producer of economic goods. The position's principal function seems to be special interest representation, whether racial (CRO, NAACP, Martin Center), religious-ethnic (EPS, NCCJ, Archdiocese, Council of Churches), sexual (WRO, CWA), legal (LBI, KIT, FFF), or occupational (AFL-CIO, Bar Association). The presence of both major political parties strengthens an interpretation of this position as containing the organized spokespersons for traditional special interest groups. While further subdivisions of this large block might be made, the gain in realism from a finer-grained structural analysis would not offset the greater complexity introduced by a larger number of structural positions.

Block IV is a health position occupied by private and public agencies concerned with disease and disability, including four of our sample associations. HOP and OBP, which might be presumed to share similar interests with these associations, were blocked into different positions. These two groups are structurally distinct from the health organizations, despite their formal representation of disabled persons. The service clubs' occupancy of the health position is understandable, given the frequency with which such organizations participate in fund-raising activities for health and medical organizations.

Identifying a common function for block V is difficult. The position contains three groups usually identified with right-wing political issues (American Legion, John Birch Society, Ku Klux Klan), but also the two environmental groups (NLS, WPO) and an emergency assistance association (DRS). To some extent this clus-

Table 8.4. Images of 12 Networks on Seven-Block Partition (combining blocks IA and IB)

Blocks	(SIAS)	Heard About	Send Information	Receive Information	Send Support	Receive Support	Send Money
I	(1)	1 1 1 1 1 – –	1 1 1 0 0 0 0	1 1 0 0 0 0 0	1 1 1 0 0 – 0	1 1 – 0 0 – 0	1 1 1 0 0 0 0
II	(1)	1 1 1 1 1 – 0	0 0 0 0 0 0 0	1 1 1 – 0 0 0	1 1 1 1 – 1 0	1 1 1 1 – 0 –	0 0 0 0 0 0 0
III	(8)	1 1 1 1 1 – –	1 1 1 1 – – –	1 1 1 1 – – –	– 1 1 1 – 1 –	– 1 1 – – – –	0 0 0 0 0 0 0
IV	(4)	1 1 1 1 1 – –	1 1 – 1 – 0 0	1 1 – 1 0 – 0	– – – – 0 – 0	1 1 – 1 0 – 0	1 1 0 1 0 0 0
V	(3)	1 1 1 – 1 – –	1 – 0 – – 0 0	1 – 0 – – 0 0	1 – – 1 – 0 0	1 – – – 1 0 0	0 1 0 0 0 0 0
VI	(9)	1 1 1 – – – –	1 1 1 – 1 – –	1 1 1 – – 1 –	1 1 1 1 – 1 –	1 1 1 – – 1 –	1 1 1 – 0 1 0
VII	(6)	1 – 1 – 1 – 0	– 0 – – 0 0 0	– – – 0 0 – 0	– – – – 0 0 0	– – – – 0 0 0	– 0 1 0 0 0 0
Density		= .75	= .15	= .16	= .19	= .16	= .02

Blocks	(SIAS)	Receive Money	Not Sympathetic	Actively Opposed	Joint Projects	Common Board	Coalitions
I	(1)	1 1 0 0 0 0 0	1 0 1 0 1 0 0	1 0 0 0 1 0 0	1 1 1 0 0 0 0	1 1 1 0 0 0 0	1 1 0 0 0 1 0
II	(1)	1 1 0 0 0 0 0	0 0 0 0 0 0 0	0 0 0 0 0 0 0	1 1 1 0 0 0 0	0 1 0 0 0 0 0	0 0 0 0 0 0 0
III	(8)	1 1 – 1 0 0 0	1 – 0 1 – – –	1 – – 0 1 0 1	1 1 1 1 – – –	1 1 1 – 0 0 0	– 1 1 1 – – 0
IV	(4)	1 1 1 1 – 0 –	– 0 0 0 1 0 0	1 0 0 0 0 0 0	1 1 1 1 0 – 0	1 1 0 1 0 0 0	1 1 1 1 0 0 0
V	(3)	1 1 0 0 0 0 0	1 – – 0 1 0 0	1 0 0 0 0 0 0	1 1 – – 1 0 0	1 0 1 – 0 0 0	1 1 – – 1 0 0
VI	(9)	– 1 – – 0 1 0	1 – – 1 1 0 0	1 1 0 1 1 – 0	– 1 1 0 0 1 –	– 1 1 1 0 1 0	1 1 1 – 0 1 0
VII	(6)	– 0 – – 0 0 0	1 0 – 0 1 0 0	– 0 0 0 1 0 0	– 0 – – 0 0 0	0 0 0 0 0 0 0	– 0 – – 0 0 0
Density		= .03	= .04	= .03	= .09	= .05	= .08

ter may be a residual category in the first main split of the seventy organizations. We will explore the structural role of this block in relation to other positions later.

The last two positions are occupied exclusively by social influence associations; they split off from the other blocks during the first partition. Block VI contains the most active neighborhood groups, including Indianapolis Neighborhood Development, Inc. (INDI), a recent umbrella organization, and Better Housing Now, whose substantive interests overlap strongly with these residentially based associations. This cluster also contains three non-neighborhood associations (Organized Blind Persons, Rights for Prisoners, Women's Political Alliance) with relationships to the other blocks structurally similar to those of the neighborhood associations.

The final block, VII, is a heterogeneous collection of three less-active neighborhood associations, health professionals, and two legal reform groups (Reform of Repressive Laws and Pro-Life Coalition). Although these associations appear to share substantive goals with groups occupying other positions, Block VII associations are structurally dissimilar and, as seen in the interblock ties, isolated from the rest of the system.

We have here inferred the functions of the eight positions from the organizations that jointly occupy these blocks, but a complete structural analysis of the interorganizational role system must examine the inter- and intra-block relationships. This examination is best done through reduction of the network data to a set of blockmodel images for each of the thirteen types of ties. Twelve of these network images appear in Table 8.4, while that for the influence attempt network merits detailed attention in Table 8.5. One modification was made to expedite presentation: power core positions IA and IB were combined into a single block, since IA contained no social influence associations. Each image represents the reduction of a 32-by-70 data matrix to a 7-by-7 matrix in which ties from only the sample social influence associations in each row block to *all* the organizations in each column block are reported. For example, Row I reports the occurrence of ties from SCS to the seven blocks, while Row III reports the density of ties

Table 8.5. Densities and Image of Influence Attempt Network ("Which organizations have policies or programs which your organization has tried to influence?")

Network	I	II	III	IV	V	VI	VII
I. Power Core (1)	.86	1.00	.59	.13	.00	.10	.00
II. Service Bureaus (1)	.47	.71	.00	.25	.00	.00	.00
III. Mixed Interest (8)	.63	.48	.39	.17	.15	.10	.00
IV. Health (4)	.40	.28	.17	.43	.04	.00	.00
V. Residual (3)	.47	.08	.00	.04	.13	.00	.00
VI. Neighborhoods (9)	.45	.35	.14	.13	.00	.15	.02
VII. Isolates (6)	.22	.04	.04	.02	.00	.03	.00

I	1 1 1 – 0 – 0
II	1 1 0 1 0 0 0
III	1 1 1 – – – 0
IV	1 1 – 1 – 0 0
V	1 – 0 – – 0 0
VI	1 1 – – 0 – –
VII	1 – – – 0 – 0

Density = .21

from all eight sample associations in the "Mixed Interest" block to the seven blocks.

In determining whether relationships exist between or within blocks, a mean density criterion was used. For example, in the original matrix for "Heard About," 1,651 of the 2,208 possible ties (ignoring self-ties) occur, a density of .748. If the social influence associations in a given block reported hearing about more than 75 percent of all the organizations in another block, a "bond" exists between these two blocks in that network. In that network's block-model image, a bond is represented by a *1*. If fewer than 75 percent of the possible ties between or within a block occur in the "Heard About" network, then no bond exists. The image contains either a *0* (no ties at all) or – (some ties occur but fewer than the mean density of the entire network).

A detailed discussion of all thirteen blockmodel images in Tables 8.4 and 8.5 is clearly beyond the scope of this analysis. Instead, we shall highlight some of the major patterns, paying special attention to the influence attempt network pattern since that relationship is most crucial to understanding the goal attainment process of the social influence associations.

Starting at the bottom, Block VII's isolation from the rest of the system is evident in the general absence of ties from the other social influence associations in the higher blocks and the sparse ties from Block VII to the organizations in the other positions. Block VII is not even internally connected in any network, indicating that it is basically a residual collection of uninvolved associations. The other associations have infrequently heard of Block VII's members and therefore do not interact with them. In turn, the isolates claim few ties to other blocks, with the exception of sending money to some interest groups, trying to influence policies of the power core, and feeling that the power core and Block V are unsympathetic and the latter actively opposes their interests. In view of its extreme structural isolation, the low average influence reputation rating of Block VII (2.45) is understandable.

The neighborhood block (VI) also achieves low salience within the system. Few other organizations have heard of them, even within their own block. But unlike the isolates, the neighborhood groups are strongly connected among themselves on other networks. They send and receive information, support, and money, and engage in joint projects and coalitions and have overlapping boards. However, the neighborhood block does not target itself as an object of attempted influence (Table 8.5), focusing instead on the power core and the service bureaus as the major influence objectives. Like other positions, the neighborhood block feels itself opposed by the power core and Block V, but it is unique in also feeling the service bureaus and health groups sometimes act against its interests.

Almost every network exhibits an asymmetric pattern: Block VI reports extensive ties to the top four blocks, yet virtually none of these ties are reciprocated (although Blocks II and III send support and approval to the neighborhood block, and SCS in Block I admits to forming coalitions with several of these associations). This asymmetry may arise from the fact that the ties are based on only the social influence associations. The neighborhood block may aim its interactions mainly at the nonvoluntary organizations in the top blocks whose interactions are not reflected in the images. Without data from these organizations about their relationships with the blocks we cannot determine whether the asymmetry is an artifact of an incomplete network. However, the neighborhood block is clearly distinct from the isolates of Block VII.

Block V, the residual cluster, receives more than a third of all the negative bonds ("Not Sympathetic" and "Actively Opposed"), exceeded only by the power core in this regard. The main reason for the animosity expressed toward Block V is the presence of the Birch Society and the Klan. Although this block is well known, it resembles the isolates of Block VII in not being otherwise well connected with the higher blocks. No other position sends information, support, or money to Block V or engages in joint projects, coalitions, or influence attempts with it. In those networks where Block V is tied to itself, it usually reflects cooperation between the two environmental groups. Block V does claim several ties to the power core as well as to the service bureaus.

The health position (Block IV) and the mixed interest block (III) display extensive mutual interactions among themselves and with the top two positions. These groups often create joint projects and form coalitions for the purpose of influencing public policies. The targets of influence attempts (Table 8.5), however, are differentiated. While both blocks try to affect the power core and the service bureaus, the health associations target on each other but not on the mixed interest groups. In turn, the mixed interest groups try to affect each others' policies but not those of the health cluster. This differentiation carries over into the money exchange networks. Mixed interest groups give money to no other blocks, but the four health social influence associations send money not only to the health block but to the top two blocks. Both mixed interest and health associations receive money from the power core, the service bureaucracies, and the health block, but the latter claims financial support from some of the mixed interest groups. Thus the health social influence associations appear to be tied into a more complex set of financial arrangements, particularly with public agencies, than the mixed interest groups, which tend to rely more upon their own memberships for money.

Generalizations about the service bureaus (Block II) and the power core (IA and IB) must be more tentative, since each contains only one of the sample social influence associations. These two associations tend to confine their interactions to the top three blocks. As recipients of bonds, both the power core and the service bureaus play similar roles for the associations in the other blocks. A major difference occurs in the two negative networks. The power core receives negative bonds from every block except the CAL in Block II. The service bureaus are seen as actively opposing only the neighborhood group. The neighborhood block seems to target more exclusively on the service bureaus (especially CAAP and the Community Services Division) in receiving money, having common board members, and creating joint projects with that block but not with the power core.

Predicting Influence

The basic premise of this chapter is that structural positions occupied by these associations can account for a portion of the influence reputation variance that cannot be attributed to the organizational characteristics investigated earlier in this chapter. As Table 8.3 demonstrates, the eight structural positions are strongly differentiated by the mean influence reputation of all seventy organizations. The means vary systematically with the intensity of interactions between blocks across multiple networks. The number of bonds a position receives from the social influence associations in all blocks is a rough index of the degree to which the associations are dependent on that block. That is, the more ties a position receives from the associations in each block, the more powerful a position is likely to be rated. The number of 1s in a given column, summed across all thirteen images, indicates the number of ties of all kinds coming from all seven blocks' social influence associations into that position. The following frequencies occur: Block I receives sixty-five of the ninety-one possible bonds; Block II receives fifty-six; Block III, thirty-nine; Block IV, twenty-six; Block V, twenty; Block VI, twelve; and Block VII only one. (The monotonic sequence is another bit of evidence helping to order the positions in a hierarchy.) These frequencies correlate almost perfectly with each block's mean influence rating for all organizations ($r = +.929$). Thus, the more successful a position's organizations are in attaining their influence objectives, the more likely that position is to be a target of interactions from the social influence associations jointly occupying the various system roles. This finding makes sense, for if the primary purpose of social influence associations is to affect changes in social values, they are unlikely to target their interactions toward the ineffectual positions in the IOR system.

The tendency for social influence associations in every part of the system to focus attention on the more powerful positions is clearly revealed in the image matrix for Influence Attempt in Table 8.5. Only the power core is the target for all seven positions (no specialization of influence efforts occurs when the two components of the power core, IA and IB, are considered separately). Fewer positions target their influence on the service bureaus; the mixed interest and health positions are each objects of attention by only two positions. No cluster of social influence associations directs sufficient influence effort at the lower three clusters to consider these latter positions as influence targets. The overall image conforms to a power hierarchy, with the intensity of influence effort by the associations proportional to the average effectiveness rating of the incumbent organizations.

We may now proceed to the central question: does a social influence association's position in the community IOR system help explain an association's ability to achieve its influence goals? If block position is measured by simply assigning numbers from one to seven, corresponding to low to high position, the linear relationship between block position and influence reputation is $r = +.706$. This covariation is greater than that between influence reputation and any other attribute measure of the associations. If the relationship between influence reputation and block position is allowed to covary in a nonlinear fashion, the relationship strengthens slightly (η^2 of .597 compared to r^2 of .483). However, the pattern of category means does not follow any discernible

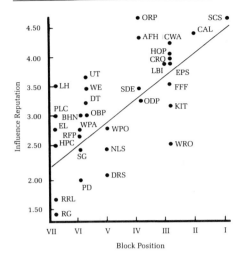

Figure 8.1. *Scatter Diagram of Relationship between Influence Reputation and Block Position*

functional form, so we will treat the covariation as though it were linear. This linearity, as displayed in Figure 8.1, permits us to use block position as a single variable in multiple regression at the cost of only one degree of freedom, compared to six degrees of freedom that the full dummy variable set would require.

When block position is added to the regression equations for both goal attainment measures, in Table 8.6, it markedly affects the prediction of influence reputation. Its net regression coefficient is almost half a standard deviation, while the beta for log-budget diminishes to slightly more than a third of a standard deviation, although it remains highly significant. Uncertainty continues to exert an important negative effect on influence reputation, but issue controversy no longer retains statistical significance. The equation now explains more than two-thirds of the variance in this goal effectiveness measure. In sharp contrast, adding block position to the equation for member ratings does not appreciably alter the ability to predict this effectiveness measure.

In sum, the blockmodel results confirm the earlier analyses of environmental effects on goal attainment. To explain success-

Table 8.6. Standardized Coefficients from Regression of Goal Effectiveness on Block Position, Organizational Characteristics, and Environmental Indicators

| | | | | Independent variables | | | |
Goal attainment	Block position	Logbudget	Tolerance	Commitment index	Uncertainty	Issue contro-versy	R^2
Member ratings	−.14	.30*	.29*	.37***	−.18	.11	.554*
Influence reputation	.48***	.36***			−.23**	.17	.683**

* p ≤ .10.
** p ≤ .05.
*** p ≤ .01.

ful influence on public policies, a social influence association's position in the community IOR system, its financial resources, and the calculability of its environment are essential. In contrast, external relationships and conditions are irrelevant to member ratings of their organizations' goal effectiveness. Internal attributes of resources and membership commitment provide the best explanation.

Chapter Nine

Conclusion

When we began research on social influence associations we were primarily interested in learning how members came to form attachments to their organizations strong enough to make collective action possible. Our purpose was to illuminate the conditions under which self-regulatory social control of moderate-sized, nominally democratic organizations is possible. Initially we thought that personal characteristics and internal organizational attributes held the key to understanding this commitment process, but the more deeply we probed into the subject, the more we came to realize that membership commitment was only part of the story we wanted to tell. Increasingly, the need to show how membership commitment contributes to an organization's capacity to achieve its social influence goals forced us to turn our attention away from solely internal attributes and toward the environmental settings within which social influence associations operate.

This evolution in our explanation of social influence association performance parallels a shift within the fields of complex organizations and social movements research toward more holistic, environmentally contingent theories. To be sure, much organizational research has focused on the relationships among internal characteristics of organizations. For example, in their impressive study of organizational structure, Blau and Schoenherr (1971) explained large variations in the structure of state employment security agencies on the basis of size alone. Size of agency was strongly related to a number of other internal characteristics that produce effective organizational control—number of hierarchical levels, number of divisions, director's span of control, and automation. These findings led to the conclusion "that in most cases internal influences predominate over external ones" (Blau and Schoenherr, 1971:166). Yet when they looked at the effect of various aspects of an agency's structure on the services supplied to clients, the structural characteristics appeared to have no more effect than did environmental conditions such as the socioeconomic and ethnic composition of the state's population.

Employment security organizations are, of course, quite different from social influence associations, and Blau and Schoenherr examined variables quite different from those we were concerned with. But there is an important congruence between both sets of findings. Their study and ours both lead to the conclusion that organizations' internal characteristics are fundamental determinants of organizational control but that the attainment of external goals—whether the placement of clients in jobs or the influencing of public policy—depends mainly on conditions in the environment. Our synthesis of internal attributes and environmental constraints emerged during the course of the research project, resulting in a relatively simple theoretical structure that accounts substantially for the patterns of observed covariation among important organizational properties.

Main Findings

Our synthesized theory contains four basic concepts: an organizational control system composed of control structures and membership commitment; organizational resources; environmental conditions; and goal attainment. Using multiple indicators of these concepts, we specified a series of relationships between variables that could be tested using simple correlational and multivariate regression methods on data from thirty-two social influence associations.

In general, the findings comport well with theoretical expectations. First, evidence points to the operation of three types of organizational control structures in generating high aggregate levels of affectual membership commitments to the collective welfare. Emphasis on purposive incentives, widespread opportunities for decision making and influence, and formal legitimacy of leaders grounded in a supralocal system were each found to have significant impact in raising membership commitment levels. Decision-making participation especially exerted a strong impact on members' commitment beliefs. Thus, at least among this type of voluntary association, social control systems composed of beliefs and structures tend toward consistency.

When an association's social control system creates a dedicated, enthusiastic membership, the organization's ability to generate high levels of resources from members and outside parties is enhanced. When members consider the association central to their life interests and view others as equally committed, the association can more readily appeal for and receive resources necessary to maintain itself and to pursue external goals. The observed covariation of membership commitment indicators with such member-based resources as internal activities, leadership, and generalized time-and-money contributions is consistent with this theoretical expectation. In addition, total financial resources—including amounts contributed from outside parties through grants and contracts—also vary strongly according to aggregate rates of membership commitment.

The discovery that a professionalized formal structure exerts a strong effect on total financial resources implies that outside funders may be more prone to invest in a type of association whose formal structure comports with societal expectations. Professionalized associations may be more legitimate among outside parties because they conform more closely to a bureaucratic standard that is seen as more mature and responsible and less risky than amateur social influence associations. Without studying how government agencies and foundations decide which associations to support, however, that interpretation remains speculative.

Formal legitimacy—the locus of authority lodged in supralocal units relative to local chapters—importantly affects the resource of membership tolerance. Memberships with stronger national bodies report less inclination to defect under hypothetical circumstances of disagreement over organizational policy. Having a tolerant membership should be an important asset for leaders engaging in influence attempts with other institutions where potentially controversial decisions must be made without consultation with the membership. If leaders felt that many members might leave under situations of policy dissatisfaction, their freedom of action would be severely circumscribed and the ability to act decisively and effectively in achieving organizational goals might be impaired.

In investigating the factors affecting organizational effectiveness, we acknowledged that goal attainment is not a unitary phenomenon. The primary measure of interest, of course, is an association's ability to influence public policies within its domain. An influence reputation indicator of effectiveness was a function of total financial assets and environmental conditions, particularly the association's location in the community interorganizational system. But a second goal effectiveness indicator, based on the membership's rating, responded to a different set of variables. Environmental conditions were unimportant, but in addition to total financial resources, tolerance and membership commitment had strong effects. These divergences in the significant predictors of influence reputation and member ratings suggest that members evaluate their association less on how well it performs in the community influence system and more according to its ability to produce large financial resources and to generate high levels of membership commitment.

Effectiveness in the community influence system, in sharp contrast, appears strongly related to the interorganizational position occupied by a group. While we did not undertake a systematic study of the determinants of position, strong ties to the politically and financially powerful organizations in the community are essential to the association's effectiveness. Isolated associations are relatively ineffective, presumably because of their inability to draw upon important community resources of information, moral support, and interorganizational cooperation for affecting institutional decision makers. The most successful associations have discovered the key to integrating themselves into positions of greater access to powerful organizational sponsors, thereby increasing the chances that these actors' assistance can be obtained in influence efforts.

Professional and Amateur Associations

While most of our theoretical expectations were supported by the empirical analyses, a major unanticipated result was the unimportance of membership resource contributions for explaining goal attainment. None of the five indicators of membership participation covaried strongly with either goal attainment measure. Other resources—tolerance and total budget—simply overwhelmed the membership resource contribution effects. However, we would be too hasty if we concluded that members' participation is completely irrelevant for organizational success. To understand conditions under which membership involvement does make an important contribution to social influence association performance, we must contrast two types of associations.

About a half century after the birth of the United States, Alexis de Tocqueville, visiting from France, observed with wonder the number and variety of associations "whose existence and growth are solely due to the initiative of individuals." In Democracy in America (1969:189) he attributed the pervasive role of associations in American life to the fact that "the inhabitant of the United States learns from birth that he must rely on himself to combat the ills and trials of life." Faced with a common problem, Americans would band together to provide for their mutual needs. Appeals for government assistance, wrote Tocqueville, would be made only as a last resort. Virtually any objective could become the focus of a voluntary effort: "There is no end which the human will despairs of attaining by the free action of the collective power of individuals" (190).

Several of the associations we studied rely primarily upon members to achieve their objectives. Locust Hills began among residents concerned with neighborhood deterioration and with the threatened flight of white families remaining in the area. To combat these trends, the group established a program of neighborhood beautification and arranged numerous social occasions to raise community awareness among the residents. Freedom From Fear was initiated by one woman's encounter with the criminal justice system's lack of sensitivity to the needs of crime victims.

The group created a counselling program in which volunteers offered assistance to crime victims and their families.

In the nearly 150 years since Tocqueville's visit, the character of voluntary associations has changed markedly. Many groups no longer hesitate to seek government assistance in pursuing their objectives, even when such objectives include altering the government's own policies. Daniel P. Moynihan, observing the "professionalization of reform," wrote that many associations are created and funded by government at the behest of social action professionals. The intended ultimate beneficiaries of such associations often have little say about organizational affairs. Specifically citing the decision-making process in the antipoverty organizations, Moynihan asserted, "Whatever exactly is meant by the term 'the poor,' it will be clear enough that they had almost nothing whatever to do with the process" (1969:34).

Many associations studied in Indianapolis rely less on their membership's resources and participation to attain their goals and more upon a professional staff's initiative. Both Uptown and Downtown are CAAP-designated organizations whose funds come predominantly from poverty-program agencies and whose activities are largely determined by contractual relationships with these funding sources. Civil Rights Organization tackles a set of social problems demanding far more time and expertise than could be obtained solely from voluntary effort. A paid staff enables this association to apply skills in fund raising and program implementation more effectively than a Tocquevillian association could.

The Tocqueville and Moynihan perspectives disagree on the importance of member participation for organizational functioning. The Tocqueville model implies that high rates of member participation are essential for goal attainment. The Moynihan model implies that member participation rates are not relevant to goal attainment, since professional activity is the crucial determinant. Professional social influence associations have proliferated in contemporary America, probably because they are more effective than amateur associations in achieving their social influence objectives (McCarthy and Zald, 1973).

To examine the importance of membership-contributed resources for organizational goal attainment, amateur associations can be contrasted with those having some incipient degree of professionalization. Our sample can be divided almost equally into a set of fifteen professionalized associations (including board-only associations with paid staffs) and a set of seventeen nonprofessionalized groups. As expected, the professional associations are more successful than the amateur groups in influencing public policies (the mean influence reputations are 3.70 and 2.80, respectively). But more important, the correlation between membership resource contributions index and influence reputation score varies markedly between the two sets of associations. As expected in the Moynihan perspective, among professional organizations influence reputation is unrelated to membership resource contributions ($r = +.04$). But, as predicted in the Tocqueville model, a strong positive relationship occurs among the amateur associations ($r = +.48$). Thus, the importance of membership participation for organizational goal attainment is conditional on the type of leadership structure of the association. This differential was obscured earlier by combining both types of association in the analysis of organizational effectiveness. If the historical trend toward greater professionalization of social movements continues, we can expect further declines in the impact of membership resources on social influence association performance. The implication of rising professionalization of these organizations for the normative self-regulation of the collectivity can best be determined by research taking a more longitudinal view than ours. But, based on the cross-sectional data we have analyzed, we view the trend away from amateur structures with some misgivings.

A Caveat

Social influence associations play a major part in the nation's political life. Apart from their significance to individuals in strengthening personal controls and providing avenues for value expression, voluntary associations significantly shape the collective decisions of the society. Standing between the state and unorganized social aggregates, social influence associations help to mobilize latent social resources and bring them to bear upon the policy deliberations of political elites. In depicting voluntary associations as effective mediators of political demands by delimited social groups, we clearly echo the imagery of the mass society theorists who ascribed voluntary organizations a crucial function in the preservation of liberal democracy (e.g., Kornhauser, 1959). Associations can restrain political elites' arbitrary actions through exposure and periodic evaluation centered around reelection efforts. Associations can enhance the level of societal self-regulation by providing their members with direct opportunities to participate in organizational governance. Associations can permit the diffusion of society-wide norms, particularly those of tolerance of opposing views and acceptance of democratic "rules of the game." Associations can shape the political agenda by raising and publicizing urgent social problems long before the mass media and the general public have become aware of them. And associations can effectively raise the tide of public concerns on topical issues to implement programmatic innovations, as we have seen countless times in such social movements as those focusing on civil rights for minorities, the aging, and the handicapped.

We suspect that all these idealizations of the mass society theory about an active complex of voluntary associations are present to some degree in the United States today. But in the course of our research, we became increasingly sensitized to an accompanying negative aspect of social influence association involvement in public policy making. Many such organizations have the capacity to paralyze the nation's ability to act decisively in certain areas of overriding public concern. In contrast to the Schumpeterian ideal in which political decision makers are relatively insulated between elections from direct pressure by the electorate, special interest organizations have proliferated in recent years to the point of subjecting the legislature and executive at all levels of government to almost continual pressure to accede to narrowly focused objectives. The combination of successful examples in the civil rights, antiwar, and consumer protection movements with legal reforms opening the decision process to greater citizen involvement undoubtedly contributed directly to this situation. Whatever the historical causes, the result is a real threat that minority special interests will triumph over wider societal values. Through effective organization and lobbying, minority opinions on abortion and gun control have been able to defeat specific candidates and to frighten other politicians into backing their policy demands. For the better part of a decade, an effective energy program to combat the changed resource situation has been snarled in Congress by producer and consumer interest groups, each pursuing their specific advantage, while the situation yearly grows more precarious for the society as a whole.

Elusive as the concept of public interest may be, we cannot help feeling that at times the societal welfare is being steadily eroded by the shortsighted pursuit of sectoral benefits that social influence associations have learned so well how to achieve. The tendency of democratic pluralist theory to view voluntary association activity as largely benign and desirable must be counterbalanced by a sober recognition that the effectiveness of such groups may be purchased at the cost of stalemate and drift on the major issues of social reconstruction facing the country today. We do not have solutions to offer in this book, but we think the situation is sufficiently troublesome to commend it as a subject for future investigation.

Appendix A

Statistical Comparison of Indianapolis
and the Nation

Table A.1. Comparison of Indianapolis SMSA and City with
Nation and All Metropolitan Areas, 1970

Social characteristic	Indianapolis		United States	
	SMSA	City	Nation	All SMSAs (N = 243)
Population (thousands)	1,100	745	203,235	1,189[d]
Percentage black	12.7	18.4	12.5	14.5[e]
Percentage foreign[a]	4.9	5.8	17.9	20.0[e]
Percentage under 18 years	36.4	35.9	34.3	33.5[e]
Percentage over 65 years	8.6	8.7	9.9	9.4[e]
Percentage born in state[b]	69.2	66.3	73.7	64.9
Median years education[c]	12.2	12.1	12.1	12.2
Percentage high school degree[c]	56.0	54.8	52.4	55.3
Percentage labor force unemployed	3.9	4.3	4.4	4.1
Percentage in manufacturing	29.2	27.9	24.4	25.7
Percentage in government	13.7	14.2	—	16.0
Percentage white-collar jobs	50.0	52.1	48.2	52.4
Median family income	$10,754	$10,754	$ 9,590	$10,474
Percentage below poverty level	6.5	7.1	13.7	8.5
Percentage over $15,000	23.9	24.9	20.7	24.6

SOURCES: Tables 47, 66, 75, 82, 108, 109, 110, 114, 115, 116, 117, 183, 184, 187, and 188 in U.S. Bureau of the Census, *Vol. I, Characteristics of the Population: 1970, Part I. United States Summary, Section 1.* Washington, D.C.: U.S. Government Printing Office, June 1973.

[a] Foreign-born plus parents foreign-born or mixed stock.
[b] Percentage of native population born in same state.
[c] For persons 25 years or older.
[d] Average for 100 largest SMSAs; other statistics based on all 243 SMSAs.
[e] Urbanized portion of SMSAs only.

Appendix B

Sampling and Interviewing

In this appendix we describe the selection of voluntary organizations and the sampling and interviewing of respondents within organizations.

Organization Sampling Frame

We constructed the sampling frame of voluntary associations in the Marion County (Indianapolis) area in the summer of 1976. We attempted to compile an exhaustive listing of all organizations meeting these criteria:

The association must not be a government agency.

It must not have economic goals as its primary objective (i.e., no unions, trade associations, or professional associations).

It must have at least twenty "members"—a majority of whom are eighteen years old and older—and not be composed solely of paid staff and "clients" receiving direct services from the organization.

The organization must have operated continuously for the last two years and must schedule at least one annual meeting for the mass membership.

The association must have as one of its primary formal goals the influencing of one or more external social institutions and not exist solely to satisfy members' affiliative-expressive interests.

At least one of the association's major objectives should fall into one of these areas: (1) health and mental health; (2) justice and legal conditions; (3) neighborhood and community; or (4) a residual "civic action" goal.

Information on organizations potentially fitting these criteria were obtained from a search of the 1975 Indianapolis telephone book; a 1974 Community Services Council directory of community service organizations; the Marion County Department of Planning and Zoning and the Indianapolis Mayor's Office lists of neighborhood groups; and interviews with informants in the Criminal Justice Planning Commission, a legal assistance center, and the Community Services Council. We used the information obtained to compile a preliminary list of organizations, omitting only groups that clearly violated one of the criteria. Next, the organizations were sorted into one of the four classifications used as sampling strata based on information about primary objective. Instances of ambiguity or multiple goals were resolved by staff conference or telephone query to the organization. Next, among voluntary associations in the health and mental health category, those with only a fund-raising or general public-education function were eliminated on the grounds that they did not attempt to influence social institutions.

At this point the list contained 21 legal and justice associations, 18 health and mental health associations, 69 civic action groups, and 185 neighborhood associations. Rather than contact every organization on the list to determine whether it met all criteria of eligibility, random samples were drawn within each stratum, organization leaders were communicated with, and the group screened for eligibility. In each stratum, the two largest organizations (by number of members) were selected with certainty, the two largest having been determined by telephone calls to half a dozen likely candidates in each stratum. If an organization failed to meet all the criteria, it was dropped from consideration and the next organization in the stratum was investigated. When an organization met all the criteria, the purpose of the study was explained and the group was invited to participate in the project.

Results of the organizational sampling process are shown in Table B.1, which displays for each of the four strata the number of groups deciding to participate and the number of contacted groups that were ineligible. (The main reasons for ineligibility were too few members, inappropriate goals, and organizational death.) Of the forty-one voluntary associations invited to participate, thirty-two (79 percent) agreed to participate and completed the project. We attempted to secure at least eight groups in each stratum, but due to a last-minute withdrawal in the health cate-

Table B.1. Participation of Voluntary Associations by Organization Classification

| Participation decision | Organization stratum | | | | |
	Legal	Health	Civic	Neighbor-hood	Total
Accepted	7	7	10	8	32
Refused	0	3	2	4	9
Ineligible	7	4	10	2	23

gory and an organizational demise in the legal category, we did not achieve this objective.

In each participating organization, a key informant—usually either the president or the executive director—was interviewed on a variety of organizational matters. Each interview, lasting from two to four hours, had a semistructured format with nonprecoded responses recorded verbatim. We gathered information on organizational decision-making processes, communication, programs and issues, interorganizational relationships, and authority relationships with supralocal bodies. Where possible, this interview information was corroborated from documentary material provided by the informant. Information from informants provided a basis for designing the interview schedule administered to samples of members and leaders and for developing the data set of organizational attributes for analysis.

Member Sampling Frame

All participating organizations either provided lists of their officers, committee or task force chairpersons, and members, or else selected systematic random samples from such lists following our instructions. Four strata were designated within each group: the president (or chairperson) and the executive director (if present); officers (including board members) and committee or task-force chairpersons; members; and volunteers (present in three associations). Only persons living in Marion County were included in the latter two categories when the organization embraced a state-wide membership (except when fewer than twenty members of one state-wide group, Organization for Retarded Persons, lived in Marion County). All persons within the first two, or "leader," strata were sampled with certainty (up to forty leaders), while systematic random samples of up to sixty members and volunteers were drawn from the eligible lists. (From pretests on four associations in Bloomington, we expected a response rate of about 50 percent, and hence sampled twice as many names as we hoped to complete interviews.) Wherever possible, we sought the following completion rate: each president; each executive director; eight or nine officers/committee chairpersons, for a total of ten or eleven leader interviews; and twenty interviews with members and volunteers, approximately half from each strata, where both existed. In several organizations fewer than thirty interviews could be completed, given the initial organization size and the response rate. In those groups, as many interviews as possible were completed. (One health organization with almost three thousand members was permitted fifty interviews.) Similarly, some organizations had too few leaders for us to complete ten interviews among the first two strata. Consequently, the total sample for these groups was composed of more than two-thirds members.

Two letters were mailed in the same envelope to half the names sampled from the membership lists in each organization. A letter from the organization president or executive director indicated the organization's willingness to participate in the project; the second letter, from us, explained the purpose of the study, insured confidentiality of responses, and informed the respondent that he or she would soon hear from a trained interviewer about a personal interview. As names of nonrespondents were dropped from the sample, new names were randomly selected from the remainder until the desired quotas were achieved or the set of sampled names was exhausted.

Interviewing

Personal interviews lasting about one hour and fifteen minutes were conducted by trained interviewers. (Two exceptions were the handful of leaders residing outside Indianapolis, who were interviewed by phone, and the members of one state-wide health organization who received an abbreviated mail-back version of the questionnaire.) About one-third of the interviews were done by first-year graduate students in sociology at Indiana University at Bloomington who were completing a required course in survey methods. The rest were conducted by residents of Indianapolis and undergraduate students at Indiana University–Purdue University at Indianapolis (IUPUI), who were specially trained and paid for their work. Interviewing took place between May 10, 1977, and September 15, 1977.

Coding of completed questionnaires was done by a paid staff of advanced graduate students in sociology at IU-Bloomington, with routine clerical help from undergraduate assistants.

Completion and Response Rates

Tables B.2 and B.3 summarize the overall interview response rates. Of the 1,310 names for which interviews were attempted, almost 83 percent were valid sample names.

The majority of the invalid names were SLIPs (Sample Listing Isn't Proper), primarily because addresses could not be found for them; a few were deleted because they had previously been interviewed as members of another organization.

Interviews were successfully completed with more than three-

Table B.2. Breakdown of Listings into Sample and Nonsample Names

Listing	(N)		Percentage	
Sample names	1,081		82.5	
Nonsample names	229		17.5	
Not a member		(43)		(3.3)
Moved		(43)		(3.3)
SLIPs[a]		(143)		(10.9)
Total	1,310		100	

[a] Sample Listing Isn't Proper.

Table B.3. Final Disposition of Sample Names

Disposition	(N)	Percentage
Interviews	820	75.9
Noninterviews	261	24.1
Refusals	(174)	(16.1)
No contact	(18)	(1.7)
Out of town	(17)	(1.6)
Other	(52)	(4.8)
Total	1,081	100

quarters of the valid sample respondents. Refusal to be interviewed was the major reason for failure to complete an interview.
The heterogeneous "other" reasons for noninterviews include ill-
ness, broken appointments, and withdrawn assignments once an
organization quota had been achieved. When only completed interviews and refusals are considered, the overall rate of completion is 82.5 percent.

Table B.4 presents the results of the interviewing process for
each organization in the project, designated by the fictitious names
assigned in this volume. The classification of interview outcomes
follows that in Tables B.2 and B.3. Column 4 combines "no contact," "out of town," and "other" reasons for noninterviews; out-
right refusals appear in column 5. The completion rate is then calculated as the ratio of completed interviews (column 6) to the sum
of columns 4, 5, and 6, while the interview rate includes only completed interviews (column 6) plus refusals (column 5) in the de-
nominator. Considerable variation in completion and interview
rates occurred across organization strata, with the neighborhood
groups having lower response rates than the other three types.
About two-thirds of the organizations had interview rates of 80
percent or higher.

Sample Weighting

Two sets of sample weights were derived from the breakdown
of completed interviews by sampling frame within organizations.
The number of completed interviews in each of the four leader-

ship and membership strata were divided into the total size in each strata. The resultant weight is the number of other persons represented by each completed interview. Because of the great disparity in organization size (one health organization contained almost 30 percent of the 10,466 persons in the population), a second set of weights was calculated in which each organization was standardized to a size of 25.6 total respondents from all strata, the average of the actual number of completed interviews per organization.

Table B.4. Results of Interviews by Organization

Organization name[a] (1)	Size of group (2)	Names[b] (3)	Ineligible[c] (4)	Refused interview (5)	Completed interview (6)	Completion rate[d] (7)	Interview rate[e] (8)
Legal-justice							
LBI	498	62	2	17	34	.642	.667
RRL	57	48	3	3	20	.769	.870
BHN	50	46	2	1	31	.912	.969
KIT	36	34	0	2	25	.926	.926
RFO	49	39	2	2	19	.826	.905
PLC	21	21	0	2	18	.900	.900
FFF	85	33	1	4	25	.833	.862
Health–mental health							
OBP	57	39	1	13	23	.622	.639
HPC	132	43	5	2	32	.780	.889
AFH	94	34	0	2	27	.931	.931
HOP	2,948	74	8	9	49	.742	.845
SDE	537	49	3	11	27	.659	.711
ORP	37	32	0	1	31	.967	.967
ODP	200	19	0	3	16	.842	.842
Civic action							
WRO	109	37	0	0	29	1.000	1.000
NLS	1,046	51	4	9	31	.705	.775

EPS	33	26	0	2	22	.917	.917
CAL	510	42	1	3	30	.877	.909
SCS	44	27	0	3	19	.864	.864
DRS	182	38	4	2	18	.750	.900
CRO	328	59	9	5	34	.708	.872
CWA	231	40	5	4	29	.763	.819
WPA	144	46	1	3	33	.892	.917
WPO	218	50	8	8	29	.644	.784
Neighborhood							
SG	374	46	12	5	11	.393	.688
EL	608	38	0	9	25	.735	.735
RG	243	32	1	7	20	.714	.741
PD	266	46	2	13	18	.546	.581
DT	69	29	1	5	20	.769	.800
LH	104	37	6	5	23	.676	.821
UT	448	43	2	12	26	.650	.684
WE	708	50	4	7	26	.703	.788
Total	10,466	1,310	87	174	820	.759	.825

[a] See Chapter Two for complete names of organizational acronyms.
[b] Sample names plus nonsample names.
[c] No contact, out of town, other.
[d] Number of interviews divided by sum of interviews, refusals, and ineligibles.
[e] Number of interviews divided by sum of interviews plus refusals.

Appendix C

Measurement of Variables

In this Appendix we present, in the order of their appearance in the text, the operationalizations of variables and scales used in the empirical analyses. Exact item wording, univariate response distributions, factor loadings, and scale intercorrelations appear in various tables.

C.1. Incentive Indices

To measure organizational incentives, we used information from a two-hour, semistructured interview with a key informant, usually the president or executive director of each association. During one segment of the interview, informants were asked to indicate what benefits they felt members received from the organization that might attract them to join and participate. Interviewers probed for solidary and material benefits as well as the purposive attractions that were usually spontaneously volunteered. Acting as coders, we independently read the entire transcript of each interview and extracted all mentions of potential solidary, material, and purposive benefits, based on the definitions of each type of incentive in Clark and Wilson's (1961) article. These empirical instances were used to construct about a dozen code categories for each of the three incentive types. These codes were then applied to each organization's transcript by two new coders as well as by us. Agreements among coders across all items within each of the three types of incentives were 96 percent for solidary, 90 percent for material, and 85 percent for purposive. We resolved differences about specific items by joint discussion. After final agreement on specific incentives in each organization, we ran a series

Table C.1. Items Used to Scale Organizational Incentives

Items	Percentage
I. Purposive incentives	
Informant explicitly mentioned goals or purposes as a benefit to members.	84
Public speakers or public educational programs.	75
Newsletter emphasizes purposes or goals.	56
Regular monitoring of legislation or administrators.	50
Past organizational success as incentive.	9
II. Solidary Incentives	
Informant did not explicitly reject social incentives.	87
Awards for service and/or prestige.	41
Regular social activities.	31
Informant explicitly mentioned sociability or friendship as incentive.	25
III. Material incentives	
Other publications or product discounts.	91
Direct services for clients.	38
Workshops, job training, or licensing programs.	38
Efforts to preserve, upgrade property values.	22
National organization magazine.	19

of Guttman scaling analyses to determine which subset of items produced the best scale. The final scale items and the percentage of organizations with these attributes are shown in Table C.1. Each item was weighted equally and summed to derive an organization's score for each of the three incentive dimensions. The coefficients of reproducibility are .84 for purposive incentives, .89 for solidary incentives, and .78 for material incentives.

C.2. Incentive Motives

Interviewers read respondents a list of twelve "reasons different people give for joining organizations" and asked them how important each reason was in their decision to join ("very important"; "somewhat important"; "not important at all"). Items were

Table C.2. Response on 16 Membership Commitment Items for Individual Members

Keyword mnemonic	Item wording	Mean	Standard deviation
Indifference:	I am indifferent about being a member of the organization.	2.16	1.01
Uncaring:	To be perfectly honest, I don't care what this organization says or does.	1.75	0.77
Importance:	What this organization stands for is very important to me.	4.37	0.70
Committed:	Personally, how committed do you feel to (organization name)?	3.47	1.25
Rescue[a]:	Suppose your local organization were in real danger of going out of existence. How much effort would you be willing to spend in order to prevent this?	3.23	0.83
Pride:	I feel a sense of pride in being a member of (organization name).	4.03	0.81
Values:	It is important to me to maintain the values of the organization.	4.02	0.72
Support:	I feel this organization would deserve my support even if I were unable to participate.	4.13	0.61
Centrality:	I feel there are very few things more important in my life than this organization.	2.11	0.92
Influence:	My membership in this organization influences most aspects of my life.	2.41	1.03
Investment:	I have put so much time and effort into this organization that it would be difficult for me to leave.	2.42	1.01
Belonging:	I feel a strong sense of belonging to this organization.	3.25	1.12
Member goals:	Most members of (organization name) are committed to the organization's goals.	3.76	0.82
Member good:	Most members feel what is good for the organization is good for them personally.	3.47	0.95
Confidence:	Most members feel confident in the organization's ability to achieve its goals.	3.71	0.80
Altruism:	Most members put the organization's goals ahead of their personal interests.	2.90	1.02

[a] Four-point scale (no effort to great deal of effort).

designed to capture solidary, purposive, and material as well as other types of demands that members might recall as having attracted them to the association. A factor analysis of all twelve reasons for joining indicated that three items loading highly on the first factor defined primarily a purposive scale (alpha = .58): opportunity to help those in need; a sense of community responsibility; and to accomplish the goals or aims of the organization. The second factor dimension seemed to combine both solidary and material reasons for joining. To permit analysis of the different effects of these two motivations, we separated the items into two scales. The solidary scale (alpha = .65) has three items: participating would be fun; opportunity to meet people with similar interests; and opportunity to have influence in community affairs. The material scale (alpha = .34) contains two elements: benefits like magazines, insurance plans, group travel; and availability of services or programs provided by the organization.

Respondents' scores on each scale were produced by assigning three points for each item answered "very important," two points for "somewhat important," and one point for "not important at all." Points were then totaled for all items in a given scale. Aggregate scores on the three motivation scales were calculated for each association by taking the mean score for each appropriately weighted sample.

C.3. Membership Commitment

The exact wording of the sixteen items chosen to designate members' commitment orientations toward their associations are listed in Table C.2, along with key-word mnemonics and their mean scores on a five-point Likert-type response scale (5 = strongly agree; 4 = agree; 3 = neither agree nor disagree; 2 = disagree; 1 = strongly disagree). Items were intercorrelated across all respondents and the correlation matrix was submitted to an exploratory factor analysis.

Briefly, the objective of factor analysis is to reduce the set of items to a smaller number of underlying, latent variables or factors that account for the total pattern of observed correlations

Table C.3. Factor Loadings from Oblique Varimax
Rotated Factor Analysis of 16 Membership
Commitment Items for Individual Members

Psychological support	Factor I	Factor II	Factor III
Indifference	−.69	−.12	−.02
Uncaring	−.74	.14	.03
Support	.47	.02	.23
Committed	.54	.34	−.01
Rescue	.53	.34	−.03
Pride	.54	.28	.08
Importance	.59	.00	.21
Values	.45	.14	.16
Centrality	−.09	.68	.21
Influence	−.01	.63	.20
Investment	.15	.61	−.03
Belonging	.34	.56	.02
Member goals	.09	−.10	.53
Member good	−.00	.05	.47
Confidence	.05	.06	.44
Altruism	−.04	.10	.44
Eigenvalues	13.43	2.68	1.79
Percentage of variance	40.4	8.5	7.2

among the indicators of membership commitment. The results tell us how many dimensions are necessary to reproduce the r-matrix; whether there is a single "general" dimension; the relative importance of each factor in contributing to the total variance in the indicators; and, through use of factor-score coefficients, how to construct differentially weighted scales of the unmeasured factors for use in substantive analyses.

The factoring method used throughout transforms a large set of observed variables into a smaller set of factors that are oblique (correlated with each other). The solution is then rotated to a new set of axes (varimax rotation) which offers the clearest substantive interpretation of the latent factors. The factor loadings for the sixteen commitment items are shown in Table C.3.

Three principal factors emerged, together accounting for more than half the total variance in the matrix. Each item loaded highly on only one factor. Factor III clearly reflects a perception of member commitment to the organization, as each of its four indicators begins "Most members. . . ." Factor II probably reflects a personal salience dimension of commitment, since the first two of its four items concern the centrality of the organization in the respondent's life. The first factor, containing the lion's share of the variance, has eight significant loadings. A common theme seems to be a generalized commitment, or loyalty, to the organization, without mention of the larger life-space context that appears in some of the second factor items. Two items, however, "Importance" and "Values," stress the salience or centrality of the organization's goals. We decided to break these two items out as a separate scale of "Goal Salience," treating the other six as a scale of "Loyalty."

Scale scores were constructed as follows. Each respondent's scale item score was standardized by subtracting the mean and dividing by the standard deviation of the sample responses. Items in a scale were weighted by factor score coefficients from the oblique factor analysis and the weighted scores summed only for those items loading highly on a given factor (i.e., the items boxed in Table C.3). Finally, for ease of interpretation, scale scores were multiplied by 100 to move the decimal point two places to the right. Thus, scores for individuals as well as organizations are positive for those most normatively oriented toward the association and negative for those least controlled by norms. Mean values are close to zero on each scale. Alwin (1973) discusses differences in such scores and factor-based scores, where each highly-loaded variable is given a weight of 1 in the scale. He finds little difference in the results.

To obtain a summary measure of commitment, a second-stage factor analysis was performed on respondents' four scale scores. A single-factor solution was extracted and this factor is interpreted as a Commitment Index. Loadings of the four scales on the index were .67, .77, .30, and .48 respectively. Index score construction followed the same linear additive procedure described above.

Table C.4. Intercorrelations, Means, Standard Deviations, and Reliabilities of Membership Commitment Scales for 32 Associations

Scale names	Goal salience	Loyalty	Personal salience	Member perception	Commitment index
Goal salience					
Loyalty	.91				
Personal salience	.79	.81			
Member perception	.70	.74	.76		
Commitment index	.95	.97	.89	.81	
Mean	-0.61	-0.55	0.32	-3.66	-0.01
Standard deviation	11.42	38.30	39.04	22.67	51.15
Reliability (α)[a]	.63	.85	.83	.57	.77

[a] Based on individual responses.

Table C.4 reports the means, standard deviations, intercorrelations, and reliabilities (Cronbach's alpha for individual responses) for scale and index scores of our sample organizations.

C.4. Decision-making Variables

We measured organizational complexity by inspecting organizational constitutions in conjunction with clarifications provided by elite informants. There were four categories.

1. Simple structure. Organization consists of a mass membership and officers, a board of directors, or both units. Hence, relatively few points of influence on decision making are potentially available to members. Eight associations fit this classification.

2. Elaborate structure. These associations have, in addition to members, officers, and board, additional decision-making units such as an executive committee (often a subset of officers and/or board) empowered to act between regular meetings and/or a system of standing committees composed of several persons who evaluate policy and program proposals and make recommendations to the group as a whole for adoption. Thus, many more points of entry into the decision-making process are potentially available to ordinary members. Nine associations fall into this category.

3. Professionalized structure. The main distinguishing attribute of these organizations is a paid executive director, frequently in charge of several paid staff members. In most cases the organization also has all the other decision units described for the elaborate structure organization. A full- or part-time paid professional provides yet another potential channel by which members may have input into the decision-making process, although some literature suggests that a professional staff may abrogate the authority of the nominally superior lay board. Nine of the sample associations with mass memberships had paid executive directors.

4. Board only. In six organizations, all persons were members

of a board of directors and no other mass membership existed. Thus, all members presumably had equal opportunity to affect decisions. (Several of these board-only groups also had paid directors, but they were classified here.)

This four-fold classification was used to create dichotomous (dummy) variables.

To determine organizational rates of *decision-making participation*, respondents were asked to nominate the issue they considered to be the most important one facing the organization in the past year, including ones which might still be active. Thus, all members of the same organization were free to nominate the same issue or entirely different ones. We then asked if members were aware of the stand the organization had taken on the issue and, if so, whether they had personally been involved in making the decision on what stand to take. We were thereby able to code members by three levels of involvement on an issue they personally considered to be most important to the organization. Coded "1" were members who were unable to think of any important issue or who did not know what stand had been taken. Coded "2" were members who knew of an issue and what stand had been taken but who said they had not participated in making the decision. Coded "3" were members who said they had participated in the decision on the most important issue, as well as persons who named an issue on which the organization had not yet taken a stand. (Many of the latter were officers or otherwise active members who were responding to our request to nominate current issues; we felt most of them were likely to participate in actually making the decision when the time came.) This three-point classification of participation on the most important issue divided the total sample almost into thirds.

To measure *total amount of influence* and *influence slope*, respondents were presented with names of each of the major positions in the organization (president/chairperson, board of directors, executive director, staff, members) and were asked: "In general how much influence do you think the following groups or persons *actually* have in determining the policies and actions in [organization's name]?" Response categories were coded: (5) a very great deal of influence; (4) a great deal of influence; (3) some influence; (2) little influence; and (1) no influence. All members' ratings of each position in the organization were averaged and treated as an objective assessment of the amount of influence exercised by that position. Tannenbaum acknowledged that "this approach to measurement has limitations; yet it seems to us more suitable than the available alternatives for the measurement of the particular concepts with which we are concerned" (Tannenbaum, 1968:24). The main error source is respondent misperception of other roles' influence, yet any alternatives to reliance on member reports would require extensive direct observation that is simply not feasible in comparative research of this magnitude.

Influence slope is the difference between the mean influence rating of the top leader (president or chairperson) and the membership influence rating. The more the leader's influence exceeds that of the members, the less democratic the association (i.e., the more centralized the control). *Total influence* is an average of the mean ratings for two or three positions occurring in nearly all associations: the president/chairperson; the board of directors; and the members. We used an average rather than a sum because four of the associations lacked one of the three positions; however, we refer to the value as the "total" amount of influence, to be consistent with prior treatments. The greater the aggregate total influence, the more widespread is control over organizational decision making.

We obtained information about the *communication* patterns among association members by asking each respondent the following question:

How often do you communicate with each of the following people about organization matters:
    President or executive director?
    Other officers, board members or committee chairpersons?
    Other members?

Response categories ranged from "rarely or never" to "once or twice a week or more." To compute numerical values for each channel of communication, we coded these verbal categories ac-

Table C.5. Correlations among Decision-making Measures for 32 Associations

	1	2	3	4	5	6	7	8	9
1. Simple structure									
2. Elaborate structure	-.36								
3. Professionalized	-.33	-.42							
4. Board only	-.25	-.32	-.30						
5. Decision participation	.10	.17	-.33	.08					
6. Total influence	.03	-.03	-.33	.39	.47				
7. Influence slope	-.17	-.19	.41	-.08	-.02	.13			
8. Average attendance	-.10	.35	-.42	.16	.39	.33	-.18		
9. Vertical communication	-.34	.30	-.16	.19	.59	.43	.04	.30	
Mean	.22	.31	.28	.19	1.99	3.55	.53	2.84	10.72
Standard deviation	.42	.47	.46	.40	.34	.18	.43	1.46	6.36

cording to the approximate number of times per year a respondent indicated communication with persons in the designated category (for example, eighteen for "once or twice a month," six for "several times per year").

In associations where all three role strata were present, eight possible channels of communication were potentially usable (we excluded presidents communicating with themselves or with an executive director). By assuming a three-tiered hierarchy with presidents at top and members at bottom, we could designate three vertical communication channels.

The content of the communication is specified in the question only as "about organizational matters." This wording clearly allows respondents a wide range of interpretation, ranging from highly instrumental advice seeking and advice giving to expression of values. While we cannot definitely conclude that normative reinforcement is the basic content of communication acts, we expect such content to figure heavily in the exchanges.

To compute organizational scores for each direction, we determined the average frequency with which each channel was used. Vertical communication consists of three types of communication: officers (or board) to the president; members to the president; and members to officers. The organizational mean communication frequencies on these three channels were simply averaged to compute the overall organizational score on vertical communication, even though typically the number of members in an organization is considerably larger than the number of officers.

Table C.5 presents the intercorrelations among the various indicators of decision making and influence as well as their means and standard deviations.

C.5. Formal Legitimacy

The measure of formal legitimacy is a Guttman scale of three dichotomous items based on content analysis of open-ended responses in the officer interviews. The scale's coefficient of reproducibility is .92. The relevant portion of the interview schedule is reproduced below:

Now we'd like to have some information that concerns the relationship of this chapter to the national (or other supra-local level) organization.

1. In what areas does the national (or other supra-local level) organization have control in setting limits and obligations on this chapter?
2. In the past, has the national (or other supra-local level) organization ever imposed a position on your organization which members felt was unwarranted?

   (IF YES) What was the issue and what was the response of leaders or members to this situation?

   (IF NO) Can the National (or other supra-local) office impose its position on this chapter if it chooses to do so?
3. Has the national (or other supra-local) body ever overturned/vetoed a decision reached by this local?

   (IF YES) What was the response of leaders or members to this situation?

   (IF NO) Can the national (or other supra-local) overturn a decision made by the local?

We assume that the potential control of local organizations by a national (or other supra-local level) organization (e.g., the ability to impose issue positions or veto local decisions) allows local leaders to use supra-local authorities as leverage in shaping local policies.

C.6. Resources

Construction of scales measuring membership resource contributions for the associations followed the same basic procedures as those for the membership commitment measures. Nineteen items in the questionnaire tapped various behavioral participation aspects. Table C.6 lists these items, along with the percentages of all respondents reporting such activity during the previous year (only a yes or no response was requested), or the means and standard deviations for three nondichotomous variables. An oblique rotated factor analysis, shown in Table C.7, produced four factors accounting for half the variance in the r-matrix. Each item loaded highly on only one factor, although four items did not load sufficiently high on any factor to be included in the resource contribution scales.

The first factor is clearly an Internal Activity scale, since its six

Table C.6. Participation in 19 Different Organizational Activities for Individual Members

Type of organizational participation	Percentage	
1. Tried to recruit new members	44	
2. Phoned or contacted other members	39	
3. Worked on special projects or workshops	34	
4. Wrote, phoned, or personally contacted government officials on behalf of the organization	32	
5. Represented the organization to other groups or to the general public	30	
6. Currently on a committee	25	
7. Provided special services to clients, patients, or members	23	
8. Hold an official position in the organization, such as officer or board member	17	
9. Gave or lent equipment or supplies	16	
10. Helped with office work	16	
11. Provided transportation on behalf of the organization	15	
12. Solicited donations	14	
13. Held a meeting at respondent's home	8	
14. Chairperson of a committee	8	
15. Wrote letters to newspapers and magazines	6	
16. Picketed or demonstrated	5	
	Mean	(sd)
17. Number of meetings of all kinds attended in last year	5.9	(13)
18. Number of hours spent outside meetings working for organization in typical month	5.4	(25)
19. Amount of money given to organization in past year, including dues	$31.7	(183)

items concern highly specific actions carried out primarily among the membership, many dealing with maintenance tasks. The second factor, involving number of meetings attended, hours spent outside meetings on organizational affairs, and money donated (including dues), cover specific actions carried out primarily among the membership, many dealing with maintenance tasks. We labelled this scale "Infra-Resources" since time and money are

Table C.7. Factor Loadings from Oblique Varimax Rotated Factor Analysis of 19 Participation Variables for Individual Members

Participation variable	Internal activity	Infra- resources	Leadership	External activity
Phoned	.38	−.09	−.34	.19
Special services	.61	.00	−.15	−.10
Supplies	.52	.10	.03	−.02
Special project	.40	−.10	−.32	.09
Give ride	.61	.06	.17	.13
Recruit	.31	−.07	−.09	.22
Held meeting	−.01	.13	−.34	.26
Office help	.14	.04	−.30	.28
Solicit	.15	.03	−.07	.26
Represent	.14	−.07	−.26	.30
Meetings	.24	.31	−.29	.13
Hours	.15	.65	−.04	.03
Donate	−.04	.63	−.03	.00
Committee	.11	.02	−.74	−.09
Chairperson	−.01	.03	−.63	.00
Officer	−.09	.07	−.70	−.01
Contact	.16	−.09	−.12	.43
Letters	−.02	.09	.02	.50
Picket	−.04	.01	.06	.50
Eigenvalues	5.49	1.47	1.43	1.12
Percentage of variance	28.9	7.7	7.5	5.9

generalized resources available to organizations for use in more focused collective actions (see Rogers, 1974). The third factor is obviously a formal leadership incumbency factor, while the fourth contains three items dealing with external influence activity.

After respondents' scale scores on these four dimensions were constructed, a second-order factor analysis disclosed that the scales loaded highly on a single summary factor, which we designated the Resource Contribution Index (scale loadings on this summary index were .43, .29, .20, and .22).

Table C.8 contains the means, standard deviations, intercorrelations, and scale reliabilities (Cronbach's alpha for individual responses) for the scale and index scores.

Table C.8. Intercorrelations, Means, Standard Deviations, and Reliabilities of Resource Contribution Scales for 32 Associations

Scale names	Internal activity	Leadership	Infra-resources	External activity	Resource Contribution index
Internal activity					
Leadership	.47				
Infra-resources	.64	.53			
External activity	.44	.20	.48		
Resource contribution index	.90	.73	.72	.62	
Mean	0.44	−3.99	0.47	−0.09	−4.31
Standard deviation	42.10	32.15	19.55	24.31	41.33
Reliability (α)[a]	.75	.72	.62	.49	.64

[a]Based on individual responses.

C.7. Tolerance

The measure of membership tolerance involves responses to the second of two questions involving hypothetical situations. The first asked, "If you were dissatisfied with a decision that your organization made concerning a *key issue*, what would be your most likely reaction?" and offered four possible responses: "(4) I would not voice my dissatisfaction and would go along with the decision"; "(3) I would voice my dissatisfaction but probably would go along with the decision"; "(2) I would try to get the decision reversed"; "(1) I would withdraw from the organization." Since so few respondents chose the last response, we used the answers to a second query, "What would be your most likely reaction if the organization continued to make unfavorable decisions?" This offered the same four response categories. The distribution across the four categories among individual members was 2 percent, 12 percent, 38 percent, and 48 percent, respectively. We assumed that organizations where members were less likely to withdraw in the face of dissatisfying policies were organizations having a greater resource of member support upon which to draw. This tolerance index was scored by assigning points from four to one according to members' responses and averaging across all respondents in an association.

C.8. Influence Reputation

In the late summer of 1978, we returned to Indianapolis to collect additional data on the sample voluntary associations. At this point we had completed most of the analysis of the internal dynamics and needed some quantitative judgments about how successful the associations had been in their efforts to influence public policies. We consulted a number of methodological reports in the community power tradition for suggestions on how to operationalize power and/or influence. While much of this literature participates in a controversy over the "best" way to identify the local community elite decision makers, we sought a simple and reliable method for attaching quantitative values to organizational rather than individual influence. Realizing that judgments might vary widely depending upon the designated criterion of effectiveness, we finally decided that informants should be asked to rate the organizations not against each other but in terms of how well each organization did in achieving the particular tasks it set for itself. The complete instructions, presented in writing to each informant, were:

Reputation for Influence

On the basis of your experience and information, please sort each organization name into the category which best describes how much *influence* the organization has had in the past couple of years on public policies in that organization's areas of interest.

Please consider in your decisions *only* how much influence an organization has in *achieving its own objectives*, and not how widespread its influence is in the entire community.

If you feel you don't know enough about a particular organization, feel free to ignore it.

The list of organizations contained seventy names, some specific organizations and some group names. We constructed this list in consultation with a sociologist at a social service organization whose main job was to evaluate voluntary associations for funding by the United Way. In addition to all thirty-two social influence associations in the study, the list included the major political, governmental, private enterprise, and other voluntary associations in the community and at the state level.

Twenty-four informants were recruited to provide evaluations. We attempted, through a snowballing technique, to identify many knowledgeable persons whose areas of expertise and participation spanned the various substantive fields in which the voluntary associations operated. By occupation, our informants include: five members of the City-County Council; five members of the General Assembly (state legislature); five staff members of four social service agencies; a staff member of the city Department of Planning and Zoning; a professor of public administration at a local university; a city reporter for the newspaper; a mayor's aide; executive directors of a hospital, chamber of commerce, a mayors'

Table C.9. Organizations' Median Influence Reputation Scores

Organization	Median score
Senior Citizens Society	4.79
American Federation of Labor-Congress of Industrial Organizations (AFL-CIO) Indiana Joint Board	4.63
American Legion	3.73
Ethnic Protection Society	3.90
Nature Lovers' Society	2.50
River Green	1.33
Society for Disease Elimination	3.50
Major Indianapolis Banks	6.71
Indianapolis Bar Association	4.93
Profile Coalition	3.00
Organization of Blind Persons	3.00
Major Broadcasting Organizations	6.00
Community Action Against Poverty of Greater Indianapolis (CAAP)	3.88
Roman Catholic Archdiocese of Indianapolis	4.43
Elm Lawn	2.75
City-County Council	6.08
Disaster Relief Society	2.13
Legal-Beagles, Inc.	3.94
Indianapolis Chamber of Commerce	5.80
Civic Advancement League	4.44
Indianapolis Division of Community Services	3.88
Indiana Council of Churches	3.63
State and Local Courts	4.88
Shady Grove	2.50
Organized Deaf Persons	3.30
Marion County Democratic Party	4.00
Indianapolis Department of Employment and Training	3.83
Poplar Drive	2.00
Indianapolis Board of Education	4.75
Indiana General Assembly (State Legislature)	6.77
Governor's Office, State of Indiana (Gov. Bowen)	6.68
Advocates for the Handicapped	4.38
Central Indiana Health Systems Agency	4.00
Indiana Hospital Association (IHA)	4.00
Better Housing Now	3.00

Organization	Median score
Major Indianapolis Industries	5.38
Conference of Christians and Jews	2.75
John Birch Society	1.80
Rights for Prisoners	2.67
Kids in Trouble	3.25
Indiana Ku Klux Klan (KKK)	1.20
Legal Services Organization of Indianapolis (LSO)	4.56
Eli Lilly Endowment	6.62
Mayor's Office, City of Indianapolis (Mayor Hudnut)	5.86
Marion County Medical Society	4.63
Martin Center	3.58
Health Outreach Program	4.08
National Association for the Advancement of Colored People, Indianapolis Chapter (NAACP)	3.69
Reform of Repressive Laws	1.64
Women's Rights Organization	2.50
Indianapolis Neighborhood Development, Inc. (INDI)	2.40
Indianapolis Star & News	6.40
Health Professionals Coalition	2.50
Locust Hills	3.50
Indianapolis Police Department	4.83
Downtown	3.13
Greater Indianapolis Progress Committee (CIPC)	5.60
Marion County Republican Party	5.78
Organization for Retarded Persons	4.73
Local Service Clubs	3.50
Wilderness Protection Organization	2.83
Uptown	3.67
United Way of Greater Indianapolis	5.94
Civil Rights Organization	4.00
Freedom from Fear	3.58
Marion County Welfare Department	4.60
Westend	3.50
Coalition of Women Activists	4.25
Women's Political Alliance	2.75
Indianapolis Department of Planning and Zoning	4.50

task force, and a local foundation; and a housewife long active in various charitable organizations.

Each informant was presented with a randomly ordered list of the seventy organizations, the written instructions, and a set of categories from one to seven with three labelled points: "(1) little or no influence"; "(4) moderate influence"; "(7) very great influence." After all assignments had been made, median values were calculated, omitting all informants who said they were unable to rate a given organization. Table C.9 presents the seventy organization names (using fictitious names where anonymity is required) and the median values.

C.9. Environmental Variables

Uncertainty

Based on information supplied by elite informants in each association, organizations were classified into high, medium, and low categories on five environmental conditions. The first two items concern the static-dynamic dimension (instability of environmental conditions):

1. Membership trends: High change (10 percent change or more in past year); medium change (1–10 percent change in past year); low change (no change in membership).

2. Stability and dependability of funding sources over past five years: High stability (stable flow of funds); medium stability (moderate fluctuations); low stability (extreme fluctuations in funding sources).

The next three items concern the complexity of environmental conditions (simple-complex dimension):

3. Number of community organizations the association works or has worked with: High number (three or more); medium number (two); low number (none or one other organization).

4. Number of opposing groups that try to limit association's activities, coded according to different functional sectors in

which opposition groups were located (government, political, social organizations, community organizations, business): High (three or more opposition sectors); medium (two); low (one or none).

5. Number of domains in which the association has goals (legal, attitudinal, social movements, financial, publicity of cause, other organizations' environments, social ecology such as urbanization): High number of domains (four to seven); medium (two or three); low (one or none).

To construct scale scores, five points were assigned to each high category, three to each medium category, and one to each low category; these were summed across all five categories. Actual scores ranged from 5 to 21, with a mean of 12.81 and a standard deviation of 3.68.

Issue Controversy

Again based on informants' reports, issue controversy is an ordinal measure of the extent to which an external situation in the past year provided an organization with an opportunity to mobilize its members to attempt to influence the agents of external institutions. Four categories (in ascending order) and their codes follow:

0. There were no important issues that required organizational action in the past year.

1. The only issues that arose were those necessitating relatively minor efforts, such as leadership contacts; no mass mobilization was needed. If an association maintained a lobbyist at the city or state level, it was classified here.

2. The organization confronted one or more issues that might call for special membership meetings or mass letter-writing campaigns. However, the issue had not reached a decision stage in the relevant external institutions. A lobbyist was not essential for classification here.

3. The organization faced an issue whose decision was pending in an external institution (such as a bill before the state legis-

lature or a city-county council) and would require mobilization of member effort.

Ten associations fell into the highest category of issue controversy. Each of these organizations had a major interest in some state legislative action, including three groups whose major priority was passage of the Equal Rights Amendment. Three associations were coded "2," twelve organizations were coded "1," and seven groups that had faced no important issues during the past year were coded "0."

C.10. Interorganizational Networks

During the summer of 1978, the leader of each organization in our sample was asked to fill out a questionnaire about the organization's relationships with all seventy organizations listed in Table C.9. The fourteen-page questionnaire consisted of a single question at the top of the page with the entire checklist of organization names below. Respondents checked off only those names that applied to contacts during the preceding two years. The exact questions, with the keyword labels, are:

1. HEARD ABOUT: Which of the following organizations have you heard anything about?
2. INFLUENCE ATTEMPT: Which organizations have policies or programs which your organization has tried to influence?
3. JOINT PROJECTS: With which organizations does your organization have joint programs or projects?
4. COALITIONS: Which organizations have joined with your organization in a common effort to attempt to influence public policies?
5. NOT SYMPATHETIC: Which organizations are unsympathetic to the objectives of your organization?
6. ACTIVELY OPPOSED: Which organizations have actively opposed or impeded the goals of your organization?
7. COMMON BOARD: With which organizations does your organization have common board members?

8. SEND INFORMATION: To which organizations do you send information about community affairs?

9. RECEIVE INFORMATION: From which organizations does your organization receive information about community affairs?

10. SEND SUPPORT: To which organizations does your organization give moral support or approval?

11. RECEIVE SUPPORT: From which organizations does your organization receive moral support or approval?

12. SEND MONEY: To which organizations does your organization give money or other material resources?

13. RECEIVE MONEY: From which organizations does your organization receive money or other material resources?

Appendix D

A Note on Statistical Methods

Since the research for this book makes extensive use of quantitative data analysis techniques, in this appendix we discuss three methods—multiple regression, path analysis, and blockmodeling—for the benefit of readers who may have only a passing familiarity with these statistical tools.

Multiple Regression

The use of regression equations has become a standard approach to quantitative data analysis in sociology in the past two decades. Several excellent treatments are available (Van de Geer, 1971; Namboodiri, Carter, and Blalock, 1975; Kerlinger and Pedhazur, 1973). We describe here in general terms how regression equation coefficients may be interpreted as tests of theoretical hypotheses.

In general terms, we use multiple regression equations to determine whether a particular dependent variable is "explained" in the statistical sense that its variation can be predicted from knowledge of the variation in two or more independent variables. The variables considered to be independent and dependent will be specified by or inferred from the research hypothesis. Designating the dependent variable by Y and two independent variables by X_1 and X_2, the typical form of a regression equation is:

$$Y = a + b_1X_1 + b_2X_2 + e$$

The values of Y for an organization are a linear (straight-line) function of the organization's values on the two X's. The exact position of the multiple regression line depends on the values of a (the intercept on the Y-axis) and the b's (slopes, or effect of a unit change in X on Y, after controlling or "holding constant" the effect attributable to the other X's in the equation). The numerical values of a and the b's in the equation are calculated from observed values of the Y and the X's, using formulae that minimize the sum of the squared differences between the observed values of Y and the estimated regression line. (This difference is represented in the equation by e, the error term, which does not have a constant coefficient, since it varies from organization to organization.)

To determine whether a particular variable X has an effect on the variation in Y, over and above the other independent variables included in the equation, a significance test for b can be performed. Each b based on sample data (the thirty-two social influence associations) can be considered an estimate taken from a sampling distribution of possible b's from all other samples of the same size from the same population (all Indianapolis social influence organizations). A standard error for each b can thus be calculated from the sample data. The most typical test of significance asks whether the sample b differs significantly from zero. Dividing the estimated coefficient by its standard error gives a t-ratio for determining the probability that the estimated b could have been drawn from a sampling distribution whose population slope is zero. We do not present these t-ratios, but we star the sample regression slope values to indicate the probability that the population slope differs from zero.

The b values in a regression equation depend upon the unit in which the X variables are measured. If these units differ (e.g., number of meetings attended versus dollars of money given), then comparisons of relative magnitudes of coefficients are difficult. Several scales were measured in arbitrary metrics based on factor score transformations, likewise rendering interpretation of the b's difficult. Therefore, we transformed the regression b's to standardized coefficients, β's (betas), by multiplying b by the ratio of the X standard deviation to the Y standard deviation. (This standardization also eliminates the need for the intercept, a, so none is reported in the text.) Each β thus represents how much of a standard deviation change in Y can be attributed to one standard deviation change in X. Direct comparisons of the importance of the X's in an equation are simple: the larger the β, the more important that X is in predicting variation in Y, holding constant the other X effects.

A final regression statistic of importance is the multiple R^2 (coefficient of determination). It reports the proportion of variation in Y which can be attributed to the combined linear effect of all the variables in the equation. In technical terms, R^2 is the ratio of (1) the variation of the Y values predicted by the equation around the mean of Y to (2) the variation around the mean of the observed values of Y. The R^2 ranges between zero (no predictive value to the equation) to 1.00 (perfect prediction). As with the individual coefficients, a statistical test (F-test) is available to test the hypothesis that the population value is zero. In the text, we star the values of R^2 to indicate the probability at which this null hypothesis may be rejected.

To summarize, the regression equation statistics used in this book tell us three things about the theoretical hypotheses tested. First, if a β is statistically significant and its sign (plus or minus) is in the expected direction, the independent variable helps explain (i.e., predict variation in) the dependent variable, as stated in the research hypothesis. Second, the relative importance among the set of independent variables in the same equation can be judged by directly comparing the absolute size of their respective β's. Third, the multiple R^2 tells us how well all the independent variables, working together in linear combination, explain variation in the dependent variable. Comparing R^2's from different equations for the same dependent variable allows us to decide which combinations of variables provide better explanations, in a statistical sense.

Path Analysis

Path analysis may be viewed as an extension of multiple regression to situations in which variables are conceived of as being causally ordered. Originally developed by Sewell Wright for ge-

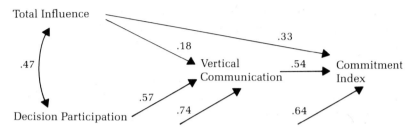

Figure D.1. Illustrative Path Model

netics, path analysis was imported into sociology in Duncan's (1966) article (see also Land, 1973; Van de Geer, 1971). If an analyst makes explicit assumptions about the temporal or causal sequence among variables, a path model can be constructed and estimates of causal effects can be obtained from a series of recursive structural equations whose numerical values are identical with standardized multiple regression coefficients. A diagram of the path model is an indispensable aid to understanding the basic purpose and interpretations of path analysis.

Figure D.1 presents a simplified version of a causal process. Two decision-making variables, total influence and decision participation are shown as antecedent to the other measures but not causally ordered. Hence, as predetermined variables within the model, their covariation is represented by a curved two-headed arrow whose value (+.47) is their zero-order correlation coefficient. Moving toward the right, the vertical communication rate is caused by both total influence and decision participation, shown by the directed single-headed arrows, and a residual factor which represents an unknown combination of other causal factors not included in the model, measurement error in variables, and random error disturbances. The numerical values attached to these three causal paths were obtained from a standardized multiple regression of vertical communication on total influence and decision participation. The betas of .18 and .57, respectively, show that the latter independent variable exercises a substantially larger direct effect on the volume of upward communication. The residual path value is calculated as the (positive) square root of the unexplained variance from the regression equation (i.e., the square root of $1 - R^2$). Upon resquaring this residual path coefficient, we see that about 55 percent of the variation in vertical communication remains unexplained in the model.

Moving further to the right in the diagram, we see that membership commitment receives causal arrows from vertical communication and total influence but not from decision participation. This causal hypothesis might have been suggested by a theory or, in the absence of an explicit hypothesis, by empirical analysis that discovered an insignificant regression coefficient from decision participation once the other two causal variables were in the equation. The model was then "trimmed" by dropping the direct path from decision participation to commitment. Comparing paths, we see that vertical communication has a somewhat greater direct impact on commitment than does total influence, but together they explain about 60 percent of the variation in the dependent measure.

The advantage of path analysis over simple regression equations lies in its ability to trace indirect causal effects in addition to the direct effects just discussed. Multiplying coefficients forward along causal paths shows how causal effects are transmitted through intervening variables. Figure D.1 nicely illustrates two different situations. First, total influence has both a direct effect on commitment (.33) and an indirect effect by raising the vertical communication rate which in turn strengthens commitment (.18 times .54 = .10 indirect effect). Thus, if the model is correctly specified, the indirect effect of total influence is about one third of its direct causal impact; a change or difference between organizations of one standard deviation in total influence will raise commitment by .43 standard deviations (.33 + .10 = .43), holding constant the effects of decision participation. Second, decision participation exerts only an indirect effect on commitment. The more decentralized the decision process, the higher the vertical communication rate, which in turn bolsters membership commitment levels. The magnitude of this indirect effect is simply the product of direct paths along the causal chain (.57 times .54 = .31), in this instance almost as much impact as the direct effect of total influence.

Blockmodeling

Blockmodeling is a method for inferring structure in multiple network data (White, Boorman, and Breiger, 1976; Boorman and White, 1976; Arabie, Boorman, and Levitt, 1978). The basic data are relationships between actors (organizations in our study), rather than attributes of actors. Ties of various types exist among the sample associations and between the associations and other organizations. Collecting all relationships of the same type, we can construct different matrices to display the interorganizational network for each type of tie. To illustrate, suppose we have reports from four voluntary associations (A, B, C, D) on sending information to each other and to three other organizations (E, F, G) not included in the study. A hypothetical matrix representing the "sent information" network might be:

	A	B	C	D	E	F	G
A		1	1	0	0	1	1
B	1		0	1	1	0	1
C	1	0		1	1	0	0
D	0	1	1		1	1	1

Entries of "1" indicate that associations in the rows sent information to organizations in the columns. Entries of "0" indicate no information was sent. Self-ties are left blank and treated as missing data. Besides the "sent information" network, other matrices representing different ties between the same set of organizations can be constructed (e.g., "received money," "met with director").

With many actors and networks (we had reports from thirty-two social influence associations on ties to seventy organizations across thirteen types of ties) deciphering an underlying structure to the interorganizational system becomes impossible without some method of data reduction. Organizations can be combined according to their similarities in the pattern of ties they have with all other organizations in all the system networks. Such "structurally equivalent" clusterings, or "blocks," can be performed by several methods (Burt, 1976, 1977a, 1977b; Sailer, 1978), but the nonsquare nature of our matrices virtually dictated that we use the iterative intercolumnar correlation algorithm—CONCOR (Breiger, Boorman, and Arabie, 1975). While CONCOR has been criticized as inefficient relative to principal components analysis (Schwartz, 1977), our attempts to use the latter method were unsuccessful while the CONCOR results were interpretable.

To use CONCOR, all networks are stacked one after the other (for 32 associations and 13 types of ties, there are 416 rows, each with 70 columns). Pairs of columns are correlated, omitting entries for self-ties. The greater the similarity between two organizations in the pattern of ties to other organizations, the higher their correlation. For pairs of nonvoluntary organizations, correlations are based on the degree of structural similarity these two organizations have in the 32 associations' relationships with both. To illustrate with the matrix above, organizations E and G correlate −.33 while F and G correlate +.58, revealing greater structural similarity between the latter pair.

After pairwise correlations have been calculated (2,415 in our data), the columns of the now square correlation matrix are again pairwise correlated. This process repeats until all entries are either +1.00 or −1.00. Organizations thus are assigned to one of two "blocks" depending on the sign of their intercorrelations. Blocks can be successively split by repeating the CONCOR algorithm. Each block is thus occupied by structurally equivalent sets of organizations and may be considered a distinct position in the interorganizational system. When to halt the partitioning depends on the analyst's purpose and feel for how well a given set of positions reveals essential information about the system's underlying structure.

Once a set of N positions or blocks has been identified, each partitioned network can be represented by an "image" matrix. Depending upon the density of ties within a block and between blocks (the proportion of actual to possible ties between organizations occupying each block), an N-by-N image of a network contains entries of "1" (a density of ties exceeding some criterion, in our case the mean density for the entire network), "−" (some ties occurring, but at a lower density than a mean network), or "0" (no ties existing between occupants of one block and another).

Since the number of blocks, N, is usually substantially smaller than the number of original actors (we identified eight blocks among seventy organizations), the images of each network are much easier to interpret.

References

Aiken, Michael, and Jerald Hage
    1966   "Organizational alienation: A comparative analysis." American Sociological Review 31 (August): 497–507.

Alba, Richard D.
    1973   "A graph-theoretic definition of a sociometric clique." Journal of Mathematical Sociology 3 (January): 113–126.

Aldrich, Howard E.
    1971   "The sociable organization: A case study of Mensa and some propositions." Sociology and Social Research 55 (July): 429–441.
    1972   "An organization-environment perspective on cooperation and conflict between organizations in the Manpower Training System." Pp. 11–37 in Anant Negandhi (ed.), Conflict and Power in Complex Organizations. Kent, Ohio: Center for Business and Economic Research.
    1976a   "An interorganization dependency perspective on relations between the employment service and its organization set." Pp. 231–266 in Ralph Kilmann, Louis Pondy, and Dennis Slevin (eds.), The Management of Organization Design. Amsterdam: Elsevier.
    1976b   "Resource dependence and interorganizational relations: Relations between local employment service offices and social services sector organizations." Administration and Society 7 (February): 419–454.
    1979   Organizations and Environments. Englewood Cliffs, N.J.: Prentice-Hall.

Aldrich, Howard E., and Jeffrey Pfeffer
    1976   "Environments of organizations." Pp. 79–106 in Alex Inkeles (ed.), Annual Review of Sociology 2. Palo Alto, Calif.: Annual Reviews.

Alutto, Joseph A., and James A. Belasco
    1972   "A typology for participation in organizational decision making." Administrative Science Quarterly 17 (March): 117–125.

Alwin, Duane
    1973   "The use of factor analysis in the construction of linear compos-

ites in social research." Sociological Methods and Research 2 (November): 191–214.

Arabie, Phipps, Scott A. Boorman, and Paul R. Levitt
1977 "Constructing blockmodels: How and why." Journal of Mathematical Psychology 17 (February): 21–63.

Argyris, Chris
1962 Interpersonal Competence and Organizational Effectiveness. Homewood, Ill.: Irwin.

Barnard, Chester I.
1938 The Functions of the Executive. Cambridge, Mass.: Harvard University Press.

Benson, J. Kenneth
1975 "The interorganizational network as a political economy." Administrative Science Quarterly 20 (June): 229–249.
1977 "Innovation and crisis in organizational analysis." Sociological Quarterly 18 (Winter): 5–18.

Benson, J. Kenneth (ed.)
1977 Special Issue-Organizational Analysis: Critique and Innovation. Sociological Quarterly 18 (Winter.)

Bierstedt, Robert
1954 "The problem of authority." In Monroe Berger, Theodore Abel, and Charles H. Page (eds.), Freedom and Control in Modern Society. Princeton, N.J.: Van Nostrand.

Blau, Peter M.
1964 Exchange and Power in Social Life. New York: Wiley.

Blau, Peter M., and Richard A. Schoenherr
1971 The Structure of Organizations. New York: Basic Books.

Blau, Peter M., and W. Richard Scott
1962 Formal Organizations. San Francisco: Chandler.

Blauner, Robert
1964 Alienation and Freedom. Chicago: University of Chicago Press.

Boorman, Scott A., and Harrison C. White
1976 "Social structure from multiple networks. II. Role structures." American Journal of Sociology 81 (May): 1384–1446.

Bowers, David G.
1964 "Organizational control in an insurance company." Sociometry 27 (June): 230–244.

Breiger, Ronald L., Scott A. Boorman, and Phipps Arabie
1975 "An algorithm for clustering relational data, with applications to social network analysis and comparison with multidimensional scaling." Journal of Mathematical Psychology 12:328–383.

Breiger, Ronald L., and Phillipa E. Pattison
1978 "The joint role structure of two communities' elites." Sociological Methods and Research 7 (November): 213–226.

Burgess, Philip M., and Richard Conway
    1973   Public Goods and Voluntary Associations: A Multi-Stage Investigation of Collective Action in Labor Union Locals. Beverly Hills, Calif.: Sage.

Burk, James S.
    1978   "Corporate attributes, position and involvement in community affairs." Unpublished master's paper. University of Chicago.

Burns, Tom, and G. N. Stalker
    1961   The Management of Innovation. London: Tavistock.

Burt, Ronald S.
    1976   "Positions in networks." Social Forces 55 (September): 93–122.
    1977a "Positions in multiple network systems, Part One: A general conception of stratification and prestige in a system of actors cast as a social topology." Social Forces 57 (September): 106–131.
    1977b "Positions in multiple network systems, Part Two: Stratification and prestige among elite decision-makers in the community of Altneustadt." Social Forces 56 (December): 551–575.
    1978   "Cohesion versus structural equivalence as a basis for network subgroups." Sociological Methods and Research 7 (November): 189–212.

Caldwell, Lynton K., Lynton R. Hayes, and Isabel M. MacWhirter
    1976   Citizens and the Environment: Case Studies in Popular Action. Bloomington, Ind.: Indiana University Press.

Cameron, Kim
    1978   "Measuring organizational effectiveness in institutions of higher education." Administrative Science Quarterly 23 (December): 604–629.

Carpenter, Harrell H.
    1971   "Formal organizational structural factors and perceived job satisfaction of classroom teachers." Administrative Science Quarterly 16 (December): 460–466.

Child, John
    1972   "Organization structure, environment, and performance: The role of strategic choice." Sociology 6 (January): 1–22.

Clark, Peter B., and James Q. Wilson
    1961   "Incentive systems: A theory of organizations." Administrative Science Quarterly 6 (September): 129–166.

Clark, Terry N.
    1968a Community Structure and Decision-Making: Comparative Analyses. San Francisco: Chandler.
    1968b "Community structure, decison-making, budget expenditures and urban renewal in 51 American cities." American Sociological Review 33 (August): 576–593.

Clarke, Harold D., Richard G. Price, Marianne C. Stewart, and Robert
Krause
    1978   "Motivational patterns and differential participation in a Ca-
           nadian party: The Ontario Liberals." American Journal of Po-
           litical Science 22 (February):130–151.

Coleman, James S.
    1973a The Mathematics of Collective Action. Chicago: Aldine.
    1973b "Loss of power." American Sociological Review 38
           (February):1–17.
    1974   Power and the Structure of Society. New York: Norton.

Collins, Randall
    1975   Conflict Sociology. New York: Academic Press.

Conway, M. Margaret, and Frank B. Feigert
    1968   "Motivation, incentive system, and the political party organi-
           zation." American Political Science Review 62 (December):
           1159–1173.

Cook, Karen S.
    1977   "Exchange and power in networks of interorganizational rela-
           tions." Sociological Quarterly 18 (Winter):62–82.

Cook, Karen S., and Richard M. Emerson
    1978   "Power, equity and commitment in exchange networks."
           American Sociological Review 43 (October):721–739.

Cummings, Larry L.
    1977   "Emergence of the instrumental organization." Pp. 56–62 in
           P. S. Goodman and J. M. Pennings (eds.), New Perspectives on
           Organizational Effectiveness. San Francisco: Jossey-Bass.

Dachler, H. Peter, and Bernard Wilpert
    1978   "Conceptual dimensions and boundaries of participation in
           organizations: A critical evaluation." Administrative Science
           Quarterly 23 (March): 1–39.

Dewar, Robert, and Jerald Hage
    1978   "Size, technology, complexity, and structural differentiation:
           Toward a theoretical synthesis." Administrative Science Quar-
           terly 23 (March):111–136.

Dornbusch, Sanford M., and W. Richard Scott
    1977   Evaluation and the Exercise of Authority. San Francisco: Jos-
           sey-Bass.

Downs, Anthony
    1957   An Economic Theory of Democracy. New York: Harper and
           Row.

Dubin, Robert
    1956   "Industrial workers' worlds: A study of the 'central life inter-
           ests' of industrial workers." Social Problems 3
           (Fall):131–142.

Dubin, Robert, Joseph E. Champoux, and Lyman W. Porter
 1975 "Central life interests and organizational commitment of blue-collar and clerical workers." Administrative Science Quarterly 20 (September):411–421.

Duncan, Otis Dudley
 1966 "Path analysis: Sociological examples." American Journal of Sociology 72 (July):1–16.

Duncan, Otis Dudley, and Leo F. Schnore
 1959 "Cultural, behavioral, and ecological perspectives in the study of social organization." American Journal of Sociology 65 (September):132–153.

Duncan, Robert B.
 1972 "Characteristics of organizational environments and perceived environmental uncertainty." Administrative Science Quarterly 17 (September):313–327.

Durkheim, Emile
 1933 On the Division of Labor in Society. New York: Macmillan.

Dye, Thomas R., and Susan A. MacManus
 1976 "Predicting city government structure." American Journal of Political Science 20 (May):257–271.

Ehrlich, Howard J.
 1967 "The social psychology of reputations for community leadership." Sociological Quarterly 8 (Summer):415–430.

Eitzen, D. Stanley, and Norman R. Yetman
 1972 "Managerial change, longevity and organizational effectiveness." Administrative Science Quarterly 17 (March):110–116.

Ekeh, Peter
 1974 Social Exchange Theory: The Two Traditions. Cambridge, Mass.: Harvard University Press.

Emerson, Richard M.
 1972a "Exchange Theory, Part I: A psychological basis for social exchange." Pp. 38–57 in Joseph Berger, Morris Zelditch, Jr., and Bo Anderson (eds.), Sociological Theories in Progress, Vol. II. Boston: Houghton Mifflin.
 1972b "Exchange Theory, Part II: Exchange relations, exchange networks and groups as exchange systems." Pp. 58–87 in Joseph Berger, Morris Zelditch, Jr., and Bo Anderson (eds.), Sociological Theories in Progress, Vol. II. Boston: Houghton Mifflin.

Etzioni, Amitai
 1968 The Active Society: A Theory of Societal and Political Processes. New York: Free Press.
 1975 A Comparative Analysis of Complex Organizations. Second Edition. New York: Free Press.

Evan, William M.
  1967   "The organization-set: Toward a theory of interorganizational relations." Pp. 173–191 in J. D. Thompson (ed.), Approaches to Organizational Design. Pittsburgh, Pa.: University of Pittsburgh Press.
  1972   "An organization set model of interorganizational relations." Pp. 181–200 in M. Tuite, R. Chisholm, and M. Radnor (eds.), Interorganizational Decision Making. Chicago: Aldine.
Faunce, William A.
  1962   "Size of locals and union democracy." American Journal of Sociology 68 (November): 291–298.
Freeman, John, and Michael T. Hannan
  1975   "Growth and decline processes in organizations." American Sociological Review 40 (April): 215–228.
Frohlich, Norman, Joe A. Oppenheimer, and Oran R. Young
  1971   Political Leadership and Collective Goods. Princeton, N.J.: Princeton University Press.
Galaskiewicz, Joseph
  1978   "Hierarchical patterns in a community interorganizational system." Paper presented at American Sociological Association meeting, San Francisco.
  1979   Systems of Community Interorganizational Exchange. Beverly Hills, Calif.: Sage.
Galaskiewicz, Joseph, and Peter V. Marsden
  1978   "Interorganizational resource networks: Formal patterns of overlap." Social Science Research 7 (June): 89–107.
Gamson, William A.
  1975   The Strategy of Social Protest. Homewood, Ill.: Dorsey Press.
Georgopoulos, Basil S., and Floyd C. Mann
  1962   The Community General Hospital. New York: Macmillan.
Goodman, Paul S., and Johannes M. Pennings (eds.)
  1977   New Perspectives on Organizational Effectiveness. San Francisco: Jossey-Bass.
Gouldner, Alvin W.
  1954   Patterns of Industrial Bureaucracy. Glencoe, Ill.: Free Press.
Gouldner, Helen P.
  1960   "Dimensions of organizational commitment." Administrative Science Quarterly 4 (March): 468–490.
Grusky, Oscar
  1963   "Managerial succession and organizational effectiveness." American Journal of Sociology 69 (July): 21–31.
Gusfield, Joseph R.
  1962   "Mass society and extremist politics." American Sociological Review 27 (February): 19–30.

Hage, Jerald
  1974   Communication and Organizational Control: Cybernetics in
          Health and Welfare Settings. New York: Wiley.
Hage, Jerald, and Michael Aiken
  1967   "Relationship of centralization to other structural properties."
          Administrative Science Quarterly 12 (June): 73–92.
Hage, Jerald, and Robert Dewar
  1978   "Size, technology, complexity, and structural differentiation:
          Toward a theoretical synthesis." Administrative Science Quar-
          terly 23 (March): 111–136.
Hammond, Phillip E., Luis Salinas, and Douglas Sloane
  1978   "Types of clergy authority: Their measurement, location, and
          effects." Journal for the Scientific Study of Religion 17 (Sep-
          tember): 241–253.
Hausknecht, Murray
  1962   The Joiners. New York: Bedminster Press.
Hawley, Amos H.
  1950   Human Ecology: A Theory of Community Structure. New
          York: Ronald Press.
Heath, Anthony
  1976   Rational Choice and Social Exchange: A Critique of Exchange
          Theory. Cambridge: Cambridge University Press.
Hickson, D. J., C. R. Hinings, C. A. Lee, R. E. Schneck, and J. M.
Pennings
  1971   "A strategic contingencies' theory of intra-organizational pow-
          er." Administrative Science Quarterly 16 (June): 216–229.
Hirsch, Paul M.
  1975   "Organizational effectiveness and the institutional environ-
          ment." Administrative Science Quarterly 20 (June): 327–344.
Hirschman, Albert O.
  1970   Exit, Voice, and Loyalty. Cambridge, Mass.: Harvard Univer-
          sity Press.
Hodgkins, Benjamin T., and Robert E. Herriott
  1970   "Age-grade structure, goals, and compliance in pre-school: An
          organizational analysis." Sociology of Education 43 (Winter):
          90–105.
Holtzman, Abraham
  1966   Interest Groups and Lobbying. New York: Macmillan.
Homans, George C.
  1950   The Human Group. New York: Harcourt Brace.
  1961   Social Behavior: Its Elementary Forms. New York: Harcourt
          Brace, World.
Hougland, James G., Jr.
  1976   Control and Policy in Protestant Organizations. Unpublished

doctoral dissertation. Bloomington, Ind.: Indiana University.

Hrebiniak, Lawrence G., and Joseph A. Alutto
1972   "Personal and role related factors in the development of organizational commitment." Administrative Science Quarterly 17 (December): 555–573.

Hyman, Herbert H., and Charles R. Wright
1971   "Trends in voluntary association memberships of American adults: Replications based on the secondary analysis of national sample surveys." American Sociological Review 36 (April): 191–206.

Indik, Bernard P.
1963   "Some effects of organization size on member attitudes and behavior." Human Relations 16 (November): 369–384.
1965   "Organizational size and member participation: Some empirical tests of alternative explanations." Human Relations 18 (November): 339–350.

Jacobs, David
1974   "Dependency and vulnerability: An exchange approach to the control of organizations." Administrative Science Quarterly 19 (March): 45–59.

Jacoby, Arthur P. and Nicholas Babchuk
1963   "Instrumental and expressive voluntary associations." Sociology and Social Research 47 (July): 461–471.

Janowitz, Morris
1975   "Sociological theory and social control." American Journal of Sociology 81 (July): 82–108.
1976   Social Control of the Welfare State. New York: Elsevier.
1978   The Last Half-Century: Societal Change and Politics in America. Chicago: University of Chicago Press.

Jurkovich, Ray
1974   "A core typology of organizational environments." Administrative Science Quarterly 19 (September): 380–394.

Katz, Daniel, and Robert L. Kahn
1978   The Social Psychology of Organizations. Second Edition. New York: Wiley.

Kerlinger, Fred N., and Elazar J. Pedhazur
1973   Multiple Regression in Behavioral Research. New York: Holt, Rinehart and Winston.

Klonglan, Gerald E., Charles L. Mulford, and Donald Tweed
1974   "A causal model of consensus formation and effectiveness." Paper presented at Midwest Sociological Society meeting, Omaha, Nebr., April 6.

Knoke, David, and David L. Rogers
1979   "A block model analysis of interorganizational networks." Sociology and Social Research 64 (October): 28–52.

Kornhauser, William
　1959　The Politics of Mass Society. New York: Free Press of Glencoe.
Kotler, Philip
　1974　Marketing Decision Making: A Model Building Approach.
　　　　New York: Holt, Rinehart and Winston.
Land, Kenneth C.
　1973　"Identification, parameter estimation, and hypothesis testing
　　　　in recursive sociological models." Pp. 19–49 in Arthur S.
　　　　Goldberger and Otis Dudley Duncan (eds.), Structural Equa-
　　　　tion Models in the Social Sciences. New York: Seminar Press.
Lane, Robert
　1959　Political Life: Why People Get Involved in Politics. New York:
　　　　Free Press.
Laumann, Edward O., Joseph Galaskiewicz, and Peter V. Marsden
　1978　"Community structures as interorganizational linkages." Pp.
　　　　455–484 in Alex Inkeles (ed.), Annual Review of Sociology 4.
　　　　Palo Alto, Calif.: Annual Reviews.
Laumann, Edward O., Peter V. Marsden, and Joseph Galaskiewicz
　1977　"Community influence structures: Replication and extension
　　　　of a network approach." American Journal of Sociology 83
　　　　(November): 594–631.
Laumann, Edward O., and Franz U. Pappi
　1976　Networks of Collective Action. New York: Academic Press.
Leary, Edward A.
　1973　Indianapolis: The Story of a City. Indianapolis: Bobbs-Merrill.
Lieberson, Stanley, and James F. O'Connor
　1972　"Leadership and organizational performance: A study of large
　　　　corporations." American Sociological Review 37 (April):
　　　　117–130.
Likert, Rensis
　1961　New Patterns of Management. New York: McGraw-Hill.
　1967　The Human Organization. New York: McGraw-Hill.
Lincoln, James R., and Gerald Zeitz
　1980　"Organizational properties from aggregate data: Separating in-
　　　　dividual and structural effects." American Sociological Re-
　　　　view 45 (June): 391–408.
Lipset, Seymour M., Martin A. Trow, and James S. Coleman
　1956　Union Democracy. Glencoe, Ill.: Free Press.
Lorrain, Francois, and Harrison C. White
　1971　"Structural equivalence of individuals in social networks."
　　　　Journal of Mathematical Sociology 1 (Spring): 49–80.
McCarthy, John D., and Mayer N. Zald
　1973　The Trend of Social Movements in America: Professionaliza-
　　　　tion and Resource Mobilization. Morristown, N.J.: General
　　　　Learning Press.

1977   "Resource mobilization and social movements: A partial theory." American Journal of Sociology 82 (May): 1212–1241.
McMahon, Anne, and Santo Camilleri
1975   "Organizational structure and voluntary participation in col-
lective-good decisions." American Sociological Review 40
(October): 616–644.
McNeil, Kenneth
1978   "Understanding organizational power: Building on the Weberian legacy." Administrative Science Quarterly 23 (March):
65–90.
March, James G., and Herbert A. Simon
1958   Organizations. New York: Wiley.
Marcus, Philip M.
1966   "Union conventions and executive boards: A formal analysis
of organizational structure." American Sociological Review 31
(February): 61–70.
Marcus, Philip M., and Dora Marcus
1965   "Control in modern organizations." Public Administration Review 25 (June): 121–127.
Marks, Stephen R.
1977   "Multiple roles and role strain: Some notes on human energy,
time and commitment." American Sociological Review 42
(December): 921–936.
Mechanic, David
1962   "Sources of power of lower participants in complex organizations." Administrative Science Quarterly 7 (December):
349–364.
Messinger, Sheldon L.
1955   "Organizational transformation: A case study of a declining
social movement." American Sociological Review 20 (February): 3–10.
Meyer, John W., and Brian Rowan
1977   "Institutionalized organizations: Formal structure as myth and
ceremony." American Journal of Sociology 83 (September):
340–363.
Meyer, Marshall W., and Associates
1978   Environments and Organizations. San Francisco: Jossey-Bass.
Michels, Robert
1949   Political Parties: A Sociological Study of the Oligarchical
Tendencies of Modern Democracy. Glencoe, Ill.: Free Press.
Miller, Jon P., and Lincoln J. Fry
1973   "Social relations in organizations: Further evidence for the
Weberian model." Social Forces 51 (March): 305–319.
Mills, C. Wright
1956   The Power Elite. New York: Oxford University Press.

Mitchell, J. Clyde
    1969   Social Networks in Urban Situations. Manchester, England: Manchester University Press.

Mohr, Lawrence B.
    1973   "The concept of organizational goal." American Political Science Review 67 (June): 470–481.

Morse, Nancy C., and Everett Reimer
    1956   "The experimental change of a major organizational variable." Journal of Abnormal and Social Psychology 52 (January): 120–129.

Moynihan, Daniel P.
    1969   Maximum Feasible Misunderstanding. New York: Free Press.

Mulford, Charles L., Gerald E. Klonglan, and Richard D. Warren
    1972   "Socialization, communication, and role performance" Sociological Quarterly 13 (Winter): 74–80.

Namboodiri, N. Krishnan, Lewis F. Carter, and Hubert M. Blalock, Jr.
    1975   Applied Multivariate Analysis and Experimental Design. New York: McGraw-Hill.

Olsen, Marvin
    1972   "Social participation and voting turnout: A multivariate analysis." American Sociological Review 37 (June): 317–333.

Olson, Mancur, Jr.
    1965   The Logic of Collective Action. Cambridge, Mass.: Harvard University Press.

Osborn, Richard N., and James C. Hunt
    1974   "Environment and organizational effectiveness." Administrative Science Quarterly 19 (June): 231–246.

Ostrom, Elinore, and Nancy Neubert
    1973   "Metropolitan reform in Indianapolis." Paper presented at American Public Administration Association meeting, Los Angeles.

Parsons, Talcott
    1937   The Structure of Social Action. New York: McGraw-Hill.
    1956   "Suggestions for a sociological approach to the theory of organizations." Administrative Science Quarterly 1 (June and September): 63–85 and 225–239.
    1958   "Authority, legitimation, and political action." In Carl J. Friedrich (ed.), Authority. Cambridge, Mass.: Harvard University Press.
    1960   Structure and Process in Modern Societies. New York: Free Press.
    1966   "The political aspect of social structure and process." In David Easton (ed.), Varieties of Political Theory. Englewood Cliffs, N.J.: Prentice-Hall.
    1969   Politics and Social Structure. New York: Free Press.

Peabody, Robert L.
    1968 "Authority." Pp. 473–477 in David L. Sills (ed.), Internation-
           al Encyclopedia of the Social Sciences, Vol. 1. New York:
           Macmillan.
Pennings, Johannes M.
    1975 "The relevance of the structural-contingency model for orga-
           nizational effectiveness." Administrative Science Quarterly 20
           (September): 393–410.
    1976 "Dimensions of organizational influence and their effective-
           ness correlates." Administrative Science Quarterly 21 (Decem-
           ber): 688–699.
Pennings, Johannes M., and Paul S. Goodman
    1977 "Toward a workable framework." Pp. 146–184 in Paul S.
           Goodman and Johannes M. Pennings (eds.), New Perspectives
           on Organizational Effectiveness. San Francisco: Jossey-Bass.
Perrow, Charles
    1968 "Organizational goals." Pp. 305–311 in D. L. Sills (ed.), Inter-
           national Encyclopedia of the Social Sciences, Vol. 11. New
           York: Macmillan.
    1970 "Members as resources in voluntary organizations." Pp. 93–
           116 in William R. Rosengren and Mark Lefton (eds.), Organi-
           zations and Clients. Columbus, Ohio: Merrill.
Pfeffer, Jeffrey
    1972 "Size and composition of corporate boards of directors: The
           organization and its environment." Administrative Science
           Quarterly 17 (June): 218–228.
Presthus, Robert V.
    1974 Elites in the Policy Process. London: Cambridge University
           Press.
Price, James L.
    1968 Organizational Effectiveness: An Inventory of Propositions.
           Homewood, Ill.: Richard D. Irwin.
    1972 Handbook of Organizational Measurement. Lexington, Mass.:
           D. C. Heath.
Pugh, Derek, David Hickson, Robert Hinings, and Chris Turner
    1968 "Dimensions of organizational structure." Administrative Sci-
           ence Quarterly 13 (June): 65–104.
Riker, William H., and Peter C. Ordeshook
    1972 Introduction to Positive Political Theory. Englewood Cliffs,
           N.J.: Prentice-Hall.
Roe, Betty Boyd, and James R. Wood
    1975 "Adaptive innovation and organizational security." Pacific So-
           ciological Review 18 (July): 310–326.
Rogers, David L.
    1974 "Sociometric analysis of interorganizational relations: Appli-

cation of theory and measurement." Rural Sociology 39 (Winter): 487–503.

Rogers, Mary F.
    1974   "Instrumental and infra-resources: The bases of power." American Journal of Sociology 79 (May): 1418–1433.

Rose, Arnold
    1967   "Voluntary associations." Pp. 213–252 in Arnold Rose, The Power Structure. New York: Oxford University Press.

Rushing, William
    1974   "Differences in profit and nonprofit organizations: A study of effectiveness and efficiency in general short-stay hospitals." Administrative Science Quarterly 19 (December): 474–484.

Sailer, Lee Douglas
    1978   "Structural equivalence: Meaning and definition, computation and application." Social Networks 1 (August): 73–90.

Salisbury, Robert
    1969   "An exchange theory of interest groups." Midwest Journal of Political Science 13 (February): 1–32.

Satow, Roberta Lynn
    1975   "Value-rational authority and professional organizations: Weber's missing type." Administrative Science Quarterly 20 (December): 526–531.

Schmidt, Stuart M., and Thomas A. Kochan
    1977   "Interorganizational relationships: Patterns and motivations." Administrative Science Quarterly 22 (June): 220–234.

Schwab, Donald P., and Larry L. Cummings
    1970   "Theories of performance and satisfaction: A review." Industrial Relations 9 (October): 408–430.

Schwartz, Joseph E.
    1977   "An examination of CONCOR and related methods for blocking sociometric data." Pp. 255–282 in David R. Heise (ed.), Sociological Methodology 1977. San Francisco: Jossey-Bass.

Selznick, Philip
    1949   TVA and the Grass Roots. Berkeley, Calif.: University of California Press.

Sills, David L.
    1957   The Volunteers: Means and Ends in a National Organization. Glencoe, Ill.: Free Press.

Simon, Herbert A.
    1964   "On the concept of organizational goal." Administrative Science Quarterly 9 (June): 1–22.

Simon, Herbert A., Donald W. Smithburg, and Victor A. Thompson
    1970   Public Administration. New York: Knopf.

Smith, Clagett G., and Oguz N. Ari
    1964   "Organizational control structure and member consensus."

American Journal of Sociology 69 (May): 623–638.

Smith, Clagett G., and Michael E. Brown
1964   "Communication structure and control structure in a voluntary association." Sociometry 27 (December): 449–468.

Smith, David Horton, Richard D. Reddy, and Burt R. Baldwin
1972   "Types of voluntary action: A definitional essay." Pp. 159–195 in David Horton Smith (ed.), Voluntary Action Research. Lexington, Mass.: D. C. Heath.

Steers, Richard M.
1975   "Problems in the measurement of organizational effectiveness." Administrative Science Quarterly 20 (December): 546–558.

Stinchcombe, Arthur L.
1965   "Social structure and organizations." Pp. 142–193 in James G. March (ed.), Handbook of Organizations. Chicago: Rand McNally.
1968   Constructing Social Theories. New York: Harcourt Brace.

Stogdill, Ralph M.
1967   "The structure of organization behavior." Multivariate Behavioral Research 2: 47–61.

Stryker, Sheldon
1977   "Developments of 'Two Social Psychologies': Toward an appreciation of mutual relevance." Sociometry 40 (June): 145–160.

Talacchi, Sergio
1960   "Organizational size, individual attitudes and behavior: An empirical study." Administrative Science Quarterly 5 (December): 398–420.

Tannenbaum, Arnold S.
1962   "Reactions of members of voluntary groups: A logarithmic function of size of group." Psychological Reports 10 (February): 113–114.
1968   Control in Organizations. New York: McGraw-Hill.

Tannenbaum, Arnold S., and Robert L. Kahn
1958   Participation in Union Locals. Evanston, Ill.: Row Peterson.

Tannenbaum, Arnold S., and Clagett G. Smith
1964   "The effects of member influence in an organization: Phenomenology versus organizational structure." Journal of Abnormal and Social Psychology 69 (October): 401–410.

Terreberry, Shirley
1968   "The evolution of organization environments." Administrative Science Quarterly 12 (March): 590–613.

Thompson, James D.
1967   Organizations in Action. New York: McGraw-Hill.

Thompson, James D., and William J. McEwen
  1958   "Organizational goals and environment: Goal-setting as an interaction process." American Sociological Review 23 (February): 23–31.
Tilly, Charles
  1978   From Mobilization to Revolution. Reading, Mass.: Addison-Wesley.
Tocqueville, Alexis de
  1969   Democracy in America. Garden City, N.Y.: Doubleday.
Van de Geer, John P.
  1971   Introduction to Multivariate Analysis for the Social Sciences. San Francisco: Freeman.
Verba, Sidney, and Norman H. Nie
  1972   Participation in America: Political Democracy and Social Equality. New York: Harper and Row.
Warner, R. Stephen
  1978   "Toward a redefinition of action theory: Paying the cognitive element its due." American Journal of Sociology 83 (May): 1317–1349.
Warner, W. Keith
  1964   "Attendance and division of labor in voluntary associations." Rural Sociology 29 (December): 396–407.
Warner, W. Keith, and William D. Heffernan
  1967   "The benefit-participation contingency in voluntary farm organizations." Rural Sociology 32 (June): 139–153.
Warner, W. Keith, and James S. Hilander
  1964   "The relationship between size of organization and membership participation." Rural Sociology 29 (March): 30–39.
Warner, W. Keith, and David L. Rogers
  1971   "Some correlates of control in voluntary farm organizations." Rural Sociology 36 (September): 326–339.
Warriner, Charles, and Jane Prather
  1965   "Four types of voluntary associations." Sociological Inquiry 35 (Spring): 138–148.
Weber, Max
  1947   The Theory of Social and Economic Organization. Translated and edited by A. M. Henderson and Talcott Parsons. New York: Oxford University Press.
  1968   Economy and Society. Edited by Guenther Roth and Claus Wittich. New York: Bedminster Press.
White, Harrison C., Scott A. Boorman, and Ronald L. Breiger
  1976   "Social structure from multiple networks. I. Blockmodels of roles and positions." American Journal of Sociology 81 (January): 730–780.

Wilken, Paul
1971   "Size of organizations and member participation in church congregations." Administrative Science Quarterly 16 (June): 173–179.

Willer, David E.
1967   "Max Weber's missing authority type." Sociological Inquiry 37: 231–239.

Wilson, James Q.
1962   The Amateur Democrat. Chicago: University of Chicago Press.
1973   Political Organizations. New York: Basic Books.

Wilson, Kenneth, and Anthony Orum
1976   "Mobilizing people for collective political action." Journal of Political and Military Sociology 4 (Fall): 187–202.

Wood, James R.
1967   "Protestant enforcement of racial integration policy: A sociological study in the political economy of organizations." Vanderbilt University, doctoral dissertation.
1972   "Unanticipated consequences of organizational coalitions: Ecumenical cooperation and civil rights policy." Social Forces 50 (June): 512–521.
1975   "Legitimate control and 'organizational transcendence.'" Social Forces 54 (September): 199–211.
1981   Legitimate Leadership in Voluntary Organizations: The Controversy over Social Action in Protestant Churches. New Brunswick, N.J.: Rutgers University Press.

Work in America Institute, Inc.
1978   "Studies in productivity." Scarsdale, N.Y.

Wright, Charles, and Herbert Hyman
1958   "Voluntary memberships of American adults: Evidence from national sample surveys." American Sociological Review 23 (June): 284–292.

Yuchtman, Ephraim, and Stanley E. Seashore
1967   "A system resource approach to organizational effectiveness." American Sociological Review 32 (December): 891–903.

Zald, Mayer N.
1969   "The power and functions of boards of directors: A theoretical synthesis." American Journal of Sociology 75 (July): 97–111.
1970a   "Political economy: A framework for comparative analysis." Pp. 221–261 in Mayer N. Zald (ed.), Power in Organizations. Nashville, Tenn.: Vanderbilt University Press.
1970b   Organizational Change: The Political Economy of the YMCA. Chicago: University of Chicago Press.

Zald, Mayer N., and Patricia Denton
1963   "From evangelism to general service: The transformation of

the YMCA." Administrative Science Quarterly 8 (September): 214–234.

Zald, Mayer N., and David Jacobs
  1978   "Compliance/incentive classifications of organizations: Underlying dimensions." Administration and Society 9 (February): 403–424.

Zeigler, L. Harmon
  1964   Interest Groups in American Society. Englewood Cliffs, N.J.: Prentice-Hall.

Zeigler, L. Harmon, and Michael A. Baer
  1969   Lobbying: Interaction and Influence in American State Legislatures. Belmont, Calif.: Wadsworth.

Author Index

Subject Index